Aquarium Fish of the World

The Comprehensive Guide to 650 Species

Atsushi Sakurai, Yohei Sakamoto & Fumitoshi Mori

English translation by Takeshi Shimizu with Neal M. Teitler

Edited by Dr. Paul V. Loiselle
Curator of Freshwater Fish
New York Aquarium

Chronicle Books • San Francisco

HIGHER LEVEL CLASSIFICATION OF FRESHWATER AND BRACKISHWATER FISHES

CLASS	**CEPHALASPIDOMORHI**	
ORDER	**PETROMYZONTIFORMES**	
FAMILY	PETROMYZONTIDAE	
	(Lampreys)	
SUBFAMILIES	PETROMYZONTINAE	
	GEOTRIINAE	
	MORDACIINAE	
CLASS	**ELASMOBRANCHII**	
ORDER	**CARCHARINIFORMES**	
FAMILIES	CARCHARINIDAE	
	(Requiem Sharks)	
	SPHYRNIDAE	
	(Hammerhead Sharks)	
ORDER	**PRISTIFORMES**	
FAMILY	PRISTIDAE (Sawfishes)	
ORDER	**MYLIOBATIFORMES**	
FAMILIES	DASYATIDAE (Stingrays)	
	GYMNURIDAE (Butterfly Rays)	
	UROLOPHIDAE	
	(Round Stingrays)	
	POTAMOTRYGONIDAE	285
CLASS	**ACTINOPTERYGII**	
ORDER	**ACIPENSERIFORMES**	
FAMILY	ACIPENSERIDAE	
SUBFAMILIES	ACIPENSERINAE	285
	SCAPHIRHYNCHINAE	
FAMILY	POLYODONTIDAE	285
ORDER	**POLYPTERIFORMES**	
FAMILY	POLYPTERIDAE	280
ORDER	**LEPISOSTEIFORMES**	
FAMILY	LEPISOSTEIDAE	285
ORDER	**AMIIFORMES**	
FAMILY	AMIIDAE	272
ORDER	**OSTEOGLOSSIFORMES**	
SUBORDER	**OSTEOGLOSSOIDEI**	
FAMILIES	OSTEOGLOSSIDAE	278
	PANTODONTIDAE	279
SUBORDER	**NOTOPTEROIDEI**	
FAMILIES	HIODONTIDAE (Mooneyes)	
	NOTOPTERIDAE	284
SUBORDER	**MORMYROIDEI**	
FAMILIES	MORMYRIDAE	282
	GYMNARCHIDAE	283
ORDER	**ELOPIFORMES**	
FAMILIES	ELOPIDAE (Tenpounders)	
	MEGALOPIDAE (Tarpons)	
ORDER	**ALBULIFORMES**	
FAMILY	ALBULIDAE (Bonefishes)	
SUBFAMILY	ALBULINAE	
ORDER	**ANGUILLIFORMES**	
SUBORDER	**ANGUILLOIDEI**	
FAMILY	ANGUILLIDAE	
	(Freshwater Eels)	
ORDER	**CLUPEIFORMES**	
FAMILIES	DENTICIPITIDAE	
	(Denticle Herrings)	
FAMILY	CLUPEIDAE (Herrings, Shads, Sardines & allies)	
	ENGRAULIDAE (Anchovies)	
ORDER	**GONORYNCHIFORMES**	
FAMILIES	CHANIDAE (Milkfishes)	
	KNERIIDAE	
	PHRACTOLAEMIDAE	
ORDER	**CYPRINIFORMES**	
FAMILIES	CYPRINIDAE	51
	PSILORHYNCHIDAE	
	COBITIDAE	64
	BALITORIDAE	59,65
	GYRINOCHEILIDAE	59
	CATOSTOMIDAE	
ORDER	**CHARACIFORMES**	
FAMILY	CITHARINIDAE	
SUBFAMILIES	DISTICHODONTINAE	27
	CITHARININAE	
FAMILIES	ALESTIIDAE	28
	HEPSETIDAE	
	HEMIODONTIDAE	33
	CURIMATIDAE	
SUBFAMILIES	CURIMATINAE	
	PROCHILODONTINAE	
	ANOSTOMINAE	32
	CHILODONTINAE	29
FAMILIES	ERYTHRINIDAE	29
	LEBIASINIDAE	
SUBFAMILIES	LEBIASININAE	
	PYRRHULININAE	40
FAMILIES	GASTEROPELECIDAE	28
	CTENOLUCIIDAE	29
	CYNODONTIDAE	
	CHARACIDAE	34
ORDER	**SILURIFORMES**	
FAMILIES	DIPLOMYSTIDAE	
	(Diplomystid Catfishes)	
	ICTALURIDAE	
	(Bullhead Catfishes)	
	BAGRIDAE	250
	CRANOGLANIDIDAE	
	(Armorhead Catfishes)	
	SILURIDAE	254
	SCHILBEIDAE	253
	PANGASIIDAE	254
	AMBLYCIPITIDAE	
	(Torrent Catfishes)	
	AMPHILIIDAE)	
	(Loach Catfishes)	
	AKYSIDAE (Stream Catfishes)	
	PARAKYSIDAE	
	(Parakysid Catfishes)	
	SISORIDAE	252
	CLARIIDAE	253
	HETEROPNEUSTIDAE	252
	CHACIDAE	253
	OLYRIDAE (Olyrid Catfishes)	
	MALAPTERURIDAE	253
	ARIIDAE	251
	PLOTOSIDAE	253
	MOCHOKIDAE	236
	DORADIDAE	251
	AUCHENIPTERIDAE	251
	PIMELODIDAE	249
	AGENEIOSIDAE (Bottlenose or Barbelless Catfishes)	
	HELOGENEIDAE	
	(Helogeneid Catfishes)	
	CETOPSIDAE	
	(Whalelike Catfishes)	
	HYPOPHTHALMIDAE	
	(Loweye Catfishes)	
	ASPREDINIDAE	253
	TRICHOMYCTERIDAE (Parasitic Catfishes & Candirus)	
	CALLICHTHYIDAE	231
	LORICARIIDAE	242
	SCOLOPLACIDAE	
	ASTROBLEPIDAE	
	(Astroblepid Catfish)	
ORDER	**GYMNOTIFORMES**	
FAMILY	GYMNOTIDAE	
SUBFAMILIES	STERNOPYGINAE	284
	RHAMPHICHTHYINAE	
	HYPOPOMINAE	
	APTERONOTINAE	284
	GYMNOTINAE	
	(Nakedback Knifefishes)	
	ELECTROPHORINAE	
	(Electric Knifefishes)	
ORDER	**SALMONIFORMES**	
SUBORDER	**ESOCOIDEI**	
FAMILIES	ESOCIDAE	284
	UMBRIDAE (Mudminnows)	
SUBORDER	**LEPIDOGALAXIOIDEI**	
FAMILY	LEPIDOGALAXIIDAE	
SUBORDER	**SALMONOIDEI**	
FAMILIES	OSMERIDAE (Smelts)	
	PLECOGLOSSIDAE	
	(Ayu Fishes)	
	SALANGIDAE	
	(Icefishes & Noodlefishes)	
	RETROPINNIDAE	
	(New Zealand Smelts)	
SUBFAMILIES	RETROPINNINAE (Southern Smelts)	
	PROTOTROCTINAE	
	(Southern Graylings)	
FAMILY	GALAXIIDAE (Galaxiids)	
SUBFAMILIES	APLOCHITONINAE	
	GALAXIINAE	
FAMILY	SALMONIDAE (Salmonids)	
SUBFAMILIES	COREGONINAE (Whitefishes)	
	THYMALLINAE (Graylings)	
	SALMONINAE (Salmons, Trouts & Chars)	
ORDER	**AULOPIFORMES**	
SUBORDER	**ALEPISAUROIDEI**	
FAMILY	SYNODONTIDAE	
SUBFAMILY	HARPADONTINAE (Bombay Ducks)	
ORDER	**PERCOPSIFORMES**	
FAMILIES	PERCOPSIDAE (Trout-Perches)	
	APHREDODERIDAE	
	(Pirate Perches)	
	AMBLYOPSIDAE (Cavefishes)	
ORDER	**GADIFORMES**	
FAMILIES	GADIDAE (Cods & Haddocks)	
	LOTIDAE (Hakes & Burbots)	
ORDER	**OPHIDIIFORMES**	
FAMILIES	OPHIDIIDAE (Cuskeels)	
	BYTHITIDAE	
ORDER	**BATRACHOIDIFORMES**	
FAMILY	BATRACHOIDIDAE	263
ORDER	**GOBIESOCIFORMES**	
FAMILY	GOBIESOCIDAE (Clingfishes)	
SUBFAMILY	GOBIESOCINAE	
ORDER	**ATHERINIFORMES**	
FAMILY	ATHERINIDAE	
SUBFAMILIES	ATHERINOPSINAE	
	MENIDIINAE	
	NOTOCHEIRINAE	
	ATHERIONINAE	
	ATHERININAE	
	BEDOTIINAE	264
	DENTATHERININAE	
	PSEUDOMUGILINAE	264
	MELANOTAENIINAE	264
FAMILY	PHALLOSTETHIDAE	
ORDER	**CYPRINODONTIFORMES**	
FAMILIES	APLOCHEILIDAE	218
	CYPRINODONTIDAE	
SUBFAMILIES	CYPRINODONTINAE	226
	VALENCIINAE	
	APLOCHEILICHTHYINAE	
	PROFUNDULINAE	
	FUNDULINAE	
	CUBANICHTHYINAE	
	FLUVIPHYLACINAE	
	EMPETRICHTHYINAE	
FAMILIES	GOODEIDAE	206
	POECILIIDAE	198
	ANABLEPIDAE	
SUBFAMILIES	ANABLEPINAE	263
	JENYNSIINAE (Jenynsiids)	
	OXYZYGONECTINAE	

Adapted from Eschmeyer, W. N., 1990, *Catalog of the Genera of Recent Fishes,*
California Academy of Sciences, San Francisco, 697 pp.

Families/Subfamilies without page citation are not included in this book.

CONTENTS

Distribution maps found on chapter title
pages are adapted mainly from Nelson,
J. S., 1984, *Fishes of the World, 2nd Ed.,* John
Wiley & Sons, Inc., New York, 523 pp. and
Berra, T. M., 1981, *An Atlas of Distribution
of the Freshwater Fish Families of the World,*
Univ. Nebraska Press, Lincoln, 197 pp.

Only genera noted or photos shown are
cited on the title page of each chapter.

AQUARIUM FISH OF THE WORLD

*Numbers show fish I.D. page.

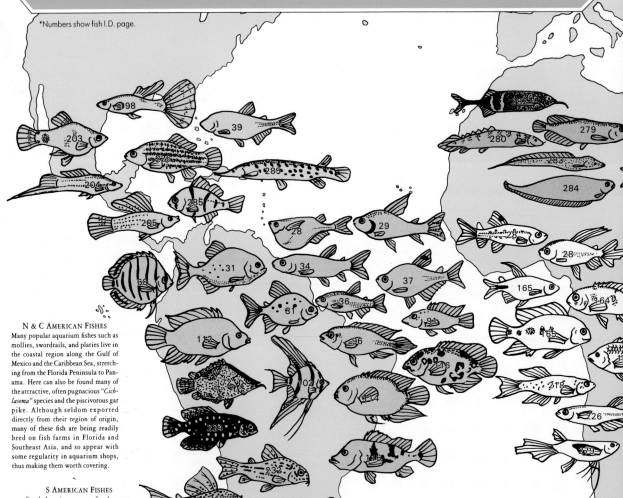

N & C AMERICAN FISHES

Many popular aquarium fishes such as mollies, swordtails, and platies live in the coastal region along the Gulf of Mexico and the Caribbean Sea, stretching from the Florida Peninsula to Panama. Here can also be found many of the attractive, often pugnacious *"Cichlasoma"* species and the piscivorous gar pike. Although seldom exported directly from their region of origin, many of these fish are being readily bred on fish farms in Florida and Southeast Asia, and so appear with some regularity in aquarium shops, thus making them worth covering.

S AMERICAN FISHES

South America accounts for the greatest number and variety of "tropical fishes." Almost all types of fishes, except for the Cyprinidae, may be found living in the waters of the large rivers—the Amazon, the Orinoco, the coastal rivers of the Guianas, and Paraná–La Plata. Among the innumerable types of fishes coming from these waters are such New World cichlids as the discus and many dwarf species, diverse numbers of catfish (the tiger shovelnose, speciose *Corydoras*, bizarre bristlenose pleco), countless characins, colorful killifishes, striking electric fishes, plus the primitive arapaima and arowana.

W AFRICAN FISHES

There are a number of lovely exotic fishes found in the tropical rain forest habitats of western Africa, including those of the Niger and Zaire (Congo) rivers. Examples include such African dwarf cichlids as *Pelvicachromis* and *Nanochromis*, medium-sized characins like the Congo Tetra and brilliantly colored killifish of the genus *Aphyosemion*. The rivers of this region are also home to the primitive bichirs and lungfish, bizarre mormyrids, many barbs and the popular upside-down catfishes.

FISHES OF THE NILE

Among the large-sized fishes inhabiting the waters of the Nile from its mouth to sources, Lakes Victoria (White Nile) and Tana (Blue Nile), are *Gymnarchus niloticus,* the arowana-like *Heterotis niloticus* and the Nile Perch. Although there are innumerable fishes within its brimming waters, overexploitation of the Nile's resources has become a problem.

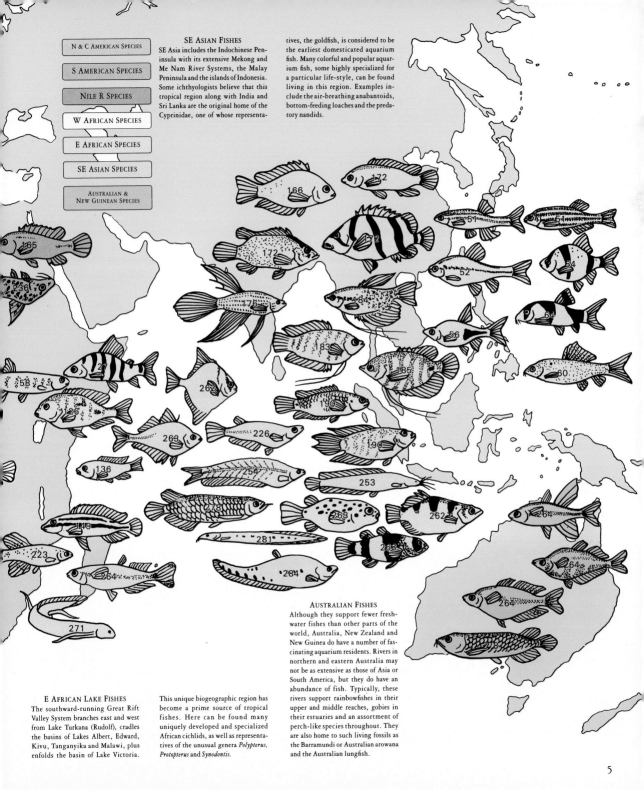

N & C AMERICAN SPECIES

S AMERICAN SPECIES

NILE R SPECIES

W AFRICAN SPECIES

E AFRICAN SPECIES

SE ASIAN SPECIES

AUSTRALIAN & NEW GUINEAN SPECIES

SE ASIAN FISHES

SE Asia includes the Indochinese Peninsula with its extensive Mekong and Me Nam River Systems, the Malay Peninsula and the islands of Indonesia. Some ichthyologists believe that this tropical region along with India and Sri Lanka are the original home of the Cyprinidae, one of whose representatives, the goldfish, is considered to be the earliest domesticated aquarium fish. Many colorful and popular aquarium fish, some highly specialized for a particular life-style, can be found living in this region. Examples include the air-breathing anabantoids, bottom-feeding loaches and the predatory nandids.

E AFRICAN LAKE FISHES

The southward-running Great Rift Valley System branches east and west from Lake Turkana (Rudolf), cradles the basins of Lakes Albert, Edward, Kivu, Tanganyika and Malawi, plus enfolds the basin of Lake Victoria.

This unique biogeographic region has become a prime source of tropical fishes. Here can be found many uniquely developed and specialized African cichlids, as well as representatives of the unusual genera *Polypterus, Protopterus* and *Synodontis.*

AUSTRALIAN FISHES

Although they support fewer freshwater fishes than other parts of the world, Australia, New Zealand and New Guinea do have a number of fascinating aquarium residents. Rivers in northern and eastern Australia may not be as extensive as those of Asia or South America, but they do have an abundance of fish. Typically, these rivers support rainbowfishes in their upper and middle reaches, gobies in their estuaries and an assortment of perch-like species throughout. They are also home to such living fossils as the Barramundi or Australian arowana and the Australian lungfish.

PREFACE

TROPICAL FISH HABITATS

Of our sun's nine planets, the earth on which we live, with its blue brilliance and teeming with life, is the most beautiful. Since its origin, the sea has been the cradle of life, nursing innumerable forms. Among the most successful are the fishes, whose present numbers may exceed three hundred thousand species. Of these, nearly one hundred thousand species live in fresh water. A large number of these inhabit the tropical and subtropical waters of South America, Africa and Southeast Asia. Many are remarkably specialized, as the photographs on the following pages will attest. Fish are all nature's gifts, living treasures of the tropical lands and waters of our bright blue planet.

SOUTH AMERICA

When I visited the Amazon, an exporter who obtains fishes from throughout the region said that each tributary river has its own distinct varieties of fishes. This explains how the waters of the Amazon can support 2,500-3,000 fish species, and why within the South American region, the total number of freshwater fish species approaches 5,000.

The Amazon has its origins in the Andes, flowing rapidly down meandering valleys on the eastern slope of this enormous mountain chain, its volume increasing as it receives the waters of its many tributaries. Its flow velocity suddenly slows down as the Amazon crosses an almost flat plain which extends some 3,000 miles (4,800 km) to the Atlantic. Dropping only about 650 ft (200 m) over this distance, the plain has a grade of but ¼ inch/mile (4 mm/km). Close to 1,000 mapped tributaries drain the approximately 2.4 million square mile (6.3 million square kilometer) Amazon Basin. Rainy and dry seasons alternate in the northern and southern portions of the Amazon Basin which straddles the Northern and Southern Hemispheres. Thus for one period of the year, water runs in from the north, and the following period, the Amazon's volume is swollen with water flowing in from the south. It is said that the waters of the Amazon equal two-thirds the volume of water carried by all the rivers of the world.

The waters of the Amazon include innumerable swamps, springs, jungle brooks, as well as larger streams filled with exposed tree roots and fallen timber. This diversity of habitats affords ample scope for the evolution of specialized life-styles, resulting in the present assemblage of more than 3,000 species. It would not be an understatement to say that almost all the fishes living within the Amazon system are fantastic. These include some of the world's largest freshwater fishes such as the Pirarucu and many of the giant predatory catfishes that live in the main channels of the larger rivers. Small forest brooks support dozens of colorful characins, while the "king" of tropical fishes, the discus, lives in oxbow lakes. The Amazon is also a treasury of fish of peculiar habits and shapes, exemplified by the mimicry of the leaffish, the flat-bodied freshwater rays and many species of knifefishes. The bountiful "mother" Amazon promises to remain a treasury of aquarium fishes forever, if protected.

AFRICA

Another big river well worth the aquarist's attention is the Zaire (Congo) River in Africa. More than 500 species have been reported from this river which stretches 2,700 miles (4,400 km) from source to mouth. As the Zaire Basin has not been fully explored by ichthyologists, the inventory of its fishes remains incomplete. Many colorful fishes also live in the brooks and rivers of the tropical rain forests or jungles stretching from the estuary of the Zaire, northwestwards to that of the Senegal. Among these are the vividly colored cichlids called "Jewel Fish" by aquarists, upside-down catfish with their peculiar swimming orientation and the weakly electric, elephant-nose fishes or mormyrids. Their mysterious behavior and morphology are no less fascinating than those of the Amazon fishes. Fishes of western Africa are not exported in numbers to compare with those of Amazonia, but aquarists' interest in this region will no doubt increase as more of its attractive fish are introduced to the hobby.

The most interesting African fishes at present available to aquarists are the cichlids native to the Great Rift Valley lakes of Tanganyika and Malawi in eastern Africa. These lakes were formed relatively recently, sometime between ten and two million years ago. So far, about 500 species in Lake Malawi and 200 in Lake Tanganyika have been recognized, and these along with the approximately 300 in nearby Lake Victoria represent the better part of around 2,000 cichlids known globally. It is certain that unknown species remain to be discovered there, and it appears likely that in many instances several distinct species have been lumped under a single name. The evolution of new species is actively in progress, so that several steps in this process may actually be observed. Accordingly, these lakes may be considered a treasury for both ichthyologists and aquarists.

Another inviting group of African fishes are the rivulins. These wonderful fishes include many species with brilliant coloration and elegant finnage. Many are annual killifishes whose eggs have the marvelous ability to survive the African dry season buried in the mud of their seasonally flooded habitats.

SOUTHEAST ASIA

As this area has long been a focus of ornamental fish exportation, many species are readily available to aquarists and enjoy much popularity. Anabantoid fishes, among them the Siamese Fighting Fish *Betta splendens,* have a labyrinth or accessory air-breathing organ. These elegant fish also show spectacular spawning behavior. Their spawning display below the foam nest provides a fresh thrill to the viewer each and every time. Cyprinid fishes dominate the fresh waters of SE Asia. Of these, Rosy and Sumatra barbs, as well as the many colorful rasboras are among the most familiar to aquarists. However, larger cyprinids such as the so-called "sharks" of the genera *Epalzeorhynchos* and *Labeo* are also popular aquarium residents.

TROPICAL FISH PRODUCING COUNTRIES

These days, 300-500 species of freshwater tropical fishes are imported annually into North America, Europe and Japan. Imports include not only the many fish collected in their native habitat, but also those cultured in such places as Sri Lanka, Singapore, Thailand and Hong Kong. Fish farmers in Florida supply significant numbers of ornamental fish to the North American domestic market and export almost as many to Europe and Japan.

SOUTHEAST ASIA

Tropical fish exported to Europe, the U.S.A. and Japan, are cultured on a large scale in Singapore, Bangkok and Hong Kong. Most are fishes native to the region, which gives Asian fish farmers a real advantage. Breeding techniques for them are quite sophisticated. Artificial stimulation of fish breeding on a large scale using hormone injections is a common prac-

tice. However, many exotic species such as livebearers, neon tetras, and most recently, Lake Malawi cichlids are also produced in SE Asia. Fish breeders in this part of the world have long been famous for their skill in producing catatechnic, or artificially selected varieties of ornamental fishes. The famous Red Royal Blue Discus is an example of such a catatechnic race developed in SE Asia.

GERMANY

Among the fishes imported from Germany are tank-bred discus and many varieties of African cichlids. These include rare species of West African dwarf cichlids, Tanganyikan cichlids such as *Tropheus* and *Lamprologus,* as well as Malawian cichlids of the genera *Aulonacara* and *Cyrtocara.* Since available water supplies in Germany are not suitable for many aquarium fishes, sophisticated techniques to adjust water chemistry in order to successfully maintain and breed "problem species" have been developed. This has led to the development of much excellent equipment and the publication of outstanding reference texts on all aspects of fish keeping. German aquarium products are also exported world-wide, while for the benefit of aquarists who cannot read German, many important works on the care and breeding of aquarium fishes have been translated into other languages.

U.S.A.

Large-scale tropical fish farms in Florida take advantage of an ideal climate and plentiful water supply to mass produce many varieties of ornamental fish. Livebearers are an important Florida export, but many egg-laying species are also bred by local fish farmers. Most of the fish produced in Florida are sold to North American buyers. However, a growing per-

centage is exported to Europe and Japan. New York and Los Angeles are also important transshipping points for fish being exported from West Africa and South America respectively.

JAPAN

At present, most freshwater tropical fishes sold in Japan are imported as local producers cannot compete with SE Asian fish farmers costwise. Other major reasons for the degeneration of tropical fish culture in Japan may be the fundamental lack of publicity and efforts to make the general public aware of the pleasure of keeping tropical fishes, along with only brief survival of non-specialist amateur aquarist clubs.

CITES,* which aims to protect animals threatened with extinction by restricting or prohibiting their trade, includes a number of endangered fishes in the appendices. Supporting trade of such fish for home aquarium sales must be opposed and not tolerated by all aquarists as such trade threatens the existence of these fish in their native habitat.

It is certain that the world of tropical aquarium fish will further develop in Japan as more unfamiliar fishes are introduced from various places throughout the world in the future. We hope that continuous efforts to develop more excellent aquarium techniques and to bring others into the aquarium hobby will lead to a breakthrough in the current status of Japanese aquarists.

Our sincere wish is that this volume will not only be read as a tabletop book, but also serve as a sourcebook for identification/ coloration comparison and understanding of the life history of tropical fishes.

*Convention on International Trade in Endangered Species of Wild Fauna and Flora (CITES).

•SCOPE AND ORGANIZATION OF THIS BOOK

This book comprises observations on the behavior and care of aquarium fishes from the fresh and brackish waters of the world. Although the term "aquarium fish" can also include marine fishes, these are not covered herein. On the other hand, this work does discuss fishes from subtropical, temperate, and even subboreal regions as well as those from tropical areas. All taxa (some 78 families of 21 orders) included in this book are listed in systematic order in the HIGHER LEVEL CLASSIFICATION table on pages 2 and 3.

There are eleven chapters in this book. Their arrangement does not reflect the evolutionary relationships of fishes. Rather, they are grouped in the order that the authors felt would best suit an atlas of aquarium fish. An overview of each family is provided at the beginning of each chapter, while an effort has been made to group similar fish together in the text. Families that comprise numerous aquarium fishes, such as CICHLIDS (Chapter 4), are further subdivided and a synopsis provided, usually by genus, for its major groups. On the other hand, Chapter 11 serves as a catchall for primitive and miscellaneous species. Also, fishes with a preference for brackish water are grouped together in Chapter 10 because of their similar maintenance needs. Therefore, each chapter can be read independently of the others without any loss of information.

Most ornamental fish behave naturally in the aquarium if their captive environment is favorable to its expression. The life-styles fishes have evolved over the long history of the earth are spectacular. At the beginning of each chapter, representative species of the family or families discussed therein have been photographed in an aquatic environment designed to allow them to express their distinctive life-styles. We have included as many such photographs as possible to give readers some idea of how these fish live in nature. Additionally, numerous photos of fish without backgrounds are included. This allows us to cover the largest possible number of species in the available space. Preference has been given to photos of representative species of each taxon. Also, many photos have been selected to allow for meristic counts such as number of fin rays and lateral line scales to be determined for the fish shown.

As noted above, representative life-styles of each group of fishes are photographically depicted at the beginning of each chapter. Information on adult length, distribution, behavior and husbandry of many species follow together with a representative selection of photos. This information will assist the reader in preparing a favorable aquarium environment for the aquarist's fish. We highly recommend using a convenient test kit to measure the pH (degree of alkalinity-acidity) and degree of hardness of a tank's water, then adjusting conditions to match the water quality preference described for the species to be placed in the aquarium.

Acknowledgements

In addition to the authors' personal observations and experience in maintaining the fishes discussed in these pages, numerous supplementary sources have been consulted during the preparation of this volume. Although the authors and titles of these publications are not cited, we do want to express sincere thanks to all of our predecessors.

We also wish to extend our gratitude to Mr. Takeshi Shimizu and Mr. Neal M. Teitler, who translated our book into English, thus making it available to aquarists throughout the world who cannot read Japanese, and to Dr. Paul V. Loiselle, who has both updated the scientific and common names of many of the fishes as well as added his own special insights during the editing process.

On behalf of the authors,

Atsushi Sakurai
June, 1992

FAMILY **CITHARINIDAE**
  SUBFAMILY DISTICHODONTINAE
    Genera *Distichodus*
      Nannaethiops
      Neolebias
      Phago
FAMILY **ALESTIIDAE**
      (African Tetras)
  Genera *Arnoldichthys*
    Brycinus
    Hemigrammopetersius
    Micralestes
    Phenacogrammus
FAMILY **HEMIODONTIDAE**
  SUBFAMILY PARODONTINAE
    Genus *Parodon*
  SUBFAMILY HEMIODONTINAE
    Genus *Hemiodopsis*
FAMILY **CURIMATIDAE**
  SUBFAMILY PROCHILODONTINAE
    Genus *Semaprochilodus*
  SUBFAMILY ANOSTOMINAE
    Genera *Abramites*
      Anostomus
      Leporinus
  SUBFAMILY CHILODONTINAE
    Genus *Chilodus*
FAMILY **ERYTHRINIDAE**
      (Trahiras)
  Genera *Hoplerythrinus*
    Hoplias

FAMILY **LEBIASINIDAE**
  SUBFAMILY PYRRHULININAE
    Genera *Copella*
      Nannobrycon
      Nannostomus
      Pyrrhulina
FAMILY **GASTEROPELECIDAE**
      (Freshwater
      Hatchetfishes)
  Genera *Carnegiella*
    Gasteropelecus
    Thoracocharax
FAMILY **CTENOLUCIIDAE**
      (Pike-Characids)
  Genera *Boulengerella*
    Ctenolucius
FAMILY **CHARACIDAE**
      (Characins)
  Genera *Acestrorhynchus*
    Anoptichthys
    Aphyocharax
    Astyanax
    Boehlkea
    Chalceus
    Crenuchus
    Exodon
    Gnathocharax
    Gymnocorymbus
    Hasemania
    Hemigrammus
    Hyphessobrycon

Inpaichthys
Megalamphodus
Moenkhausia
Nematobrycon
Paracheirodon
Petitella
Phoxinopsis
Prionobrama
Pristella
Roeboides
Tetragonopterus
Thayeria
Triportheus
  SUBFAMILY GLANDULOCAUDINAE
    Genus *Pseudocorynopoma*
  SUBFAMILY SERRASALMINAE
      (Piranhas & allies)
    Genera *Colossoma*
      Metynnis
      Myleus
      Mylossoma
      Serrasalmus
  SUBFAMILY CHARACIDIINAE
    Genus *Characidium*
  SUBFAMILY STETHAPRIONINAE
    Genus *Poptella*

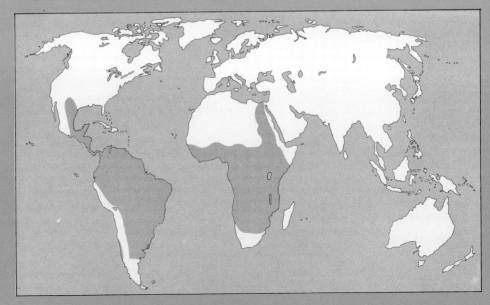

A *Paracheirodon axelrodi, Hyphessobrycon griemi,* etc. Cardinal, flame and other tetras swimming in a well laid out, planted community tank.

A *Distichodus affinis.* Silver Distichodus. Fishes of this genus are representative of medium- to large-sized African characoids.

CHARACOIDS

Over 1,300 species of characoid fishes are known to science. These highly diverse fishes are distributed from Mexico to South America and throughout tropical Africa. Characoids (Order Characiformes) are closely related to carps and minnows (Order Cypriniformes). They differ from them in having teeth in the jaws and in most cases, an adipose fin. On the other hand, characoids lack the pharyngeal teeth and barbels characteristic of the Cypriniformes.

Characoids display diverse feeding habits. Some species are carnivorous, attacking other fish, devouring them entirely or else feeding on their prey's fins or scales. Yet others feed on invertebrates or are herbivores. Habitat preferences also vary greatly, from rapidly moving waters to stagnant marshes. Their life-styles are also diverse. Midwater, surface and even bottom-dwelling species are known. Not surprisingly, characoids fill a wide range of ecological niches and exhibit many different anatomical and behavioral specializations.

In the aquarists' world, characoids from South America, most notably from the Amazon Basin, have long been popular. These range from the small tetras to the medium- and large-sized types represented by the Pink-Tailed Characin and the genera *Metynnis* and *Colossoma*. There are also many characteristically impressive characoids in and around the Zaire River in Africa.

Introduced on the following pages are nine families of characoids including the Citharinidae, Hemiodontidae and Anostomidae.

B *Brycinus longipinnus*. Long-Finned African Tetra.

C *Phenacogrammus interruptus*. Congo Tetra.

D *Distichodus sexfasciatus*. Short-Nosed Clown Tetra.

E *Arnoldichthys spilopterus*. Red-Eyed Characin.

AFRICAN CHARACOIDS

Large-sized, representative forms such as the piscivorous and aggressive Tiger Fish or the African Pike, and the pugnacious, but strikingly beautiful, Clown Tetra, add an element of wildness to the aquarium. However, as these large fishes are strongly territorial, they do not exist peacefully with others. On the other hand, when they are kept by themselves, their conspicuous characteristics and beauty can be well appreciated.

Small-sized African characoids include the Congo and Yellow Congo Tetras. They are mild tempered, prefer to school and do best when kept in a large, well-planted community aquarium.

A *Serrasalmus calmoni*. Dusky Piranha. Sharp teeth and strong jaws are the Piranha's main assets. They're skittish and predatory in an aquarium.

B *Colossoma* sp. Red Pacu.

C *Mylossoma aureum*. Golden Mylossoma.

D *Semaprochilodus taeniurus*. Colored Prochilodus.

E *Chalceus macrolepidotus*. Pink-Tailed Chalceus.

NOTES ON PIRANHAS

There are many stories about piranhas, some of which are true and others which are overstated. Through care in aquaria, much of the mystery surrounding them has been cleared up as information has been accumulated and understanding of their behavior has further developed. The authors had the opportunity to angle for piranha in the Amazon, about an hour upstream from Manaus. At every cast of the bait, the piranha bit as it began to sink. Yet, at the same time before our very eyes, boys were bathing in the same water. Piranhas in this location were said to be safe as no one had been attacked by them. Of the possible sixteen known species, four are said to be dangerous, and the behavior of even these varies in degree depending upon their habitat.

Piranhas have the power with their strong jaws and razor sharp teeth to cut through the bones of fish in a single bite. They can even cut through a steel angling hook, $\frac{1}{32}$ in. (1 mm) in diameter. In the Brazil-ian state of Mato Grosso, over 1,200 cattle are reportedly eaten annually. Some states in the U.S. prohibit the import of these ferocious fish. In nature, piranhas can be found living in most of the rivers of South America, east of the Andes. They are particularly common in the Amazon and its tributaries.

When first placed in an aquarium, they seem to be rather timid. Once they become accustomed to the tank, their original appetite returns and they can swallow a goldfish or loach in a single horrendous bite. Caution is needed in handling piranhas. The authors have heard of a case where someone's finger was bitten off while he was replacing turbid water.

A *Carnegiella marthae* (left). Black-Winged Hatchetfish. *C. strigata* (right). Marble Hatchetfish.

B *Metynnis hypsauchen*. Plain Metynnis young.

A *Nannostomus espei*. Barred or Espe's Pencilfish.   **1** Pair spawning on a Ruffled Swordplant.

CHARACOID BREEDING TECHNIQUES AND SPAWNING BEHAVIOR

There are three major types of spawning behavior in characins. Pairs of the first type spawn by dashing about together or quivering side by side and then laying either adhesive or non-adhesive eggs on water plants or sand. Included in this type are the small-sized characoids known as tetras, and many medium to large

2 Exhibiting elegant markings.

species such as the Pink-Tailed Characin. Although there are differences among the many species, this spawning behavior is the most representative of the group.

When the spawning season arrives, prepare a suitable, well-aerated aquarium and cover the entire bottom with Java moss or synthetic yarn mops. As most characins are sensitive to water quality, be sure to check pH and hardness as well as water temperature. After spawning is completed, remove the parents

1 ♂ (above) enticing ♀.

2 Pair picking spawning site.

B *Nannobrycon eques.* Three-Striped Pencilfish. **3** Moment of spawning.

4 Eggs attached to underside of leaf.

and add a bit of methylene blue to keep the eggs from fungusing. Eggs hatch within 1-3 days, and the fry become free swimming within 4-5 days after that. Begin feeding them at this point.

The second type, as exemplified by the pencilfishes, lays eggs on the underside of leaves. A small aquarium with broad-leaved water plants such as Amazon Swordplants is recommended for spawning. Parents should be removed after spawning as they may eat the eggs.

The genus *Copella* is an example of the third type which spawns side by side, laying eggs on stones or leaves. Since the male cares for the eggs and young fry, he should be left with the eggs after spawning.

B 1 Male positions the female under a leaf by poking her on the dorsal side.
2 If satisfied, she somersaults and pretends to spawn. They do not clean the spawning site as do cichlids.
3 Side by side, spawning commences on the underside of a leaf.
4 Eggs, 1/2 in. (1 mm) in diameter and numbering 30-100, are laid on the leaf.

A *Leporinus affinis*. Banded Leporinus.

B *Hemiodopsis fowleri.* Slender Hemiodus.

C *Exodon paradoxus.* Bucktoothed Tetra.

D *Leporinus* sp.

E *Abramites hypselonotus.* Headstander.

F *Anostomus anostomus.* Striped Headstander.

G *Leporinus maculatus.* Dwarf Leporinus.

A *Paracheirodon innesi.* Neon Tetra. One of the most popular tropicals, it shares this position with guppies and angelfish. A school swimming is always eye catching.

B *Inpaichthys kerri.* Blue Emperor.

C *Petitella georgiae.* False Rummy Nose Tetra.

D *Nematobrycon palmeri*. Emperor Tetra.

E *Hyphessobrycon erythrostigma*. Bleeding Heart Tetra.

F *Megalamphodus sweglesi*. Red Phantom Tetra.

G *Moenkhausia pittieri*. Diamond or Pitter's Tetra.

H *Nannostomus trifasciatus*. Three-Lined Pencilfish.

I *Astyanax fasciatus mexicanus*. Blind Cave Tetra.

NATIVE HABITAT OF TETRAS

Brooks flowing through the Amazonian jungle are the native habitats of the small characins known as tetras. Light shines through the foliage. These slow-flowing waters are brown, but clear, the bottom covered with decaying leaves, slightly acidic (pH 5.5-6.3), around 0°DH hardness and a rather low temperature of about 72-75°F (22-24°C). Intermittent thick clumps of underwater plants can be found in the brooks, while heavy growths of grass or bushes line their banks. Tetras may also be found in the main stem of the Amazon as well as in its associated oxbow lakes.

J *Copella metae*. Black-Banded Copella. 2 in. (5 cm). Formerly known as *Pyrrhulina nigrofasciatus*. Distributed throughout the Amazon River, which supports a number of undescribed species of this genus.

2 Black Phantom Tetra.

Although small characins can be kept in small aquaria, it is recommended that they be placed in large aquaria along with quite a few other fish of related species so that they can be observed behaving as they would in their native habitat. In nature they form schools. Mild-tempered and attractive in all aspects of figure, shape and coloration, they may be more charming when kept in groups rather than by themselves. Most species prefer slightly acidic, soft water. The aquarium should be set up with a combination of clumps of water plants and a few open spaces, the latter for free-swimming activity. This would be at best, similar to the jungle waters of the Amazon.

While some species swim near the surface, others tend to move along the bottom. During some periods, some may establish a territory while courting a female. Others may circle with extended fins. When we observe such enchanting aquaria, we are apt to lose track of the passage of time.

A 1-2 Spawning Black Phantom Tetras. Male and female fully spread their fins as they near the finely leaved plants, quiver as they come close together, and then quickly break apart. At this moment, the non-adhesive eggs are discharged and sink into the fine foliage below.
B Beckford's Pencilfish spawns weakly adhesive eggs among finely leaved aquatic plants or on the bottom. As they don't care for the eggs, but rather eat them after spawning, separation is necessary.
C Head-and-Tail-Light Tetras spawn while dashing through plants to which the spawn adhesive eggs attach.
D Spawning Black Tetras. Lay 300-1,500 transparent, adhesive eggs in a single spawning that cling to water plants.
E An unidentified pair of *Pyrrhulina* species laying eggs on a broad leaf. Eggs are either simultaneously fertilized as the pair are positioned side by side, or the male ejaculates sperm shortly thereafter. The male remains and cares for the eggs until they hatch.

A *Megalamphodus megalopterus*. Black Phantom Tetra. **1** Just discharged eggs sinking.

B *Nannostomus beckfordi.* Beckford's Pencilfish.

C *Hemigrammus ocellifer.* Head-and-Tail-Light Tetra.

D *Gymnocorymbus ternetzi.* Black Tetra.

E *Pyrrhulina* sp. spawning. ♂ (front).

A *Boulengerella lateristriga*. The so-called South American Pike Characin.

B *Phago maculatus*. African Fin-Eating Characin.

C *Ctenolucius hujeta*. The so-called South American Freshwater Needlefish.

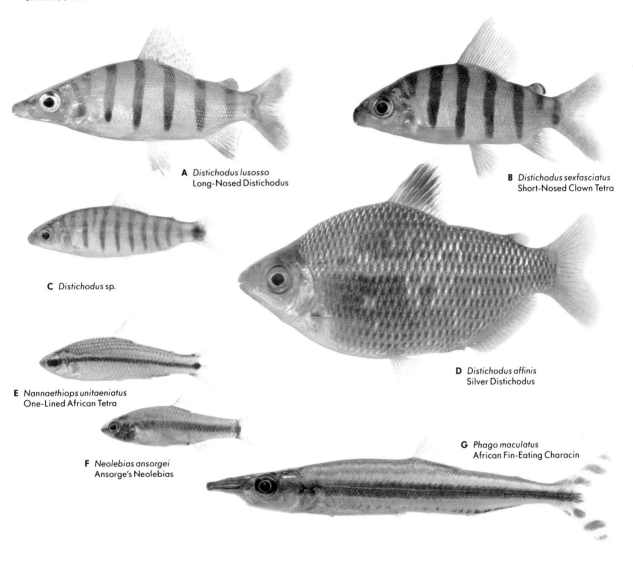

A *Distichodus lusosso*
Long-Nosed Distichodus

B *Distichodus sexfasciatus*
Short-Nosed Clown Tetra

C *Distichodus* sp.

D *Distichodus affinis*
Silver Distichodus

E *Nannaethiops unitaeniatus*
One-Lined African Tetra

F *Neolebias ansorgei*
Ansorge's Neolebias

G *Phago maculatus*
African Fin-Eating Characin

A Needs a large aquarium as they can reach a max. length of 28-32 in. (70-80 cm). Zaire R. Beautiful stripes when young become more uniformly black as it matures. Pugnacious, so requires care in selecting tank mates. No record of breeding.

B 24-28 in. (60-80 cm). Lower to middle reaches of Zaire R. Beautiful, hardy and care is easy. Although it prefers live food such as blood worms, it is mainly herbivorous, requiring slightly boiled spinach or lettuce. As with the above species, it is best kept by itself.

C Similar to young *D. fasciolatus*, but lacks that species' black spots. Seems to be a distinct species. Habitat is believed to be in W. Africa.

D 8 in. (20 cm). Zaire R. When young, the red dorsal, pelvic and anal fins combined with its slightly inclined swimming manner, present a pretty picture. As it grows, the body blackens and silver scales become highly reflective, offering an appearance of elegant simplicity.

E 2½ in. (6.5 cm). Niger to Zaire R Basin. Mild-mannered, this fish can coexist with many South American characins. Not sensitive to water quality, but sudden changes of water should be avoided.

F 1½ in. (3.5 cm). Central Africa. Prefers slightly acid water. When in good physical condition, the fins are scarlet. Can be bred in aquaria. Male holds female in a sigmoid position as they spawn.

G 6¼ in. (16 cm). Niger. Piscivorous; both bill-like jaws have 22 teeth which help it eat the fins of other fish or whole small fish. On the other hand, it is quite nervous, staying mainly in the corner of the aquarium. A large aquarium with a number of refuges is recommended. It is fairly rare, as imports are few.

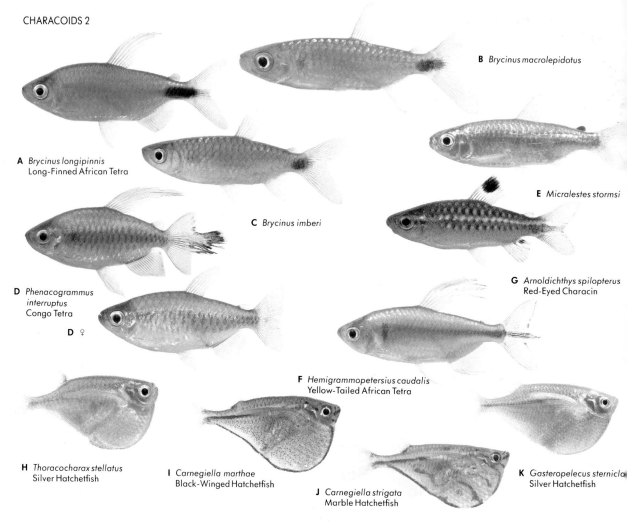

B *Brycinus macrolepidotus*

A *Brycinus longipinnis*
Long-Finned African Tetra

E *Micralestes stormsi*

C *Brycinus imberi*

D *Phenacogrammus interruptus*
Congo Tetra

D ♀

G *Arnoldichthys spilopterus*
Red-Eyed Characin

F *Hemigrammopetersius caudalis*
Yellow-Tailed African Tetra

H *Thoracocharax stellatus*
Silver Hatchetfish

I *Carnegiella marthae*
Black-Winged Hatchetfish

J *Carnegiella strigata*
Marble Hatchetfish

K *Gasteropelecus sternicla*
Silver Hatchetfish

A 5 in. (13 cm). Western Africa. Prefers neutral to slightly acid water. Hardy, care is easy. Good-looking midwater swimmer, it coexists well with other fishes. Strongly herbivorous, it may eat plants in the aquarium. Breeding in aquaria is easy, and in its early stages, fry will eat brine shrimp.

B 12-16 in. (30-40 cm). Nile to Zaire R. Pugnacious by nature, it will attack the same or other species even when it is just 2 in. (5 cm) long. Solitary care or in a school of same-sized fish is recommended. As it is rather high-priced however, the latter method may be difficult. Readily eats any food including flakes.

C 9 in. (23 cm). Cameroon to Kasai. Prefers slightly acidic water. Previously placed in the genus *Alestes*. Lately, many have been exported. Sexing is difficult, and breeding in aquaria has not been accomplished. Aggressive by nature, it should be kept by itself or in a school of same-sized congeners. Herbivorous, they eat aquarium plants.

D ♂ 3¼ in. (8 cm), ♀ 2¼ in. (6 cm). Central Africa, Zaire R Basin. When maintained as a school of adults within a well-planted aquarium, they will exhibit a show of overwhelming beauty, their rainbow colors constantly changing as they move about. Prefer slightly acid, soft water. Omnivorous, they breed readily in aquaria, with eggs hatching within 4-5 days.

E 2 in. (5 cm). Zaire R Basin. Named for the red adipose fin. Prefers slightly acid, soft water. Few of this active, mild-tempered species are imported separately. Rather, they appear as "contaminants" mixed in with other types of fish. As there are many attractive, small species within *Micralestes*, future imports of these desirable aquarium fish can be expected.

F 2¼-2¾ in. (6-7 cm). Zaire R. Named for its yellow tail, it is imported mixed with the Congo Tetra. Rather rare, it prefers slightly acid, soft water. Readily eats flakes or live foods such as blood worms. A somewhat nervous, delicate fish.

G 4 in. (10 cm). Niger R. Pugnacious, it does not coexist peacefully with other small-sized characins. It should be kept in small groups of its own kind in a splendid, landscaped (wood, rocks, many plants) aquarium. The tank needs to be covered as it frequently jumps. Although it prefers insects such as flies, it readily accepts blood worms and flakes. No record of breeding in aquaria.

H 2¾ in. (7 cm). Stagnant lake, pond, swamp waters of Amazon Basin. A large, well-planted aquarium with a wide open space above the plants is recommended. As in the wild it eats insects that have fallen into the water, flies or ants are preferred, but will become accustomed to flakes. Prefers slightly acid water.

I 1½ in. (3.5 cm). Negro R, Orinoco R, Peru, Venezuela. Lives in slow-flowing waters of jungle brooks, ponds and lakes. When threatened, they can jump 10-16 ft (3-5 m) from the water surface.

J 1¾ in. (4.5 cm). Western Guiana to the lower reaches of the Amazon. Like other hatchetfish, it prefers slightly acid, soft water. Sexing is difficult, breeding behavior is not well known, but this egg-scatterer has been recorded to have spawned on the stems of *Myriophyllum*.

K 2¼ in. (6 cm). Guiana and lower reaches of the Amazon. Prefers slightly acid, soft

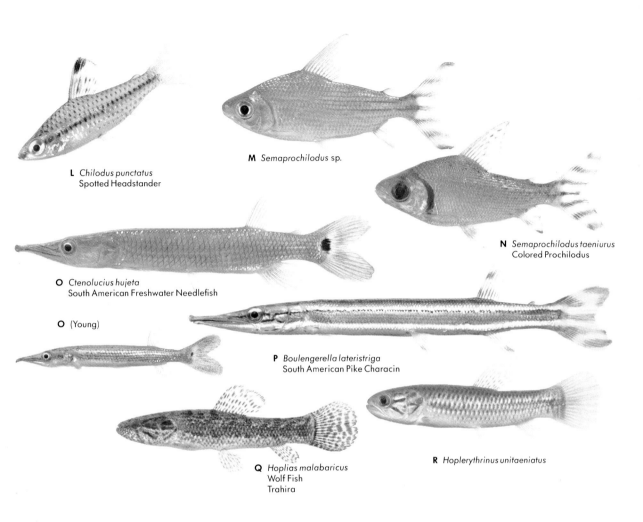

L *Chilodus punctatus*
Spotted Headstander

M *Semaprochilodus* sp.

N *Semaprochilodus taeniurus*
Colored Prochilodus

O *Ctenolucius hujeta*
South American Freshwater Needlefish

O (Young)

P *Boulengerella lateristriga*
South American Pike Characin

Q *Hoplias malabaricus*
Wolf Fish
Trahira

R *Hoplerythrinus unitaeniatus*

water. Coexists best in a well-planted aquarium with bottom-swimming fishes, because when kept with active, top-swimming fishes, its appetite appears to diminish. Rather hardy, its care is easy. Breeding in aquaria has not been accomplished yet.

L 3½ in. (9 cm). Widely distributed in northern South America—Venezuela, Guiana, Peru, Brazil. Prefers slightly acid water. Eats blood worms and sometimes, soft grasses. Breeding is rather easy. Lays 400-500 rather large (½-⅒ in. or 2-2.5 mm in diam.) eggs. Fry begin eating brine shrimp after becoming free-swimming, moving with the head inclined downward.

M, N 12-16 in. (30-40 cm). Guiana to Amazon. Fishes imported under this name also include those in the genus *Semaprochilodus*. Members of this genus feature a compressed body and lips that turn inside-out when the mouth is opened. The mouth has file-like teeth which are used for grazing on moss. Those with many spots on the body are commonly called "Spotted Prochilodus," while those without, "Silver Prochilodus." Actual identification is difficult, however, due to the lack of readily distinguishable diagnostic characters. Rather mild-mannered in aquaria. Basically herbivorous, they will also take live food. Prefer neutral to slightly acid water. Frequently jump out of the tank. If conditions are favorable, they're long-lived. No breeding yet recorded.

O 28 in. (70 cm). Magdalena R in Colombia, Venezuela, Panama. Also known as the "Silver Gar" after its shininess when young. Piscivorous, it's a voracious eater that will consume a fish half its size. A large, wood and rock-scaped aquarium is recommended. Should be kept by itself or only with other large fish. Doesn't tolerate new water, so

only ⅓ should be replaced at any one time. External sexual characteristics are not distinguishable. Spawnings have been reported in Germany and Japan. Eggs are sprayed out over the water surface, sinking and adhering to leaves and rocks. At 82°F (28°C), eggs hatch within two days, and the larvae become free-swimming after 4-5 days.

P 20 in. (50 cm). Negro R. Live in ditches thick with reeds, eating small fish or aquatic insects. In aquaria, they are highly skittish, darting against the glass at even the slightest sound, frequently dying from injuries to the snout thus incurred. It is recommended that they be kept in a large tank stocked with plant and woody refuges. Tank placement should be in a quiet spot where they will not be startled. Other same-sized or larger peaceful fish may be placed in the same tank.

Q 20 in. (50 cm). Widely distributed from Costa Rica and Panama to Ecuador, South America. Piscivorous, ambushes approaching small fish in the ditch from behind reeds or rocks. Coloring and markings vary greatly among the young, but these fade to a uniformly brown pattern during its rather uninteresting growth. No breeding recorded.

R Said to reach 40 in. (1 m) in their native habitat. South America. Piscivorous and voracious. Active and has black lines on sides when young. Inhabiting small brooks or ponds, they have been observed moving across land at night. Due to the activity of the special respiratory area on the anterior portion of the swim bladder, they are able to live in water with a low oxygen content.

29

A *Metynnis roosevelti*
Spotted Metynnis

B *Metynnis hypsauchen*
Plain Metynnis

C *Myleus rubripinnis*
Redhook Metynnis

D *Metynnis argenteus*
Silver Dollar

E *Mylossoma aureum*
Golden Mylossoma

F *Serrasalmus nattereri*
Red-Bellied Piranha

A 2 in. (5 cm). Maximum length unknown. Amazon Basin. Metynnis are strongly herbivorous, frequently nibbling on aquatic vegetation. Grow quickly and have a good appetite when raised in schools of about ten individuals. Breeding in aquaria is difficult, but has been accomplished.

B 7 in. (18 cm). Widely distributed in Amazon Basin. Prefer slightly acidic, hard (10-15°DH) water. Omnivorous. Boiled lettuce or spinach should be included to provide for their mainly herbivorous diet. Breeding is easy. Under favorable conditions, a pair will spawn side by side, quivering near stones or wood on which about 2,000 eggs will be released. Larvae begin eating brine shrimp at a very early stage.

C 6-8 in. (15-20 cm). Amazon Basin. Most popular metynnis, it has an identifiable red, modified hook to the anal fin. Sometimes eat aquarium plants, but spinach or other vegetable matter should be fed as a regular part of the diet. Prefers slightly acidic, hard water. Can be bred, but requires skill.

D 8 in. (20 cm). About twenty species of *Metynnis* are known, most reaching about 8 in. (20 cm) at maturity, medium-sized for characins. This species, from the Amazon Basin and Guiana, is not so popular. Vegetable matter plus foods formulated for carp are recommended for its diet.

E 10 in. (25 cm). Amazon Basin, Paraguay, La Plata R. Prefers slightly acidic, soft

G *Colossoma* sp.
Red Pacu

H *Colossoma bidens*
Black Pacu

water. Mild-mannered, it can be kept with other fishes of the same size. Nibbles on aquatic plants. Male has an anal fin larger than that of the female. No record of being bred in an aquarium.

F 12 in. (30 cm) in nature, 8 in. (20 cm) in aquaria. Widely distributed throughout tropical South America. Prefers slightly acidic, soft water, but can tolerate alkaline conditions. Feed small live fish, cut-up fish or steamed chicken. Does not peacefully coexist with other species, but it is recommended that they be kept in schools of ten or more in a large aquarium. Two pair off from the school for spawning, and afterwards, the male guards the eggs.

G 28 in. (70 cm). Amazon Basin. *Colossoma* spp. unlike the carnivorous piranha, are strongly herbivorous, and in fact, are caught in the Amazon by using citrus fruit for bait. A very large aquarium is needed as they soon outgrow the normal home one.

H Max. size unknown, but seem to reach or exceed size of the Red Colossoma. Amazon Basin. Eats almost any food including pellets and small fish. Fish of this genus have a relatively long life, said to exceed ten years.

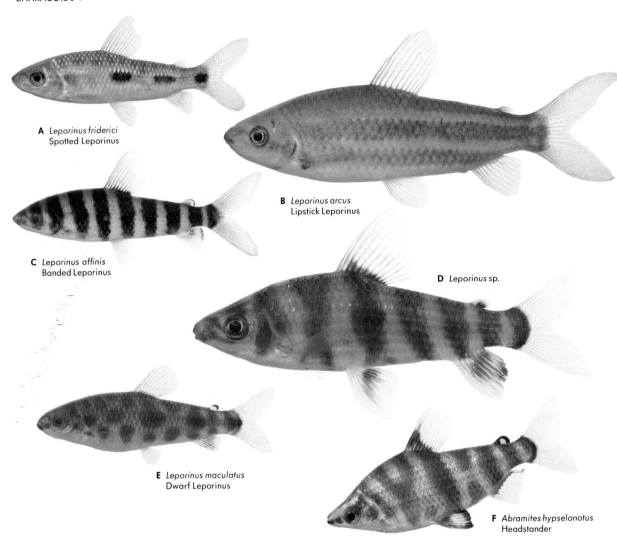

A *Leporinus friderici*
Spotted Leporinus

B *Leporinus arcus*
Lipstick Leporinus

C *Leporinus affinis*
Banded Leporinus

D *Leporinus* sp.

E *Leporinus maculatus*
Dwarf Leporinus

F *Abramites hypselonotus*
Headstander

A 14 in. (35 cm). Guiana to the Amazon Basin.

B 8 in. (20 cm). Paraguay, Uraguay, Bolivia, Ecuador, Colombia and Mato Grosso State, Brazil. Kept in a large aquarium, it will swim actively, have distinct body coloration, but as it grows, the stripes will fade out to a dull black. Herbivorous, it may eat the aquarium plants. No record of breeding in aquaria.

C 12 in. (30 cm). Wide distribution from central to northern South America. In nature, usually school over sandy pool bottoms, catching floating aquatic insects and grazing on bottom algae. Keep them in a large, wood and rock aquascaped tank. No plants are necessary as they may be eaten. Breeding has not been recorded.

D 4 in. (10 cm). *Leporinus* sp. Max. size unknown. Because its stripes and coloration resemble those of *Abramites*, it is uncertain whether this species is *L. desmotis* or not.

E 6 in. (15 cm). Amazon Basin to Guiana. Schools above bottom of pebble-covered ponds, among other fishes. Prefers slightly acidic, rather hard water. Herbivorous, it also eats live or prepared foods. In community tanks, it may nibble on the fins of other fish. Breeding is difficult, but has been reported in Japan.

F 4-5½ in. (10-14 cm). Guiana, Amazon Basin. Schools along grassy shores. Care is easy. Mild-tempered except when ripe, at which time it becomes aggressive. Prefers slightly acidic, soft water. Herbivorous, should be fed ample amounts of vegetable matter such as boiled spinach or lettuce. No record of breeding.

G 6 in. (15 cm). Abundant in the Amazon Basin, Negro R. Prefers neutral to slightly acid, soft water. Feed live foods such as blood worms, but will take dry foods. As it is strongly herbivorous, the recommendation is that the aquarium should not be planted. A very hardy, elegant species, it has a long life. Aquarium spawning has not been accomplished.

H 10 in. (25 cm). Amazon Basin to Guiana. Prefers neutral to slightly acidic, soft water. Like others of the genus, it is herbivorous and may eat planted aquatic vegetation. No record of breeding.

I 8 in. (20 cm). Western Guiana to upper reaches of the Amazon. Abundant in grassy,

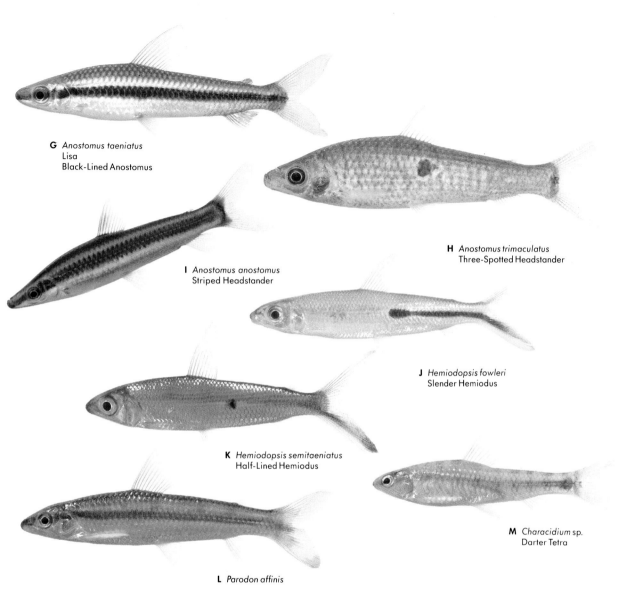

G *Anostomus taeniatus*
Lisa
Black-Lined Anostomus

H *Anostomus trimaculatus*
Three-Spotted Headstander

I *Anostomus anostomus*
Striped Headstander

J *Hemiodopsis fowleri*
Slender Hemiodus

K *Hemiodopsis semitaeniatus*
Half-Lined Hemiodus

M *Characidium* sp.
Darter Tetra

L *Parodon affinis*

stagnant waters. Prefers neutral to slightly acidic, soft water. Highly territorial behavior, aggressive towards others, but not as much when a group is kept in a large aquarium with numerous woody alcoves. They may nip at the tips of other fishes' fins, especially those with long or flowing finnage.

J 5 in. (13 cm), 9½ in. (24 cm) max. Amazon Basin. Prefers slightly acidic, soft water, and to feed on live foods such as blood worms. An active mid-water swimmer, so a large tank with a wide open space and grassy refuges is recommended. Coexists well with other fish of about the same size.

K 6-8 in. (15-20 cm). Guiana, Amazon Basin. Rather plain, but as it is active, mild-tempered and easy to care for, it can be considered attractive. Readily eats any type of food such as pellets, flakes or blood worms. As with others of this genus, the tendency to jump makes a tank cover a necessity.

L 6 in. (15 cm). La Plata R, Parana R, Paraguay Basin. Most of the characins are surface to midwater swimmers, but this species prefers the bottom of deeper waters. Its

quick movement as a blood worm is caught on the bottom of the tank gives one a feeling of the essence of characin activity.

M 2¾ in. (7 cm). Orinoco to La Plata R, South America. Prefers neutral, well-oxygenated water. Charming behavior of darting about the aquarium floor, nibbling at food. Likes live food such as blood worms, best. Lays about 150 eggs as it spawns in a pair side-by-side at the bottom. As the newly hatched, bottom-dwelling larvae have very small mouths, infusoria is the food of choice.

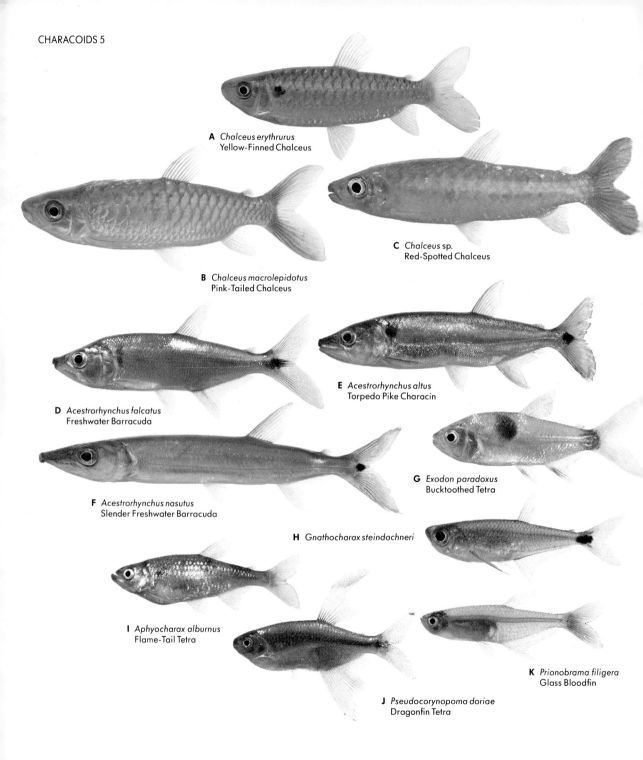

A *Chalceus erythrurus*
Yellow-Finned Chalceus

C *Chalceus* sp.
Red-Spotted Chalceus

B *Chalceus macrolepidotus*
Pink-Tailed Chalceus

E *Acestrorhynchus altus*
Torpedo Pike Characin

D *Acestrorhynchus falcatus*
Freshwater Barracuda

G *Exodon paradoxus*
Bucktoothed Tetra

F *Acestrorhynchus nasutus*
Slender Freshwater Barracuda

H *Gnathocharax steindachneri*

I *Aphyocharax alburnus*
Flame-Tail Tetra

K *Prionobrama filigera*
Glass Bloodfin

J *Pseudocorynopoma doriae*
Dragonfin Tetra

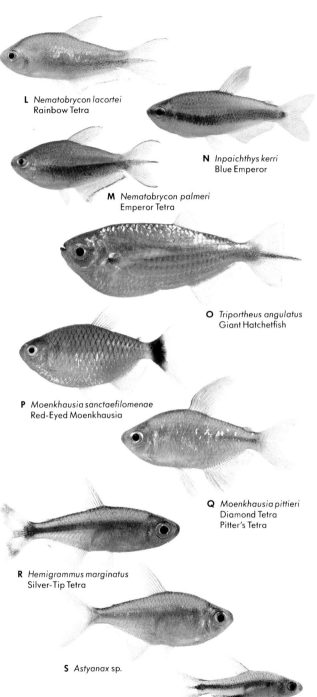

L *Nematobrycon lacortei*
Rainbow Tetra

N *Inpaichthys kerri*
Blue Emperor

M *Nematobrycon palmeri*
Emperor Tetra

O *Triportheus angulatus*
Giant Hatchetfish

P *Moenkhausia sanctaefilomenae*
Red-Eyed Moenkhausia

Q *Moenkhausia pittieri*
Diamond Tetra
Pitter's Tetra

R *Hemigrammus marginatus*
Silver-Tip Tetra

S *Astyanax sp.*

T *Phoxinopsis typicus*

A 8 in. (20 cm). Amazon Basin. So named because of the yellow-colored pelvic and anal fins. The dorsal and caudal fins are red like other members of the Chalceus genus.

B 10 in. (25 cm). Guiana to Peru. Solitary care or ten fish in a large aquarium is recommended as they tend to attack each other when there are less than ten fish in the same tank. On the other hand, they're not so aggressive towards other types of fish so can be placed with medium to large fishes, especially those that swim in mid-water or near the surface. Breeding is difficult. More than 2,000 eggs of ¹⁄₃₂-¹⁄₂₀ in. (0.8-1.2 mm) diam. are laid as the pair dash about. Larvae should be fed brine shrimp as soon as they become free-swimming.

C 8 in. (20 cm). Very similar to *C. macrolepidotus*, but is distinguished by the red spots along its side.

D Longer than 8 in. (20 cm). Positive identification is not possible as published species descriptions are sketchy, but this species appears to belong to the *A. falcatus* complex. Piscivorous, should be fed small minnows, goldfish, etc.

E Longer than 8 in. (20 cm). Amazon Basin, Paraguay R. Among the many "Torpedo Pike" characins imported, this species is the most popular. Not sensitive to water quality, but prefers slightly acid to neutral pH and 6-10°DH. Feeds on small fish– minnows, etc. Breeding in the aquarium has been recorded.

F Longer than 8 in. (20 cm). Northern Amazon Basin. Easily distinguishable from the above two species by its narrower body depth and absence of a black spot behind the upper operculum.

G 7 in. (18 cm). Guiana to Brazil. Lives in grassy-lined brooks. Prefers slightly acidic, soft water. Best kept in sizeable groups of its own kind or as solitary specimens, as adults are aggressive, eating scales off of other fish.

H 2¼ in. (6 cm). Guiana, upper reaches of Orinoco R, Amazon Basin. Prefers slightly acid, soft water. Best kept in a school, housed in a well-planted aquarium.

I 2 in. (5 cm). Brazil, Peru, Bolivia. Mild-mannered, suited for a community tank, it prefers floating foods, but readily accepts any type.

J 3¼ in. (8 cm). Southern Brazil, Uraguay, Argentina. To maintain this fish in the best physical condition, rather cool, 68-72°F (20-22°C) water is best.

K 2 in. (5 cm). Amazon Basin, especially around Madeira R. Sensitive to water quality, water should be slightly acidic and soft. Omnivorous. Breeding is easy when correct water quality is maintained. Eggs hatch within 3 days. Due to their small size, fry should be fed infusoria.

L 2¼ in. (6 cm). Calima region of Colombia. Prefers slightly acidic, soft water. Live food such as blood worms best, but will eat dry foods. Should be kept in a well-planted, woodscaped aquarium.

M 2 in. (5 cm). San Juan Basin, Pacific slope of Colombia. Slightly acidic, soft water preferable. Eats anything, making care easy. Will readily spawn in soft water kept at around 79°F (26°C). Scatters 50-100 eggs onto fine-leaved plants. Remove parents after spawning. Eggs hatch in 48 hours. Fry become free-swimming in 3-4 days, and should be fed infusoria the first week, followed by brine shrimp from the second.

N 1½ in. (4 cm). Mato Grosso State in Brazil. Not sensitive to water quality, but prefers relatively cool temperatures of 64-72°F (18-22°C). Care and breeding are easy.

O 8 in. (20 cm). Guiana, Orinoco R, Madeira R, lower reaches of the Amazon. Plain but pleasant in appearance, this fish swims in a midwater school. Exists peacefully in a community tank stocked with same-sized fish. Tank needs to be covered as it's a jumper. No breeding recorded.

P 2¼ in. (6 cm). Paraguay, Paranaiba R. Lives in brooks, swamps and marshes. Hardy, care is easy. Omnivorous, requires plants in its diet. Easily bred; it may lay more than 2,000 eggs in one spawning. Larvae should be fed infusoria the first two days, brine shrimp thereafter.

Q 2¼ in. (6 cm). Lake Valencia and vicinity in Venezuela. Omnivorous, needs plants in its diet, but care is easy. When the male's ready to spawn, its body develops a shiny black appearance.

R 2 in. (5 cm). Around Santarém, northern Brazil. Diagnostic character of note is the caudal fin marking.

S 1½ in. (4 cm). Maximum size unknown. Imported mixed in with other Amazonian species. Its mouth shape identifies it as a member of this genus.

T 1¼ in. (3 cm). Imported from the Amazon Basin, its locality is unknown as no related species are known from South America. Care is difficult as it does not eat well.

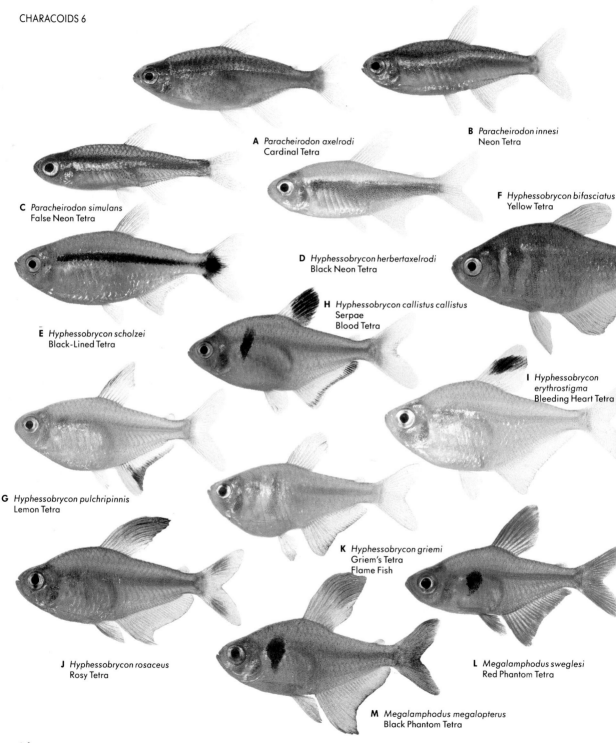

A *Paracheirodon axelrodi*
Cardinal Tetra

B *Paracheirodon innesi*
Neon Tetra

C *Paracheirodon simulans*
False Neon Tetra

F *Hyphessobrycon bifasciatus*
Yellow Tetra

D *Hyphessobrycon herbertaxelrodi*
Black Neon Tetra

E *Hyphessobrycon scholzei*
Black-Lined Tetra

H *Hyphessobrycon callistus callistus*
Serpae
Blood Tetra

I *Hyphessobrycon erythrostigma*
Bleeding Heart Tetra

G *Hyphessobrycon pulchripinnis*
Lemon Tetra

K *Hyphessobrycon griemi*
Griem's Tetra
Flame Fish

J *Hyphessobrycon rosaceus*
Rosy Tetra

L *Megalamphodus sweglesi*
Red Phantom Tetra

M *Megalamphodus megalopterus*
Black Phantom Tetra

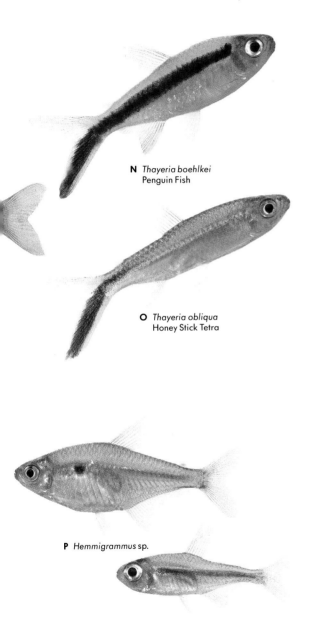

N *Thayeria boehlkei*
Penguin Fish

O *Thayeria obliqua*
Honey Stick Tetra

P *Hemmigrammus* sp.

Q *Hyphessobrycon heterorhabdus*
Flag Tetra

A 1½-2 in. (4-5 cm). Amazon Basin. Lives in jungle brooks and ponds. Prefers slightly acidic, soft water. Red abdominal band is longer and wider than in the following two species. Presents a stunning atmosphere when a school is kept by itself in a well-planted aquarium. Easily eats any type of food, but breeding is difficult.

B 1¼-1½ in. (3-4 cm). Amazon Basin. Lives in jungle brooks and ponds. Slightly acidic, soft water at cool temperatures of 70-73°F (21-23°C) preferred. Bred in a small aquarium, a pair scatters eggs on fine-leaved plants such as *Cabomba* or *Nitella*. Remove parents after spawning. Under strong aeration, eggs hatch within 12-24 hours. Due to small size of larvae, feed them infusoria.

C 1 in. (2.5 cm). Negro R. Prefers slightly acidic, soft water. Distinguished from the true Neon Tetra by its narrower body depth and blue line extending to the base of the caudal fin.

D 1¼-1½ (3-4 cm). Mato Grosso State, Brazil. Not sensitive to water quality, but prefers slightly acidic, soft water. Water temperature should be around 77°F (25°C). Does well in a small school, housed in a community tank with many other small characins. Prefers worms or other live food, but takes dried food as well.

E 1½ in. (4 cm). Near Para, Brazil. Hardy, and since it will not attack other small characins, is well suited for a community tank.

F 2 in. (5 cm). Coastal area of southeastern Brazil. Care is easy as it is hardy and not sensitive to water quality. Breeding is also easy.

G 1½-2 in. (4-5 cm). Widely distributed throughout the Amazon Basin. Not sensitive, but prefers neutral to slightly acidic, soft water. Mild-tempered and hardy, it peacefully coexists with other small characins. Spawning is easy. It lays 100-200 eggs at a time which hatch out within a day. Larvae tend to stay hidden and grow slowly.

H 1½ in. (4 cm). From Paraguay up to Mato Grosso State, Brazil. Found in slow-flowing rivers and jungle brooks, it prefers slightly acidic, soft water. If water quality is suitable, breeding is not so difficult. Spawns by circling and dashing about, laying brownish eggs. Due to the small size of the larvae, first food should be egg yolk infusion and infusoria.

I 3¼ in. (8 cm). Upper reaches of the Colombian Amazon. Prefers slightly acidic, soft water. A beautiful, relatively large-sized tetra, it is difficult to keep it in good physical condition. It is recommended that this species be maintained in a school of seven or more individuals placed in a well-planted aquarium that has many refuges.

J 1½ in. (4 cm). Essequibo R, Guyana & Guaporé R.

K 1½ in. (4 cm). Around Rio de Janeiro. Found in slow-flowing rivers or forest ponds. Care is easy as it is not sensitive to water quality, but to bring out its uniquely beautiful coloration, slightly acidic, aged water is needed. Easily bred, 100-200 eggs will be laid in a single spawning. Due to the small size of the early larval stages, they should be fed infusoria.

L 1½ in. (4 cm). Upper reaches of the Colombian Amazon. Prefers slightly acidic, soft water, but is fairly difficult to keep in top physical condition. A school of seven or more individuals is recommended to be placed in a large, well-planted aquarium that also houses other mild-tempered fishes. Breeding is fairly difficult, while growth of the larvae is slow.

M 1½ in. (4 cm). Mato Grosso, Brazil. Not sensitive, but prefers slightly acidic, soft water. It is recommended that this fish be kept in a school of a few individuals as a solitary one tends to be skittish and has a poor appetite. Breeding is rather easy when a young female is combined with a mature male that has well-developed finnage. Eggs hatch within 1-2 days, but growth of the larvae is slow.

N 2½ in. (6 cm). Grassy shallows or forest brooks of the upper reaches of the Amazon. Prefers slightly acidic, soft water. This fish's unique manner of swimming makes it an attractive addition to a community tank for which it is well suited. A mild-mannered characin, but to avoid weak teasing, it is recommended that a school be maintained. Spawning is easy, with more than 1,000 eggs being laid at one time. Even so, the larvae can eat brine shrimp from the time they hatch.

O 3¼ in. (8 cm). Lives in the bottom humus strata of grassy jungle brooks in the lower reaches of the Amazon.

P 1¼ in. (3 cm). Amazon Basin. Common, but rather nondescript species which has been occasionally identified as *H. stictus*.

Q 1¾ in. (4.5 cm). Lower reaches of the Amazon, Tocantins R. Prefers slightly acidic, soft water. Sometimes the fish will have encysted skin parasites that will give the upper part of the body a golden irridescent appearance.

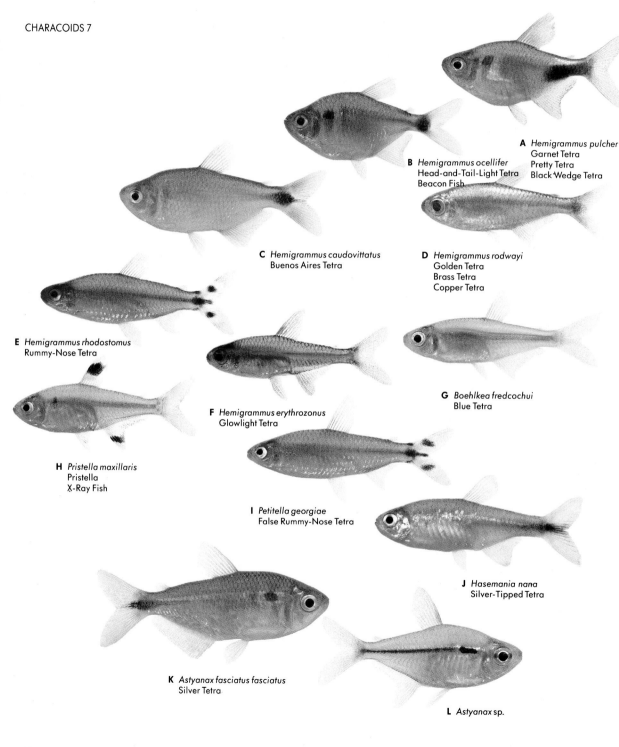

A *Hemigrammus pulcher*
Garnet Tetra
Pretty Tetra
Black Wedge Tetra

B *Hemigrammus ocellifer*
Head-and-Tail-Light Tetra
Beacon Fish

C *Hemigrammus caudovittatus*
Buenos Aires Tetra

D *Hemigrammus rodwayi*
Golden Tetra
Brass Tetra
Copper Tetra

E *Hemigrammus rhodostomus*
Rummy-Nose Tetra

F *Hemigrammus erythrozonus*
Glowlight Tetra

G *Boehlkea fredcochui*
Blue Tetra

H *Pristella maxillaris*
Pristella
X-Ray Fish

I *Petitella georgiae*
False Rummy-Nose Tetra

J *Hasemania nana*
Silver-Tipped Tetra

K *Astyanax fasciatus fasciatus*
Silver Tetra

L *Astyanax* sp.

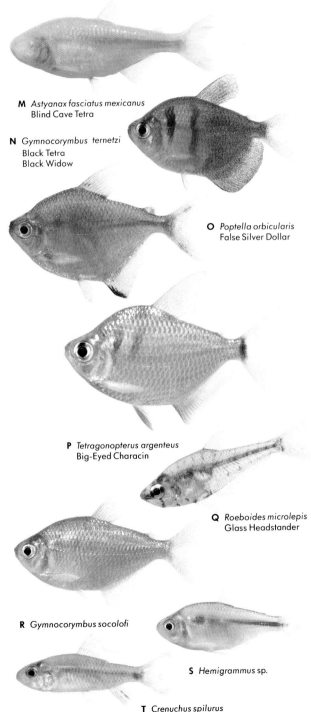

M *Astyanax fasciatus mexicanus*
Blind Cave Tetra

N *Gymnocorymbus ternetzi*
Black Tetra
Black Widow

O *Poptella orbicularis*
False Silver Dollar

P *Tetragonopterus argenteus*
Big-Eyed Characin

Q *Roeboides microlepis*
Glass Headstander

R *Gymnocorymbus socolofi*

S *Hemigrammus* sp.

T *Crenuchus spilurus*
Sailfin Tetra

A 2¼ in. (6 cm). Upper and middle reaches of the Amazon. Not sensitive to water quality, but at low temperatures is liable to pick up white spot disease. Readily eats dry or live foods. Mild-tempered, it is well suited for a community tank. Easily bred.
B 1¾ in. (4.5 cm). Widely distributed throughout the Amazon. Prefers slightly acidic, soft water. The spawning tank, in which 200-1,000 eggs will be laid at one time, should be kept at 82°F (28°C). Eggs hatch by the next day, and the larvae become free-swimming by the next day. They should be fed mashed yolk for the first 2-3 days, and brine shrimp afterwards. Fry grow fast, developing the characteristic shiny eye and caudal fin base spot coloration in about one month.
C 2¾ in. (7 cm). Near Buenos Aires. Hardy and easily cared for, it is herbivorous so likes to nibble on water plants. It also has a tendency to nip long fins of other fishes.
D 1½ in. (4 cm). Guiana. Mild-tempered, and care is easy. This fish's golden coloration might be caused by encysted skin parasites contracted in the natural habitat.
E 2 in. (5 cm). Markings on the caudal fin distinguish it from *Petitella georgiae*, the False Rummy-Nose. Also, the whole head, not just the snout, becomes red when water conditions are right for the fish to reach top physical shape. Prefers slightly acidic water, and is sensitive to change in water quality. It is also quite susceptible to white spot disease. Easily eats any type of food live or dry. Aquarium breeding is considered very difficult.
F 1¼ in. (3 cm). Only in the Essequibo R, Guyana. Schools in the shady portion of jungle brooks or ponds. A good community tank fish, it is hardy and mild-tempered. School care in a well-planted aquarium with woodscaping is recommended. It easily breeds in the manner of the Neon Tetra.
G 2 in. (5 cm). Upper reaches of the Amazon. Unaged water should be avoided. Blue flanks become intensified in slightly acid water. It is beautiful fish that is both active and peaceful. No record of aquarium breeding.
H 1¾ in. (4.5 cm). Guiana to the lower reaches of the Amazon. A mild-mannered fish well suited for a characin community tank. Care and breeding are easy.
I 1½ in. (4 cm). Lower reaches of the Amazon. A mild-tempered, yet skittish fish, the red snout tends to fade if it is not in the best physical condition. Keeping it in a small school housed in a well-planted aquarium with slightly acidic water may induce spawning. Eggs hatch within 30-36 hours.
J 1½ in. (4 cm). Southeastern Brazil.
K 6 in. (15 cm). Colombia, Venezuela, Guiana. Not sensitive to water quality, but a little should be changed on a regular basis. It is recommended that it be kept with same-sized fish or those a bit bigger, but not with smaller ones. Easily breeds, the eggs hatching out in 1-1½ days, and larvae becoming free swimming in 5 days.
L 1½ in. (4 cm). Maximum size unknown. Lake Tefé in the Amazon Basin.
M 3¼ in. (8 cm). Lives in subterranean cave lakes and streams scattered throughout central Mexico. Not sensitive to water quality, but prefers rather cool temperatures of 64-73°F (18-23°C). Eats any type of food. It is recommended that it be kept by itself in an aquarium with fine sand spread on the bottom. Breeds easily when a pair is kept in the abovementioned cool temperature. Larvae hatch out within 4-5 days, become free swimming in 6 days, and have a vestigial eye which soon disappears. *Anoptichthys jordani* is a junior synonym of *A. f. mexicanus.*
N 2 in. (5 cm). Wide distribution throughout Central America. As it prefers shade, it is found in abundance in waters below thickets and in slow-flowing brooks in forests. Best kept in slightly acidic, soft water. Posterior half of the body is blackest when young. It gives an excellent appearance when swimming in a school with its head slightly raised. Most important for easy breeding is to keep the tank at 86°F (30°C). Possibly due to continuous inbreeding in cultured stocks, many individuals lack the strong black posterior.
O 4¾ in. (12 cm). Guiana, Paraguay, Amazon Basin.
P 4¼ in. (11 cm). Guiana, Amazon Basin, Sao Francisco R. Care is easy as it readily eats any type of food.
Q 1½ in. (4 cm). Named for its manner of swimming with head inclined downwards, several species with this characteristic are usually found together as "Headstanders" in the same import. Although hardy, mild-tempered and easy to care for, they are rather plain-colored, so few imports are made.
R 2¼ in. (6 cm). Northern part of the Amazon Basin. A rather large-sized tetra which belongs to the same genus as the Black Tetra.
S 1½ in. (4 cm). Maximum size unknown. Care is easy, and water should be of neutral pH.
T 2-2¼ in. (5-6 cm). Western Guiana, middle reaches of the Amazon. Lives in grassy shores. Rather delicate, it should be kept in a densely planted tank that has a number of hiding places, and is filled with slightly acidic, soft water. Prefers live foods such as smaller fish and blood worms.

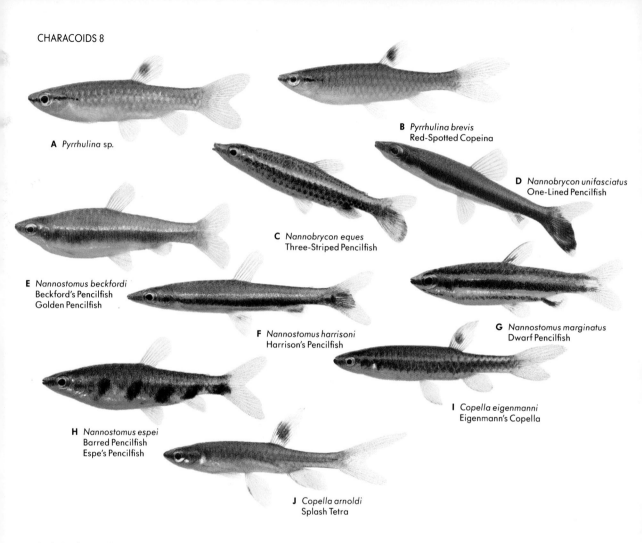

A *Pyrrhulina* sp.

B *Pyrrhulina brevis*
Red-Spotted Copeina

C *Nannobrycon eques*
Three-Striped Pencilfish

D *Nannobrycon unifasciatus*
One-Lined Pencilfish

E *Nannostomus beckfordi*
Beckford's Pencilfish
Golden Pencilfish

F *Nannostomus harrisoni*
Harrison's Pencilfish

G *Nannostomus marginatus*
Dwarf Pencilfish

H *Nannostomus espei*
Barred Pencilfish
Espe's Pencilfish

I *Copella eigenmanni*
Eigenmann's Copella

J *Copella arnoldi*
Splash Tetra

A 2¼ in. (6 cm). Widely distributed throughout the Amazon Basin.
B 2¼ in. (6 cm). The most popular fish in this genus, it has several red spots behind the gill cover. Sold as the "Red-Spotted Copeina" in most aquarium shops. As this species is sensitive to changes in water quality, it is best to avoid purchasing just-imported individuals.
C 2 in. (5 cm). Guiana, middle reaches of the Amazon. Lives in shallow shores lined with heavy reed growth. It prefers slightly acidic, soft water. Best foods include daphnia, blood worms and mosquito larvae. Doesn't feed off of the bottom of the tank.
D 2½ in. (6.5 cm). Upper and middle reaches of the Amazon, Negro R, Orinoco R, Guiana. Found in heavily reed-lined shallows, it prefers slightly acidic, soft water. Body coloring fades when water conditions are not favorable. Feeds on live food floating on the surface of the water. Breeding is rather difficult, but spawns like other pencilfish.
E 2 in. (5 cm). Guiana, Negro R, middle reaches of the Amazon. Lives in shallow brooks or on shorelines with a humus bottom. Slightly acidic, soft water preferred. Accepts a wide range of food such as daphnia, blood worms and commercial dry types. A ripe pair easily spawns in a small aquarium filled with fine-leaved plants such as *Myriophyllum*.
F 2¼ in. (6 cm). Guiana, upper and middle reaches of the Amazon. Found in jungle ponds and brooks that have a humus bottom. Small school maintenance is recommended. Live foods such as mosquito larvae and daphnia are best.

G 1¼ in. (3 cm). Guiana, lower reaches of the Amazon. Lives in jungle brooks with a humus bottom. Prefers slightly acidic, soft water. When a pair is ripe during the breeding season, they will intermittently lay clutches of eggs every day or two in a small tank filled with finely leaved plants. Since they will eat the eggs, remove the pair each time, as soon as they finish laying the clutch of eggs.
H 1½ in. (4 cm). Guyana, upper reaches of the Mazaruni R and its branches. Care is easy as it is rather hardy once acclimated and will readily eat dry food. Spawns by laying eggs on the underside of broad-leaved plants. It seems that these imports come during their spawning season.
I 2¼ in. (6 cm). Middle and upper reaches of the Amazon, Guiana. Prefers slightly acidic, soft water. Care is rather easy, but the aquarium must be covered as it is a frequent jumper. Spawning habits are unknown.
J ♂ 3½ in. (9 cm), ♀ 2¾ in. (7 cm). Para, Amazon. Prefers neutral to slightly acidic water. Very unique spawning behavior; pair jumps out of the water and spews eggs onto the underside of an overhanging leaf or surface. A few eggs are laid each jump until a dense mass of more than 100 eggs are in place. It is said that the male stays below the eggs, using his caudal fin to splash the mass every 15 minutes or so. Fry hatch in about three days, and fall into the water. In a half-filled aquarium, they have been reported to jump up and spawn on the underside of an inclined plate of glass.

CYPRINIDS

2

FAMILY	CYPRINIDAE
	(Minnows & Carps)
Genera	*Balantiocheilos*
	Barbus
	Brachydanio
	Carassius
	Chela
	Cyprinus
	Danio
	Epalzeorhynchos
	Esomus
	Garra
	Hampala
	Labeo
	Labiobarbus
	Leptobarbus
	Luciosoma
	Morulius
	Opsaridium
	Osteochilus
	Probarbus
	Puntius
	Rasbora
	Tanichthys

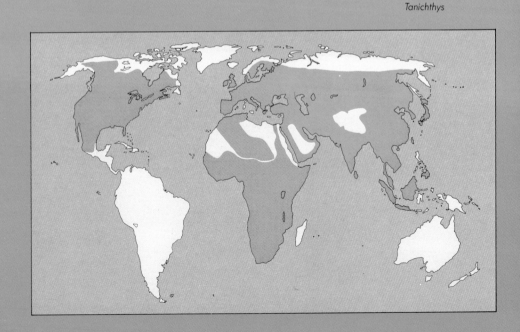

CYPRINIFORM FISH

This order which includes the carps and minnows (of which some 1,700 species in at least 220 genera have been identified) is naturally distributed throughout the world except for the South American and Australian continents, plus such places as Madagascar. The cyprinid fishes dominate in the freshwaters of Asia, just as the characoids do in South America. They lack teeth in the jaws, but possess them in the throat. The form, position and number of these "pharyngeal teeth" are characters extensively used in the taxonomic identification of cyprinids. Other such characters include barbels and the absence of an adipose fin.

Most fishes of the speciose polyphyletic genera *Barbus* and *Puntius* are of small to medium size, pretty and very popular among aquarists. Many of the large-sized species, however, are important food fishes. Although most of the cyprinids are schooling fishes, this tendency is stronger in the larvae. On the other hand, even juveniles of some species like the Red-Tailed Black Shark are highly territorial and require a large aquarium. While they will not peacefully coexist with others of the same species, they do so with fishes of other species or genera. Most cyprinids are basically herbivorous, and will eat plant-based artificial foods. In an aquarium, some will also eat the aquatic plants, as well as blood worms or other similar live foods.

Nuptial coloration is exhibited by many of the species, the male taking on quite a splendid beauty during the breeding period. Frequently newly imported fishes are not very attractive as their bodies are quite emaciated and their coloration, faint. After an extended period of proper care, however, they become incredibly beautiful. Although the basic maintenance requirements for this group are rather easy, keeping cyprinids in topnotch condition requires considerable effort.

A *Balantiocheilos melanopterus.* Bala Shark. This large-sized cyprinid can grow up to 16 in. (40 cm) in length, and can provide many hours of keen appreciation. Its mild demeanor allows it to be kept with other tropicals of about the same size in a tank larger than 4 ft. (120 cm) in length.

A *Puntius sachsi*. Golden Barb. Widely distributed throughout SE Asia, *Puntius* species are all quite interesting, easy to care for and coexist well with other tropicals.

B *Epalzeorynchos bicolor.* Red-Tailed Black Shark.

C *Barbus fasciolatus.* African Banded Barb. 2¼ in. (6 cm). Zimbabwe. This small, pretty barb with a delicate appearance is difficult to keep, transports poorly, and only rarely exported.

A *Puntius tetrazona* var. Albino Tiger Barb. **1** Moment of spawning with ♂ embracing ♀.

CYPRINID SPAWNING BEHAVIOR

2 Pair's prenuptial chase.

Many species of the carp family are prolific egglayers, characterized by a short interval between spawns. Some species, however, have not yet been bred in an aquarium, while others are known to require special water conditions to induce spawning. Spawning behavior may be divided into three categories:

1. Using his dorsal and caudal fins, the male embraces the female, while non-adhesive eggs are released, falling to the bottom of the tank.

2. Essentially the same spawning behavior, but adhesive eggs are released and become attached to water plants.

3. The pair swim side-by-side, laying eggs on the underside of wide-leaved plants.

Category 1 includes Zebra and Pearl Danios. As the ripe female and active male will eat the eggs even while spawning, the pair should be placed in a large-mesh net which has been suspended in the aquarium. In this way, eggs can fall through the net and escape the parents' cannibalism. Covering the tank bottom with large-diameter gravel or marbles is also recommended as an egg-saving measure.

Included in category 2 are the Sumatra and Rosy Barbs, and the Giant Danio. The spawning tank should be densely planted (*Myriophyllum,* etc.) or furnished with nylon yarn spawning mops. After the eggs have been laid, the parents should be moved to another aquarium. A bit of methylene blue and aeration should be added to the tank housing the eggs, which will hatch in 2-3 days.

Rashora hengeli and *R. heteromorpha* belong to category 3. A ripe male and female will be seen somersaulting, pushing eggs onto the undersides of wide-leaved plants such as Amazon Swords or Cryptocorynes. The pair should be removed after spawning. These fishes

B *Brachydanio frankei* var. Long-Finned Leopard Danio.   **1** Pair laying eggs as they swim side by side.

are especially sensitive to water quality which should be maintained at pH 5.5-6.5 and 0-3°DH (slightly acidic and soft).

Some fishes such as the White Cloud Mountain Minnow rarely eat their eggs, and will spawn more or less continually in a well-planted aquarium without any special effort on their keeper's part.

A Spawning Albino Tiger Barbs. As the male embraces the ova-laden female, the eggs are laid and fertilized. A total of 200-500 eggs are laid in clutches of 3-6 in a single spawning.
B 1-2 Leopard Danios spawning. Danios are fast swimmers even in an aquarium, and their spawning occurs in a flash. Six to ten eggs are extruded, fertilized and scattered as the pair darts next to each other.

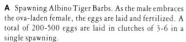

2 ♂ (right) in pursuit of ♀.

A *Puntius tetrazona*. Tiger Barb. Active schooling fascinates aquarists.

B *Puntius oligolepis.* Checkered Barb.

C *Puntius nigrofaciatus.* Black Ruby Barb.

D *Opsaridium christyi.* Copper-Nose Minnow.

E *Chela laubuca.* Indian Hatchetfish. 2¼-2¾ in. (6-7 cm). India, Burma, Malaysia, Sumatra. Abundant in rice fields and brooks. Just imported fish are usually weak and therefore liable to become diseased as a result of a sudden change in water quality. Once acclimated though, they eat well and become quite healthy. Very easy to care for and breed.

A *Rasbora heteromorpha*. Harlequin Fish or Red Rasbora.

B *Rasbora trilineata*. Scissortailed Rasbora.

C *Pseudogastromyzon myersi*.

D *Gyrinocheilus aymonieri*. Chinese Algae Eater.

E *Garra waterloti*. African Stoneroller. 4¾ in. (12 cm). Western Africa. This *Garra* species lives in fast-moving mountain streams, and is rarely exported. Care is easy, and as it has a mild demeanor, it will peacefully coexist with other tropicals in a medium-sized, or larger, tank.

F *Garra* sp. 1½ in. (4 cm), maximum length unknown. Sri Lanka. This small, rarely exported species is quite useful in an aquarium as it eats the algae off water plants, and seems to thrive on this food source.

50

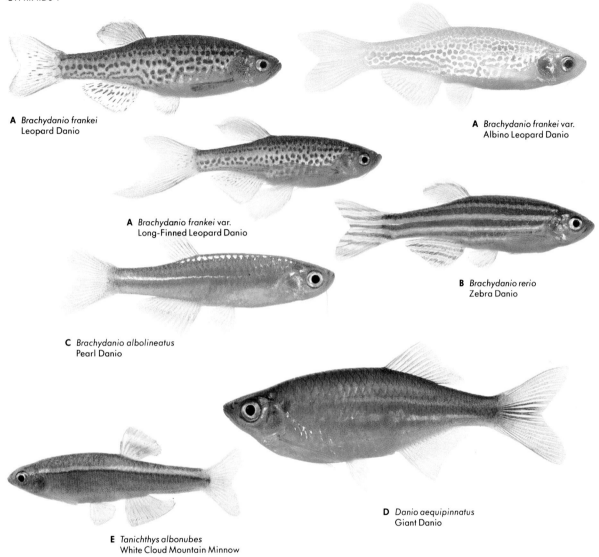

A *Brachydanio frankei*
Leopard Danio

A *Brachydanio frankei* var.
Albino Leopard Danio

A *Brachydanio frankei* var.
Long-Finned Leopard Danio

B *Brachydanio rerio*
Zebra Danio

C *Brachydanio albolineatus*
Pearl Danio

D *Danio aequipinnatus*
Giant Danio

E *Tanichthys albonubes*
White Cloud Mountain Minnow

A 2 in. (5 cm). Introduced into N. America and Japan in 1963, this "species" is said to be a color form of the Zebra Danio that was fixed in Czechoslovakia. This explanation appears to be reinforced by the fact that a Leopard x Zebra cross produces fertile offspring, while crosses with other species of *Brachydanio* result in sterile young. Two variants developed from this form are shown at right and below.

B 1¾ in. (4.5 cm). Eastern India. Living in rice fields, stagnant water and slow-flowing brooks, it has long been popular with beginners. Although wild caught fish have a beautiful brilliance that has appeared to have faded in successive generations of cultured stock, such stock is still attractive when swimming within a school in a well-planted aquarium. The light horizontal stripes in males tend to be yellowish while those in females are whitish. Recently a long-finned variety has become popular.

C 2¼ in. (5.5 cm). India, Burma, Thailand, Sumatra, Malay Peninsula. Found in rice paddies and still regions of brooks. Although it may be kept in a small tank, a large,

heavily planted one is recommended as this species is an active swimmer and likes plenty of space. It readily eats any type of food. Care and breeding are easy.

D 4¾ in. (12 cm). Western India, Sri Lanka. Readily eating any type of food, it is not sensitive to water quality. Although too active to be kept with other fish, it is quite dynamic in appearance. When kept under good conditions and well fed with live foods, it easily spawns. A large spawning tank is recommended. Its eggs adhere to the water foliage.

E 1½ in. (4 cm). Canton, Hong Kong (China). Well tolerates low temperatures, so it can be kept in an unheated tank. Small, pretty and hardy, care and breeding are easy. Parents do not eat the eggs or larvae. When a school of about ten adults is maintained in a densely planted aquarium, production of larvae is easy. Newly hatched larvae should be fed infusoria or strained yolk, and brine shrimp from the first week on.

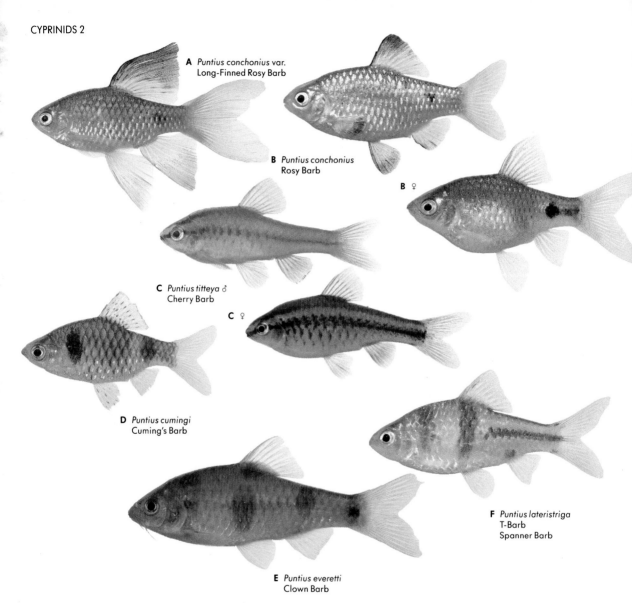

A *Puntius conchonius* var.
Long-Finned Rosy Barb

B *Puntius conchonius*
Rosy Barb

B ♀

C *Puntius titteya* ♂
Cherry Barb

C ♀

D *Puntius cumingi*
Cuming's Barb

F *Puntius lateristriga*
T-Barb
Spanner Barb

E *Puntius everetti*
Clown Barb

A-B 2 in. (5 cm). Northeastern India. Not sensitive to water quality, but does prefer conditioned water, as sudden transfer to new water may result in it becoming diseased or dying. Periodic partial replacement of water is therefore recommended. It is a beautiful, active, midwater swimmer that readily eats any type of food and breeds easily.

C 2 in. (5 cm). Sri Lanka. Living in the shaded grassy or bushy banks of brooks, it prefers slightly acidic water of around 72°F (22°C). School maintenance in a heavily planted tank is recommended. Breeding is easy, with small fish laying about 200 eggs which hatch out in about 24 hours.

D 2 in. (5 cm). Sri Lanka. Found in brooks running through forested mountains, it will eat most anything, and is both hardy and easily cared for. When kept in a school, top physical conditioning will be maintained. A partial replacement of the water may induce it to spawn.

E 4 in. (10 cm). Singapore, Borneo. Slightly acidic, aged water is recommended as

alkaline conditions cause the fish's coloration to fade and possibly early death. To condition a pair for spawning, separate the male and the female for 3-4 weeks during which they should be fed plenty of live and vegetable-based foods. The breeding tank's water needs to be slightly acid, soft and aged. A pair will lay 500-2,000 eggs. As larvae are especially sensitive to water quality, be careful when making partial water replacement.

F Max. 7 in. (18 cm), smaller in aquaria. Thailand, Singapore, Malaysia, Java, Sumatra, Borneo. Prefers soft, slightly acidic aged water. Frequent, partial water replacement is recommended, thus avoiding sudden water changes. Breeding is easy, but a large tank is required as the pair will lay 2,000-3,000 eggs.

G 4¾ in. (12 cm). Malaysia, Borneo, Sumatra, Bangka. Prefers slightly acidic water. Hardy, care is easy as it readily eats any type of food. An active, beautifully striped fish that fits well into a community tank. Breeding is said to be very difficult.

H 1½ in. (4 cm). Sumatra. Slightly acidic, soft water is best. Care is easy as the fish is

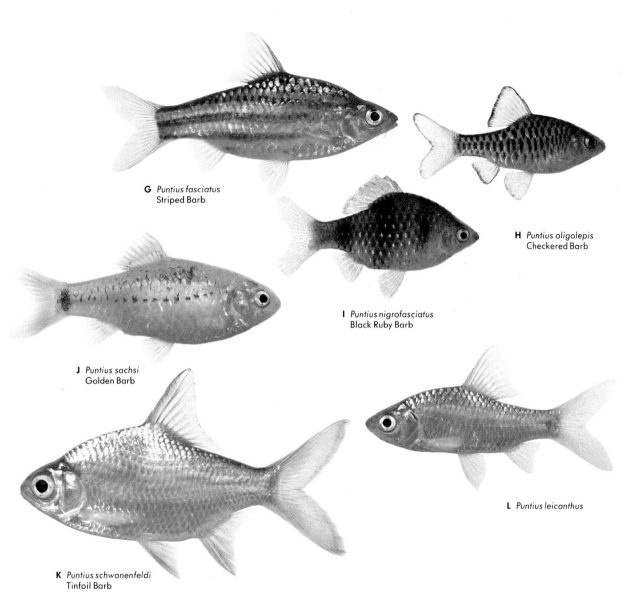

G *Puntius fasciatus*
Striped Barb

H *Puntius oligolepis*
Checkered Barb

I *Puntius nigrofasciatus*
Black Ruby Barb

J *Puntius sachsi*
Golden Barb

K *Puntius schwanenfeldi*
Tinfoil Barb

L *Puntius leicanthus*

hardy and readily eats all foods. Mild-tempered, it coexists well in a community tank. Breeding is rather easy. Parents are cannibalistic, so remove them after spawning is completed. 100-200 eggs are laid. The fry hatch out after 2 days, and should be fed infusoria.

I 2 in. (5 cm). Southern Sri Lanka. Although distribution is limited, this species is said to be abundant within the region's slow moving rivers. Prefers slightly acidic, soft water. Water replacement requires great care as the fish is liable to become diseased if the water quality is not favorable. 300-500 eggs are laid in a single spawning. Feed infusoria to the larvae.

J 2¼ in. (6 cm). Southern China and Vietnam. Slightly acidic, soft aged water is necessary, as the fish is especially sensitive to unaged water. Even so, care is easy as it is hardy and readily eats any type of food. Breeding is also easy, with the 200-300 eggs laid hatching out in 24-30 hours. Free swimming after 3 days, the larva should be fed infusoria or strained yolk the first 2-3 days.

K Can reach 16 in. (40 cm) in nature. Indonesia, Thailand. Not sensitive to quality, but does require aged water. Readily eats live and dry foods as well as lettuce, it needs a large aquarium as it is a large, active swimmer. Breeding in such big aquaria is easy. A few thousand eggs are laid in a single spawning. Larvae should be initially fed brine shrimp.

L 4 in. (10 cm). Thailand, Indochina. Living in slow-flowing waters, this mid-sized barb does well in a 25 gallon (100 liter) tank. Care is easy as it eats all live and dry foods, but breeding is said to be difficult.

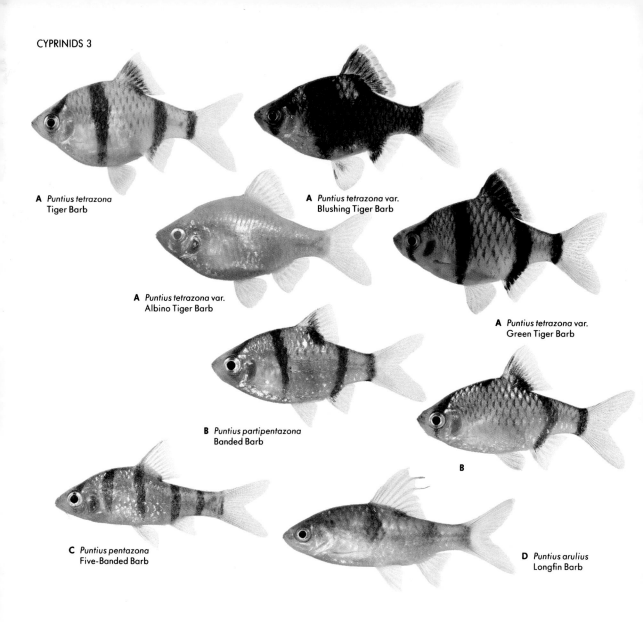

A *Puntius tetrazona*
Tiger Barb

A *Puntius tetrazona* var.
Blushing Tiger Barb

A *Puntius tetrazona* var.
Albino Tiger Barb

A *Puntius tetrazona* var.
Green Tiger Barb

B *Puntius partipentazona*
Banded Barb

B

C *Puntius pentazona*
Five-Banded Barb

D *Puntius arulius*
Longfin Barb

A 2¼ in. (6 cm). Sumatra, Borneo. Known in earlier aquarium literature as the Sumatra Barb. Prefers slightly acidic water. This small, pretty barb is an active schooling fish that has long fascinated avid aquarists. Inquisitive and spirited, it coexists moderately well with other fishes, but is known for being mischievious because of its periodic behavior of nipping at fins (especially long ones). This may be a consequence of successive inbreeding. Breeding is easy with 300-1,000 eggs being laid in a single spawning. Free-swimming larvae readily catch brine shrimp. Cultivated variants include the Green, Albino and Blushing Tiger Barbs shown here.

B 2 in. (5 cm). Malay Peninsula. Slightly acidic, soft water preferred. Distinguished from the above by the narrower second band which sometimes is incomplete (right photo). Although care and breeding are the same as the above, this fish is rather weak and difficult to breed. Only rarely exported.

C 2 in. (5 cm). Malay Peninsula, Borneo. Slightly acidic, soft water is best. Highly suited for community aquaria, it is active, but mild mannered. On introduction, it is very liable to die, but once acclimated, becomes hardy. Breeding is rather easy. Larvae should be fed infusoria.

D 4¾ in. (12 cm). Southeastern India. Prefers slightly acid, soft water. Coexists well with other species in a large, well-planted, woodscaped aquarium. It is active, beautiful and breeds easily when this proper water quality is maintained.

E 5 in. (13 cm). Sri Lanka, India, Burma. Prefers neutral to slightly acid water. It has two wide vertical black bands on the body until it reaches about 2 in. (5 cm), at which point the bands begin to fade and only the posterior spot is left. Active, care is easy, it eats any type of food. Best suited to be kept with other fish of about the same size. Breeding is also easy.

F 1½ in. (3.5 cm). Thailand, Malaysia, Sumatra. A small, active swimmer in the aquarium, care is easy. It likes blood and other aquatic worms. Outside of Japan, few

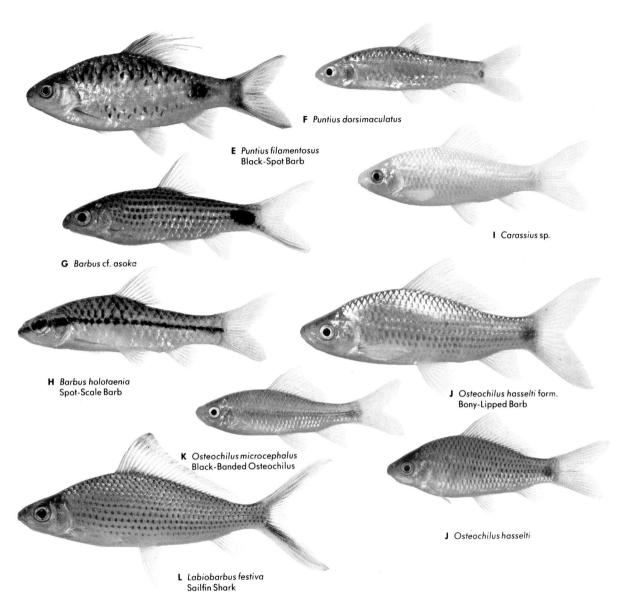

F *Puntius dorsimaculatus*

E *Puntius filamentosus*
Black-Spot Barb

G *Barbus* cf. *asoka*

I *Carassius* sp.

H *Barbus holotaenia*
Spot-Scale Barb

J *Osteochilus hasselti* form.
Bony-Lipped Barb

K *Osteochilus microcephalus*
Black-Banded Osteochilus

J *Osteochilus hasselti*

L *Labiobarbus festiva*
Sailfin Shark

cases have been reported of the fish being bred in large aquaria.
G 3¼ in. (8 cm), max. size unknown. Despite its mouth being inferior and the diagnostic markings, distinctive, positive identification could not be made. It is a bottom feeder and prefers blood and other aquatic worms. Tolerant of water quality, it is easy to care for.
H 4¾ in. (12 cm). Zaire to Cameroon, branches of the Zaire R. Sensitive to water quality, it prefers slightly acidic, soft conditions. Mild-tempered, it has been found to coexist well with same size fishes from SE Asia. Feeds on aquatic worms and flake foods. No record of breeding.
I 6 in. (15 cm). Although at first glance this fish appears to be a carp-goldfish (*Cyprinus* x *Carassius*) hybrid, it is actually an albinistic form of *O. hasselti*. A dealer in Singapore said it is found wild in Sri Lanka. It has a unique attractiveness, and care is easy.

J Reaches more than 24 in. (60 cm) in nature, but only 8 in. (20 cm) in aquaria. Thailand, Indonesia. One of the larger Cyprinidae offering qualities similar to those appreciated in the Black Shark. Its file-like teeth are adapted to scraping off plant growth from underwater rocks. Care is easy as it prefers pellets or other dry foods.
K 8 in. (20 cm). Thailand, Malaysia, Indonesia. Rarely seen, it is found among batches of loaches and rasboras. Similar to the above species, it has a longitudinal stripe running along its side while the above has a black spot on its caudal peduncle. Likes to eat the algae off the aquarium glass.
L 12 in. (30 cm). Malay Peninsula. The large dorsal fin is a good diagnostic character. It is a quick bottom swimmer and powerful jumper that likes blood worms and other large foods. No record of breeding.

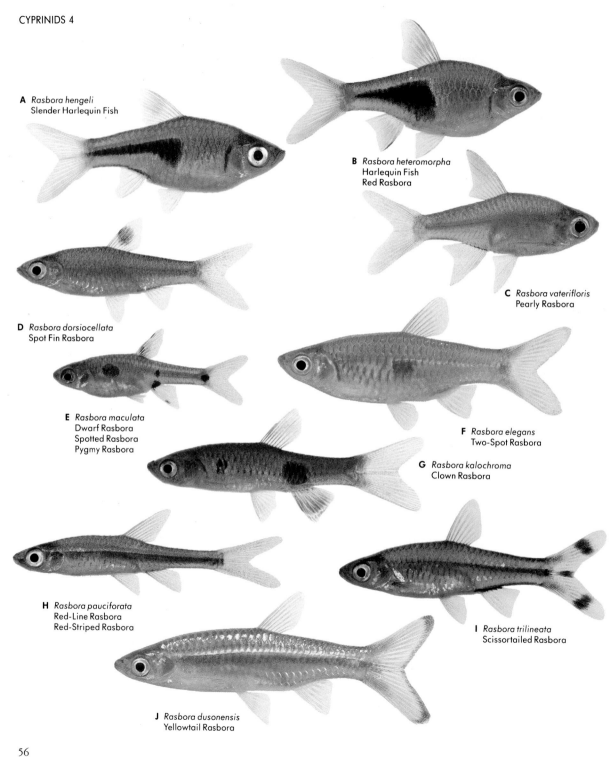

A *Rasbora hengeli*
Slender Harlequin Fish

B *Rasbora heteromorpha*
Harlequin Fish
Red Rasbora

C *Rasbora vaterifloris*
Pearly Rasbora

D *Rasbora dorsiocellata*
Spot Fin Rasbora

E *Rasbora maculata*
Dwarf Rasbora
Spotted Rasbora
Pygmy Rasbora

F *Rasbora elegans*
Two-Spot Rasbora

G *Rasbora kalochroma*
Clown Rasbora

H *Rasbora pauciforata*
Red-Line Rasbora
Red-Striped Rasbora

I *Rasbora trilineata*
Scissortailed Rasbora

J *Rasbora dusonensis*
Yellowtail Rasbora

K *Rasbora sumatrana*
Sumatran Rasbora

L *Rasbora daniconius*
Golden-Striped Rasbora

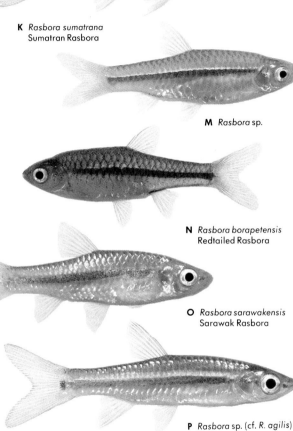

M *Rasbora* sp.

N *Rasbora borapetensis*
Redtailed Rasbora

O *Rasbora sarawakensis*
Sarawak Rasbora

P *Rasbora* sp. (cf. *R. agilis*)

tions are not favorable. The pair spawns over a grassy area, the eggs sinking to the bottom. Parents are quite cannibalistic, so they should be removed immediately, as soon as the spawning is completed. Egg hatch within about 40 hours, and the larvae become free swimming in 5 days.

D 2¼ in. (6 cm). Slow-flowing brooks in the Malay Peninsula and Sumatra. Prefers slightly acidic, soft water. Highly suited for well-planted community tanks, it is mild-tempered and swims in schools. Breeding is easy under favorable water conditions.

E ¾ in. (2 cm). Malay Peninsula, Sumatra, Borneo. Lives in stagnant, grassy waters. Prefers slightly acidic, soft water (pH 6.0, 0.5-2.5°DH). Too tiny for community aquaria, it is best kept as a single species group in a small tank. It spawns easily when water conditions are right. Eggs are laid on fine-leaved plants such as *Myriophyllum* and *Nitella*. Larval care is easy; they should at first be fed infusoria.

F 5 in. (13 cm). Malaysia, Indonesia. Slightly acidic, soft water preferred. It is best kept with other medium-sized fishes as it is an active, mid-water swimmer. Readily eats any type of food. The ♂ is smaller, and the spots, sharper than the ♀. Breeding is rather easy.

G 4 in. (10 cm). Malaysia, Singapore, Indonesia. Lives in acid waters over mulm bottoms, and should be kept in tanks with aged acidic, soft water. It is susceptible to *Ichthyophthirius* attack when water conditions are unfavorable. In good conditions, it swims actively and the red coloration is strong. No record of aquarium breeding.

H 2¾ in. (7 cm). Brooks of eastern Sumatra. Sensitive to water quality. It prefers slightly acidic, soft water (pH 6.2, 2-3°DH). Fish in good condition have a brilliant red line, even stronger than that of the Glow Light Tetra. Breeding is difficult, but possible. Eggs are scattered over aquatic grasses.

I 4 in. (10 cm). Malay Peninsula, Sumatra, Borneo. Prefers slightly acidic, soft water. Care is easy as it is hardy and readily eats any type of food when maintained under proper water conditions. Breeding is easy, but dependent on proper water quality. In a single spawning, 500-1,000 eggs are laid. At first, the larvae should be fed infusoria or strained yolk.

J 6 in. (15 cm). Thailand, Malaysia, Sumatra, Borneo. Slightly acidic, soft water preferred. This rarely imported and not so popular rasbora is relatively large-sized, active and quite beautiful. It readily eats any type of food.

K 5 in. (13 cm). Thailand, Malaysia, Indonesia. A large-sized rasbora similar to *R. elegans*, it is an active swimmer and does best in a medium-sized tank. Although it prefers slightly acidic, soft water, it is able to adapt to most any water quality. It readily eats any type of food including dry and live foods. Large specimens may be caught in Thailand from January to March.

L 1½ in. (4 cm), max. size about 2¾ in. (7 cm). Thailand. The wide, straight, longitudinal mid-body black stripe diagnostically running all the way to the nose, has a golden stripe running its length. Its body is rather high and rounded in appearance. Usually exported as a "contaminant" in shipments of more colorful species.

M 4 in. (10 cm). Thailand, Burma. Appears to prefer slightly acidic, soft water. Hardy, it readily eats all types of food. When exported, it is usually mixed in with other rasbora species.

N 2 in. (5 cm). Thailand, Malaysia. One of the most popular small rasboras. Even though it will become acclimated to any water quality, slightly acidic, soft water is preferable to bring out the bright red tail coloration. Mild-tempered, it is well suited for a community tank of small fish. Readily eats aquatic worms, dry foods and any other type of foods.

O 3¼ in. (8 cm). Thailand, Malaysia, Indonesia. A rare species, it is exported mixed in with batches of the Gold-Lined Rasbora. It has a wide black longitudinal stripe running the length of the body. Care is easy, and it eats any type of food.

P 1¾ in. (4.5 cm), max. size unknown. Malay Peninsula, Southern Thailand, Borneo. Found mixed in with Scissor-Tailed Rasboras imported from Thailand. Has no black blotches on the caudal fin.

A 1¼ in. (3 cm). Swamps and brooks around Telanaipura, Sumatra. Prefers slightly acidic, soft conditioned water. Like many other rasboras, it is sensitive to water quality. Eats blood and other aquatic worms as well as flake foods. Lays a few eggs on the underside of leaves.

B 1½ in. (4 cm). Southern Thailand, Malay Peninsula, Sumatra, Java. Prefers slightly acidic, soft water. Willingly eats any type of food including flakes, blood and other aquatic worms. Easy to care for, it is both hardy and mild-mannered. Under favorable water conditions (pH 5.3-5.7, 1.5-2.5°DH), spawns easily. Swimming side by side, the pair lays eggs on the underside of broad-leaved aquatic plants (Amazon Swords, Cryptocorynes, etc.). The pair should then be removed to a separate tank. After hatching out a day later, the larvae become free swimming in 3-4 days. For the first 2-3 days, the fry should be fed infusoria or strained yolk; later, switch to brine shrimp. As the larvae are highly sensitive to new water, caution should be taken during water replacement.

C 1½ in. (3.5 cm). Slow-flowing mountain brooks in Sri Lanka. Aged, slightly acidic, soft water preferred. Mild-tempered, it is a good schooling fish for community aquaria. Breeding is difficult as the female will not become gravid when water condi-

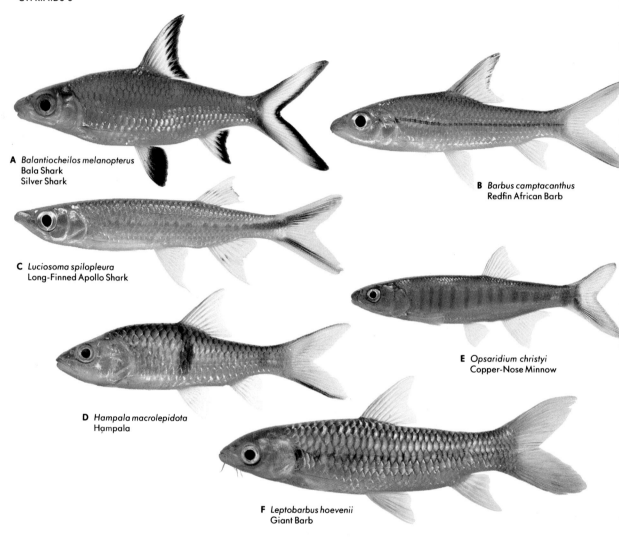

A *Balantiocheilos melanopterus*
Bala Shark
Silver Shark

B *Barbus camptacanthus*
Redfin African Barb

C *Luciosoma spilopleura*
Long-Finned Apollo Shark

E *Opsaridium christyi*
Copper-Nose Minnow

D *Hampala macrolepidota*
Hampala

F *Leptobarbus hoevenii*
Giant Barb

A 16 in. (40 cm). Thailand, Sumatra, Borneo. The Thai variant has a golden brown band on the fins where white is seen here. Said to prefer neutral to slightly alkaline water, it is not sensitive to water quality. Hardy, rather large-sized and mild-tempered, this fish can be kept in a community tank, but it definitely needs a large one. A powerful jumper that must be kept in a tightly covered tank. SE Asian fish farmers have been reported to have bred it by using hormones.

B 6¼ in. (16 cm). Widely distributed throughout West African rivers. This African barb has been bred in Singapore and is now becoming popular. It readily eats blood worms or dry food, but requires frequent feedings or else it becomes quite lean. Frequent nipping at each other is observed.

C 10 in. (25 cm). Indonesia, Malaysia, Thailand, Viet Nam. Prefers slightly acidic, soft water, but is tolerant of changes in water quality. Very aggressive towards others of the same species. A fast-swimming predator that should never be kept with fish small enough to be eaten. A tank cover is necessary as it's a jumper. Breeding method is unknown.

D 10 in. (25 cm). Thailand, Burma. A medium-sized cyprinid with a large mouth, it prefers dry carp foods and grows quickly. Highly predatory towards fish small enough to be easily swallowed. When young, it has a black band running down mid-body, and a bright orange tail. However, when it reaches about 8 in. (20 cm), the body becomes uniformly blackish. A powerful jumper that needs a large aquarium to prosper in captivity.

E 5 in. (13 cm). Zaire R. Although not sensitive to water quality, it prefers temperatures in the 72-75°F (22-24°C) range. This infrequently exported, mild-tempered species resembles *Zacco platypus,* a colorful Japanese cyprinid, also rarely exported. As it is a ready jumper, a tank cover is needed. Carnivorous, foods such as small insects and blood worms are preferred. No breeding record.

F Exceeds 20 in. (50 cm) in length. Thailand. Hardy, omnivorous and easy to care for, it maintains a natural beauty from larvae through adult when kept in a large tank with wide open spaces. A powerful jumper that must be kept in a well-covered tank. Eaten in Thailand, it hasn't been bred in captivity.

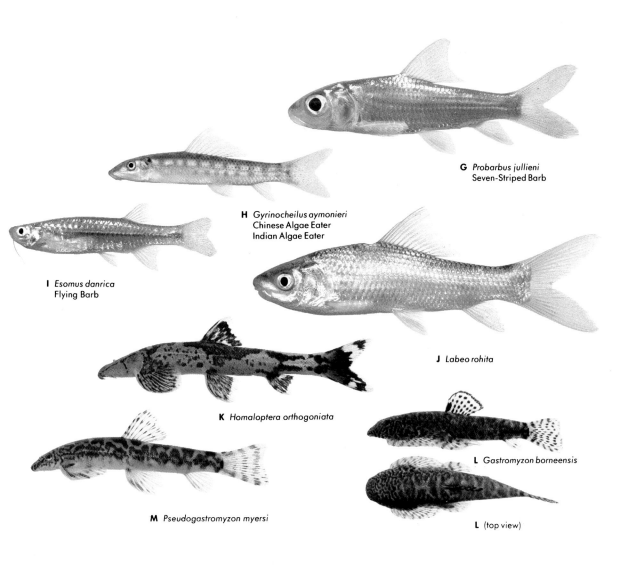

G *Probarbus jullieni*
Seven-Striped Barb

H *Gyrinocheilus aymonieri*
Chinese Algae Eater
Indian Algae Eater

I *Esomus danrica*
Flying Barb

J *Labeo rohita*

K *Homaloptera orthogoniata*

L *Gastromyzon borneensis*

M *Pseudogastromyzon myersi*

L (top view)

G Exceeds 40 in. (1 m) in nature, but at most, 28 in. (70 cm) in aquaria. Thailand, Malay Peninsula. Although it prefers worms which it picks out of a sandy bottom, even pellets will be eaten. As this mild-tempered, yet large-sized fish grows quickly, soon exceeding 12 in. (30 cm), it soon requires a very large aquarium.

H Reaches 10 in. (25 cm) in nature. Thailand. Not sensitive to water quality, it does prefer neutral to slightly alkaline conditions. When young, it has a mild demeanor, but is rather inactive. It is thus no less attractive and useful as an addition to a community setup than other algae-eating species. However, individuals over 4 in. (10 cm) in length do become aggressive. Breeding method is unknown.

I 6 in. (15 cm) in nature, less in aquaria. Thailand, Sri Lanka, India. Tolerant of varied water quality, it is an active swimmer so a cover is needed to prevent it from jumping out of the tank. Aquatic worms such as blood worms are the preferred food. Breeding is easy, and the yellow eggs are laid among thick patches of aquatic grass.

J 6 in. (15 cm), can grow to 24 in. (60 cm). This rarely exported cyprinid was originally introduced from India to SE Asia for food fish culture. Its lips are well

adapted for scraping algae.

K 4 in. (10 cm). Fast-moving SE Asian waters. This hillstream, and the two other loaches (see next chapter) below are not cyprinids. Sometimes called the "Rocket Fish," it is tolerant of varied water quality, but prefers strong aeration and temperatures of 72-75°F (22-24°C). Found sucking on stones and wood, it feeds on live foods when available, plus needs a diet heavy in vegetable matter.

L 2¼ in. (6 cm). Fast-moving SE Asian, Chinese, Hong Kong waters. A sucker-mouthed loach that superficially looks like a "Pleco," its care is easy. Usually found sucking on stones, in captivity it prefers to eat boiled spinach.

M Fast-moving SE Asian and Chinese waters. This mild-mannered, sucker-mouthed loach eats algae off stones, and requires a primarily vegetable diet for long life.

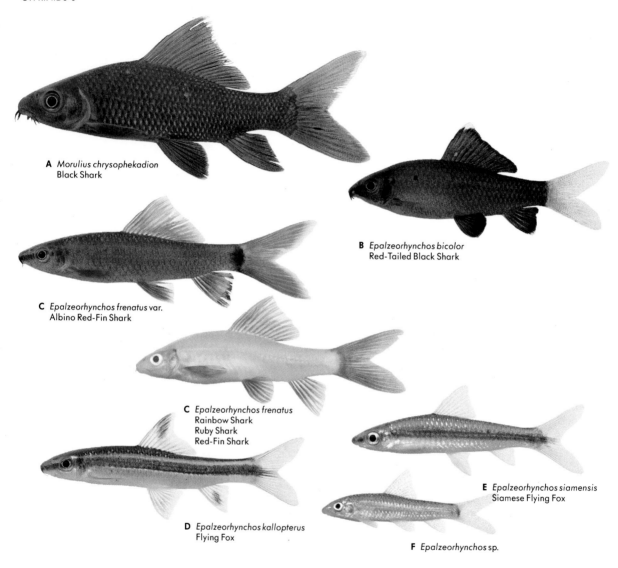

A *Morulius chrysophekadion*
Black Shark

B *Epalzeorhynchos bicolor*
Red-Tailed Black Shark

C *Epalzeorhynchos frenatus* var.
Albino Red-Fin Shark

C *Epalzeorhynchos frenatus*
Rainbow Shark
Ruby Shark
Red-Fin Shark

D *Epalzeorhynchos kallopterus*
Flying Fox

E *Epalzeorhynchos siamensis*
Siamese Flying Fox

F *Epalzeorhynchos* sp.

A 8 in. (20 cm). SE Asia. Prefers neutral water. Beautiful, yet quite pugnacious, it sometimes chases to death not only companions of the same species, but also larger fish of other species. Accordingly, solitary care is recommended. Not too hardy, care is rather difficult. No spawnings have been reported.

B 4¾ in. (12 cm). Me Nam R in Thailand. Prefers slightly alkaline (pH 7.5), hard (10°DH) water. Readily eats any type of food, but occasional feedings of boiled lettuce or spinach is recommended. Although it can be kept in a community tank with members of other genera, it is very aggressive towards *Labeo* or other *Epalzeorhynchos* species. Breeding is quite difficult.

C 4¾ in. (12 cm). Thailand, Mekong R. Prefers slightly alkaline, rather hard water. Aggressive towards other *Epalzeorhynchos* or *Labeo* species, it can be maintained in a large community tank with members of other genera. However, when a number are together in a large aquarium, they will not become territorial, but rather school together. No record of breeding. An albino form is also available.

D Grows to 6 in. (15 cm) in nature, 4¾ in. (12 cm) in aquaria. Sumatra, Java, Borneo. Not so sensitive, but prefers soft water. Needs a large tank as it is territorial towards members of the *Epalzeorhynchos-Labeo* complex, but gentle towards other genera. Prefers live foods such as aquatic worms, but also efficiently eats the algae off the glass in aquaria. No breeding record.

E 5½ in. (14 cm). Thailand. Prefers slightly alkaline water, but readily adapts to any water conditions. Omnivorous, devouring live foods such as blood and other aquatic worms, it's well known as an effective (especially thread) algae eater. Care is easy. The pair bangs against each other during spawning, scattering the eggs onto the sandy bottom.

F 1 in. (2.5 cm), max. size unknown. There are currently five known species of Flying Foxes recognized from Thailand where this specimen comes from. This one, however, is quite distinct from the two species cited above. Care is easy as it readily eats aquatic moss.

LOACHES

3

FAMILY	**COBITIDAE** (Loaches)
SUBFAMILY	**BOTIINAE**
Genus	*Botia*
SUBFAMILY	**COBITINAE**
Genera	*Acantophthalmus*
	Acantopsis
FAMILY	**BALITORIDAE**
	(Hillstream Loaches)
SUBFAMILY	**NEMACHEILINAE**
Genus	*Noemacheilus*
SUBFAMILY	**BALITORINAE**
Genera	*Gastromyzon*
	Homaloptera
	Pseudogastromyzon
FAMILY	**GYRINOCHEILIDAE**
	(Algae Eaters)
Genus	*Gyrinocheilus*

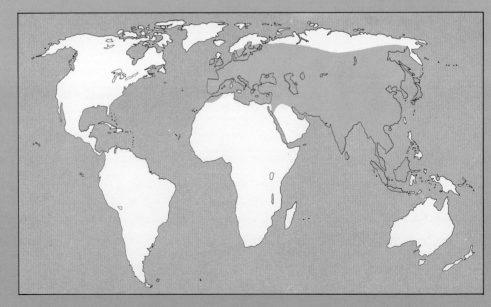

A *Botia eos* (immature). Rarely exported, it is named after the Greek goddess of the dawn, Eos.

COBITID FISH

Members of the loach family are found distributed throughout northern Africa (Morocco, Ethiopia), Europe and all over Asia. The greatest number of species, however, is found in SE Asia. Most of these fishes are relatively small, and search for food along the bottom of the tank using their barbels which contain taste buds. They are therefore useful as cleaners of the aquarium. They mainly tend to be nocturnal, and so may stay hidden behind rocks or in the sandy bottom during the daytime, though acclimated individuals do become diurnal. One of the genera, *Botia,* includes a number of beautiful species which are well appreciated in the hobby.

Other interesting structures characteristic of many loaches include a mildly toxic hinged spine(s) below the eye, and a part of the intestine acting as an auxiliary respiratory organ. Aquarists should take note of the former structure to avoid being "stung" through carelessness. The latter structure allows the fish to take in oxygen directly from the air through the intestine and thus to survive in water with a low oxygen content. One such is *Misgurnus anguillicaudatus,* the Japanese Weatherfish, which gulps air at the surface and discharges the unabsorbed portion through its anus. Some species are also known to be able to emit sounds which have been observed during their territorial or spawning behavior. Breeding, however, is difficult. Very ripe females are often seen, but spawning only rarely occurs. SE Asian fish farmers are reported to have successfully spawned loaches by using hormone injections.

B *Noemacheilus botia.*

C *Botia macracanthus.* Clown Loach.

D *Noemacheilus* sp. Spotted or Mottled Loach.

E *Botia lohachata.* Pakistani Loach.

F *Botia beauforti.* Beaufort's Loach.

G *Botia sidthimunki.* Dwarf Loach.

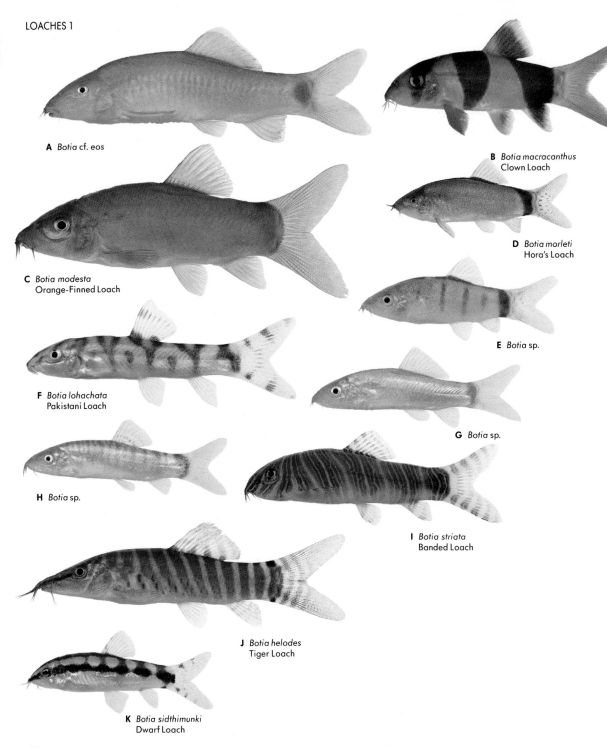

A *Botia* cf. *eos*

B *Botia macracanthus*
Clown Loach

C *Botia modesta*
Orange-Finned Loach

D *Botia morleti*
Hora's Loach

E *Botia* sp.

F *Botia lohachata*
Pakistani Loach

G *Botia* sp.

H *Botia* sp.

I *Botia striata*
Banded Loach

J *Botia helodes*
Tiger Loach

K *Botia sidthimunki*
Dwarf Loach

L *Botia beauforti*
Beaufort's Loach

M *Botia rubipinnus*
Red-Finned Loach

N *Noemacheilus botia*

O *Noemacheilus sp.*

A 2¼ in. (6 cm). Native to Thailand, this species is rarely exported. Though this species has the small eyes and quite narrow vertical bands characteristic of *B.eos,* this identification is tentative.

B Exceeds 12 in. (30 cm) in nature, but 6 in. (15 cm) at most in aquaria. Indonesia, Sumatra, Borneo. Tolerant of varied water quality, it prefers new, well-aerated water. A good community tank fish best kept with same-sized cyprinids, it is an active daytime swimmer. Although blood and other aquatic worms are preferred, it does readily eat dry foods. Regrettably it hasn't been bred under aquarium conditions, but it's been reported that SE Asian farmers have bred it by using hormone injections.

C 4 in. (10 cm). Thailand, Viet Nam, Malaysia. Lives in slow-flowing rivers. Rather nervous, it usually remains hidden in a refuge during the daytime when kept by itself. When maintained in a school however, it's quite active. No breeding record.

D 4 in. (10 cm). Thailand. Not sensitive, but prefers slightly acidic, soft water. It is pretty in its simplicity, but usually remains hidden. Well-suited as an aquarium cleaner, this fish eats blood and other aquatic worms, plus food detritus.

E 1¼ in. (3 cm), max. size unknown. Found mixed in with the above species, it differs by having a slightly longer body. This loach might occupy the same habitat and distribution as Hora's Loach, however.

F 2¾ in. (7 cm). India, Pakistan. Lives in slow-flowing rivers. Nocturnal by nature, usually remaining hidden within grasses or rock caves, it becomes diurnal after reaching about 2 in. (5 cm) in length. A strong swimmer, this loach has a tendency to squeeze into the tubing of bottom filtration/aeration systems. Live foods such as aquatic worms are preferred.

G 1½ in. (4 cm), max. size unknown. Found in Thailand mixed in with a batch of *B. morleti,* its identification is uncertain, but may be a young *B. eos.*

H 1½ in. (4 cm), max. size unknown. Found in Thailand, it has about 12-14 fine, rather indistinct vertical bands running down both sides. It may be a young *b. leconti* or an undescribed species.

I 2¾ in. (7 cm). India. Hardy and beautiful, it lives in slow-flowing brooks. Voraciously eats aquatic worms. No record of it being bred in an aquarium.

J 8 in. (20 cm). Thailand, Malaysia, Singapore, Java, Sumatra, Borneo. Nocturnal, remaining hidden within a refuge during the daytime, once accustomed to its surroundings it becomes diurnal and makes sounds requesting food from its owner. Possessing a voracious appetite, this loach will eat any type of food; live, including smaller fishes, and even pellets or flakes. Not yet bred.

K 1½ in. (4 cm). Thailand. Prefers slightly alkaline, soft water. Live foods such as aquatic worms are preferred, but also readily eats food detritus. A good community fish to be kept with small cyprinids, it looks very pretty in an aquarium when it swims in a school. Regrettably it hasn't been bred yet.

L 8 in. (20 cm). Thailand, Malaysia, Singapore, Java, Sumatra. Prefers well-aerated, slightly acidic, soft clean water. A nocturnal fish, it usually stays hidden during the daytime. Aquatic worms such as blood worms are favored. Best kept as a group in a large tank outfitted with a number of woody hiding places.

M 3¼ in. (8 cm). Thailand. Similar to, and easily confused with *B. leconti* which is also rarely exported. *B. rubipinnus* has a smaller eye and a somewhat deeper, but definitely shorter, body. Constant feeding of live foods is required to maintain a healthy individual.

N 4¾ in. (12 cm). Northern India. Not sensitive, but prefers slightly alkaline water. It has a feeding habit like the Japanese Weatherfish, sucking in bottom sand that contains food, and then expelling the sifted sand through its gill slits. This loach's markings are much nicer and more distinct than its Japanese cousin. Good quality dry food as well as live foods are readily eaten. As it is not mischievous with other fishes, it is well suited as a community tank cleaner.

O 4¾ in. (12 cm). Westward from Burma through India and Pakistan. Identification is uncertain as this fish may be a marking variant of the above. Care of this genus is very easy, and they prefer live foods such as blood and other aquatic worms. Possibly spawning in aquaria has been unsuccessful due to the fish being under stress, but hormone injection-induced breeding has been accomplished.

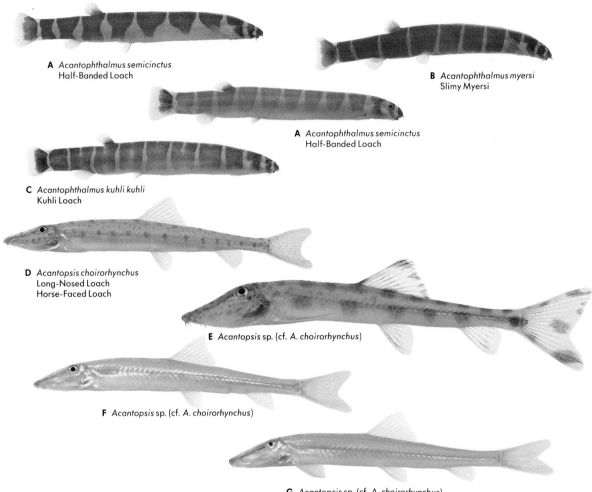

A *Acantophthalmus semicinctus*
Half-Banded Loach

B *Acantophthalmus myersi*
Slimy Myersi

A *Acantopsis semicinctus*
Half-Banded Loach

C *Acantophthalmus kuhli kuhli*
Kuhli Loach

D *Acantopsis choirorhynchus*
Long-Nosed Loach
Horse-Faced Loach

E *Acantopsis sp.* (cf. *A. choirorhynchus*)

F *Acantopsis sp.* (cf. *A. choirorhynchus*)

G *Acantopsis sp.* (cf. *A. choirorhynchus*)

A 3½ in. (9 cm). Indonesia. Lives on the muddy bottom of shallow, meandering brooks situated at the foot of mountains. The tank water should be slightly alkaline (about pH 6.5), and the bottom filled with fine sand. Sharp (such as coral) sand must be avoided to prevent injury to the fish's body. They prefer company, so this species should be kept in a group of ten or more. Nocturnal, its beautiful coloring and pattern cannot be fully appreciated as it usually remains hidden in a refuge during the daytime. Useful as an aquarium cleaner because it eats food detritus, it should also be fed live aquatic worms. An exporter has reported that stock kept a long time in a large tank had spawned. This suggests that the possibility of breeding it in an aquarium is worth the effort. To do so, the group should be kept in a large tank with the water depth kept to around 4 in. (10 cm). The lighting should be subdued, and the fish well supplied with food at all times. A long wait may be required, but when the male entwines the female and the floating eggs are released, it is surely a sight to see.

B 3¼ in. (8 cm). SE Thailand. Prefers slightly acidic, soft water. A nocturnal fish, it usually remains hidden in a refuge or the sandy bottom, and so can be rarely appreciated. Hardy, readily eating any type of food, care is easy. Breeding is feasible if the conditions mentioned for the above Half-Banded Loach are maintained.

C 3¼ in. (8 cm). About seven species of the genus *Acantophthalmus* are known, and they are all imported under the general common name of "Kuhli Loach." As there are many variations in markings, collecting them is quite interesting.

D-E-F-G 8 in. (20 cm). SE Asia, Java, Sumatra, Borneo. Lives in the sandy bottoms of both rapid and slow-moving waters and prefers neutral or slightly acidic water. An aquarium should have fine sand on the bottom to which aquatic plants have become firmly attached, interspersed with woody and stone refuges. Feed it blood or other aquatic worms. Although only one species has been described in this genus, there are many pattern variants including spots on the side, complete absence of same, plus some with distinct blotches. Whether this represents simply marking variation, geographical diversity, or different species, will require further close study.

CICHLIDS

4

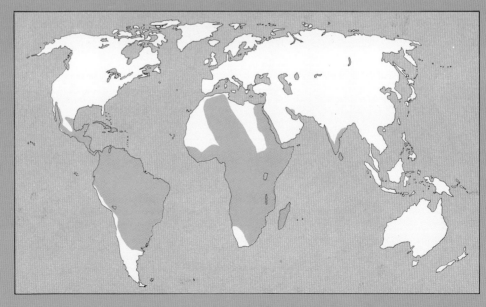

DISCUS

Discus are widely distributed throughout the northern Amazon Basin. Most of them are not found living in the main, rapidly flowing tributaries, but rather, in the intermittent waters of river-bed lakes, around sunken logs in stagnant brooks and among aquatic grasses or floating plants that lie within the shade during the daytime. The temperature of these slightly acidic, soft waters (around pH 6, below 1° DH) tends to range between 77-82° F (25-28°C). Although they are said not to be found living in alkaline waters, in SE Asia they are raised in soft to slightly hard (4-8° DH), alkaline water. Therefore, it can be shown that over the long term, Discus can become acclimated to even alkaline water.

Coloration and markings of Discus tend to vary with their habitat. Considering the vastness of the Amazon Basin, it is quite reasonable to assume that geographical isolation has given rise to different populations. Further careful research may eventually give different weight as to whether these variations are simply color morphs, subspecies or full species, but at present, the authors have adopted the conclusions of Dr. L. P. Schultz that there are two species of *Symphysodon*: *S. discus* and *S. aequifasciata,* and that there are three subspecies of the latter. On the other hand, further color variations in *S. aequifasciata* may become the basis for more subspecies. Recently, Dr. W. E. Burgess has proposed a new subspecies of *S. discus.*

In the Amazon Basin, Discus are collected by using a strong light to mesmerize the fish and then catching them with a dip net, or encircling the habitat with a net and then drawing it in closer, removing wood or other obstructions as it is drawn tighter.

A *Symphysodon aequifasciata aequifasciata*. Green Discus.

A Green Discus. 6 in. (15 cm). Lake Tefé, Tefé R, Purus R, Santarém. The nine dark green vertical bands on a ground of light or yellowish brown are distinct in young fish but tend to fade as they mature. There are many color variants including a wide spectrum of green or blue side markings. Discus with clear vertical bands across the entire body are known as the "Royal Green." This was the base stock from which color improvements were made, but it is still worthy of appreciation in its original form, especially when one sees a male in full nuptial coloration. Discus with red spots on the sides are called the "Peruvian Green," while those with sharp green vertical bands are known as the "Tefé Green." Breeding Discus is easy.

A Peruvian Green Discus. ◗

A *Symphysodon discus.* Heckel Blue Discus.

A Heckel Blue Discus. 6 in. (15 cm). Amazon R, Purus R, Madeira R, Xingu R. Nine vertical bands run down the sides with the ones crossing the eye and about the middle being especially wide. Light blue lines run horizontally across the entire grayish brown body. Abundant in the Amazon Basin, it is quite difficult to care for in aquaria as it is quite sensitive to poor water quality. It is best kept as a school. Breeding is said to be very difficult.

B 6 in. (15 cm). Leticia, Purus R. Usually the blue horizontal lines cover the brown body, but in some individuals, these lines become discontinuous or are restricted to the head region. The Royal Blue Discus with strong blue lines is believed to be the stock from which the Red Royal Blue Discus was developed in SE Asia. Care is rather easy.

C Brown Discus. 6 in. (15 cm). Around Belém and Manaus, Urubu R, Purus R. Blue horizontal stripes cover a pale to dark brown body. The eye is bright red. Most Brown Discus imported into Europe, North America and Japan come from SE Asia, and have a strong reddish hue to the body which is believed to come from the live foods they are fed. This hue may fade when the food source is changed. Like most other discus, care and breeding are quite easy.

B *Symphysodon aeqnifasciata haraldi.* Royal Blue Discus. ◗

C *Symphysodon aequifasciata axelrodi.* Brown Discus. Type imported from Belém. ◗

A *Symphysodon aequifasciata* var. Royal Blue Red Discus. **1** Type produced in SE Asia.

IMPROVED DISCUS TYPES

There are many improved races now available for the appreciation of aquarists, including the Royal Blue Red Discus from SE Asia and the Turquoise Discus from the U.S. or Germany. These were developed through artificial selection and hybridization with the objective of expanding the area covered by the cobalt blue coloration, the fish's most fascinating feature. Among the five subspecies of two species, it was probably from the Royal Green and Royal Blue Discus strains of *S. aequifasciata* that the improved types were derived. Such selection has concentrated on strengthening the blue coloration and making the lines clearer. Producing such improved types is painstaking work which requires many hours and an ability to cull extremely carefully. Many other improved strains, such as a Red Turquoise Discus, will probably be produced in the future.

2 This improvement derived from *S. aequifasciata* is not appreciated as much as the Turquoise Discus.

A 1-2 Royal Blue Red Discus. 7 in. (18 cm). Produced in great numbers in SE Asia, this beautiful discus has brilliant blue or green stripes running across a bright red ground color. There is a professional breeder in Bangkok specializing in the Royal Blue Red Discus that has about one hundred mated pairs producing quite a few offspring. His fish were derived from improved Royal Green and Royal Blue Discus strains of *S. aequifasciata*. Bangkok water varies in pH from slightly acid to alkaline depending on the season, while its hardness runs from 4 to 8° DH. A once or twice daily change of about ⁷⁄₁₀ of the water combined with strong aeration may be best, especially as they are very sensitive to nitrites. Just-imported Royal Blue Discus have a very colorful red body, but this pigmentation tends to fade over time. On the other hand, the blue or green stripes become more distinct. This is due to the type of food they are fed. In Southeast Asia the fish are fed ova of giant freshwater prawns as well as mosquito larvae and daphnia. To maintain the red body coloration, it is recommended that the fish be fed foods with a high carotenoid pigment content, such as krill. Young fish are also given male sex hormones to bring out the blue stripes and make them more distinct, so when this supplement is discontinued, the coloration will fade out over time. However, as these fish mature, the distinctive coloration may return.

A *Symphysodon aequifasciata* var. Wattley Turquoise Discus. "Wattley third-strain" fish are very popular among dedicated aquarists.

B *Symphysodon aequifasciata* var. German (Cobalt Blue). Turquoise Discus. This might become the most popular type in the future.

A Wattley Turquoise Discus. 7 in. (18 cm). American professional breeder Jack Wattley selected his original stock from about a thousand fish collected in the Amazon. From these, he developed three improved types. The first type has discontinuous blue lines, while the second type was sent to Germany and became the stock from which the German (Cobalt Blue) Discus was produced. The "third-strain" shown on the page to the left is characterized by its broad turquoise stripes which become even more brilliant after the fish reaches 2 in. (5 cm). As the fish grows further, these stripes become even more distinct and the ground color fades. One of the characteristics of the Wattley Turquoise Discus lines is that they have been well-fixed, so that young are very much duplicates of their parents in coloration. Care and breeding require skillful technique.

B German (Cobalt Blue) Turquoise Discus. 7 in. (18 cm). A number of famous German breeders such as Dr. Eduard Schmidt-Focke have developed a number of discus with beautiful markings and coloration including the Brilliant Turquoise, the Broken Turquoise and the Full-Color Turquoise. Dr. Schmidt-Focke developed his strain from early Green and Blue Royal Discus stocks introduced into Germany. Later on, some features from the Wattley Turquoise, from which the German (Cobalt Blue) Discus was developed, were introduced. Its strongest feature is the brilliant blue. On the other hand, the Germans have developed a Red Turquoise Discus with a red to brick-red ground color which was introduced through hybridization with discus from the Trombetas River which have a predominantly red coloration. This line has very rosy prospects. However it is far from being fixed.

A *Symphysodon aequifasciata* var. Royal Blue Red Discus. **1** Cleaning the wood spawning site.

2 Pair about to spawn (♀ below).

DISCUS SPAWNING METHOD

Raise a group of 2-2¼ in. (5-6 cm) fish in a separate tank. When they reach about 4 in. (10 cm), watch for them to pair off, and a pair that begins pecking on the glass is ready to spawn. This pair should be moved to a large tank (50 gallons or more) in which a large plastic tube, piece of slate or wood has been placed. The pair will then clean this site and then begin spawning. About 100-200 eggs will be laid and hatch out within 2-3 days. In 4-5 days afterwards, the larvae will attach themselves to the sides of their parents. The skin of the parents secretes a milky mucus which serves as the fry's first food. As they get a little larger, they will swim away from the parents. At this time they will begin eating brine shrimp, and grow to over ¾ in. (2 cm) in just one month.

A 1 A mated pair. They will spawn on a plastic pipe, slate, wood or even the glass walls of the tank. On the day they spawn, the oviduct (♀) and spermiduct (♂) extend, making sexing possible.
2 The pair prefers a spawning site that has an irregular or unglazed surface such as an inverted flower pot. They will begin spawning once the site has been meticulously cleaned.
3 You can see the female's oviduct which extends about ⅛ in. (3-4 mm) on the day of spawning. She lays about 100-200 eggs in rows of 10-20, starting from below and working her way up. These eggs hatch within 3-2 days, and 4-5 days later the brood attaches to the sides of the parents.

4 Blowing water over the eggs for aeration.

3 Female laying eggs (note extended pink oviduct).

77

DISCUS CARE

Waters of the Amazon where discus are found are slightly acid (pH 6.5), soft (0-3°DH) and range in temperature around 77-82°F (25-28°C). Wild-type stocks and those cultured in Germany are said to prefer these water conditions. Yet in Southeast Asia, discus are raised in alkaline water that is around 82-91°F (28-33°C). Their tolerance to alkalinity makes them adaptable to most N. American and Japanese water conditions. If the degree of water hardness is too high, however, either a reverse osmosis unit or an ion exchange resin filter should be used to produce water of the desired softness.

Discus are, however, sensitive to water pollutants, especially nitrites. Although nitrites can be changed to relatively harmless nitrates by microbial filtration, sufficient aeration and partial water changes remain important elements of discus maintenance. In SE Asia, breeders do not use filtration, but partial water changes are performed once or twice daily. Keeping only a few fish in a large tank will help prevent pollutants from building up too rapidly, and keep labor requirements down.

Varied foods such as blood worms, mosquito larvae and processed beef hearts will keep discus healthy. Food debris that falls to the bottom should be removed immediately so it doesn't spoil.

A There are three important points in discus care: keep the fish as a group in a large tank, keep nitrite content low by daily partial water replacement and give them a well balanced diet. Fishes produced in SE Asia and the German Turquoise are well acclimated for aquarium care and thus easy for beginners to raise if they adhere to these three points. On the other hand, wild-type stocks, the Heckel Blue and Green Discus, do not readily eat dry foods. Even well-experienced breeders have trouble maintaining good coloration in their fish as discus react to many conditions negatively, such as fading for a period after frequent water changes. To keep such discus in top shape requires tedious, daily care and a really deep affection for one's fish.

A *Symphysodon aequifasciata* var., *Symphysodon aequifasciata axelrodi.* Royal Blue Red Discus & Brown Discus pair with fry eating mucus "milk" off parents' sides.

AEQUIDENS GROUP CICHLIDS—ACARAS

Most of the cichlids in this group were formerly included in the genus *Aequidens*. Acaras are distributed mainly within the tropical region of South America, and range in size from the small Flag Cichlid to the large Port Acara. Their mild-tempered nature has made them popular aquarium fishes for a long time, especially as they coexist easily with same-size fish in a large community tank. Since they don't uproot plants, except occasionally during breeding season, they can be kept in a nicely aquascaped aquarium.

ACARA SPAWNING BEHAVIOR

Of the three types of acara spawning behavior, the most general one has the fish laying adhesive eggs on flat stones followed by bi-parental care of the developing eggs and free-swimming juveniles. With the second type (as in *A. coeruleopunctatus*), the pair spawns on fallen leaves. This allows them to move the eggs to safety if an enemy threatens or their location begins to dry up. Both parents defend the mobile young. The third type, characteristic of all *Bujurquina, Tahuantinsuyoa*, as well as two *Aequidens* species, is primitive or delayed mouthbrooding. Eggs are deposited on a flat surface, but one or both parents carry the newly hatched fry in their oral cavity until they are free swimming. Both parents care for the mobile young, who are allowed to re-enter the adults' mouth when seriously threatened.

Adults are not sensitive to water chemistry, but slightly acidic, soft water is preferable during spawning and juvenile care. As they prefer new water, frequent water changes are desirable.

A 1-2 The pair locks jaws to test each other's strength prior to spawning.
3 After the spawning site, fallen leaves or a flat rock, is selected, the pair cleans it with their mouth.
4 Moving along the stone, the ♀ lays her eggs. The ♂ will follow in the same manner to fertilize them.
5 As if the ovipositor has some ability to sense the presence of eggs, the ♀ lays the ova row next to row, never on top of one another.
6 Both ♂ and ♀ circulate water over the eggs to keep them supplied with oxygen and help prevent bacterial attack.

A *Aequidens pulcher*. Blue Acara.   **1** Prenuptial strength contest.

2 Locking jaws as a test.

3 ♀ cleaning the spawning site.

4 Spawning begins.　　　　　**5** Closeup of ovipositor during egglaying.　　　　　**6** Pectorals circulate water over eggs.

7 The pair may prepare several depressions in advance in which to rear their young. Before these fry become free swimming, their parents may periodically move them from hole to hole.

8-9 Once the yolk sac is depleted, the fry will become free swimming. At this stage, they should be fed brine shrimp. The pair will stand guard as their fry feed. If danger approaches, the parents will make a quick motion to signal their young, who will drop down to the tank bottom as the pair hovers over them.

8 Pair cares for their young.

9 ♀ guarding her free-swimming fry as they search for food. ▶

A 1 The Paraguay Acara spawns on flat surfaces such as stones or fallen leaves like many other acara species. However, the juveniles will be kept in the oral cavity of the parents. Four species within this genus are known to be such primitive mouth-brooders. This photo shows the fry at the moment of hatch being sucked into the parent's mouth; the egg case remaining attached to the stone.

2 ♀ with her buccal cavity filled with her young.

3 Fry spend about their first week within the oral cavity, at the end of which their yolk sac has been absorbed and they emerge from the mouth searching for food. It has been observed that for another week they will retreat into their parent's oral cavity for the night or should danger approach.

A 1 Sucking up newly hatched fry.　　　　**2** Mouthbrooding ♀.

3 *Bujurquina vittata*. Paraguay Acara ♀ spews out about 150 young.

B *Cichlasoma portalegrense.* Port Acara.

C *Cleithracara maronii.* Keyhole Cichlid.

D *Laetacara curviceps.* Flag Acara.

E *Aequidens* sp. (cf. *A. rivulatus*). Orange-Trim Acara.

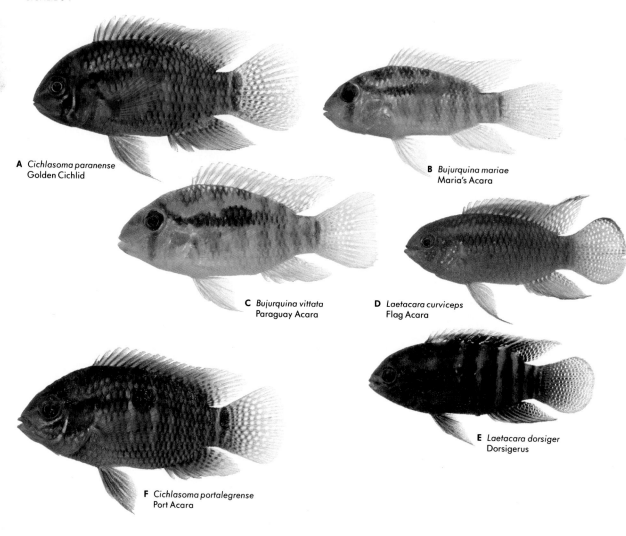

A *Cichlasoma paranense*
Golden Cichlid

B *Bujurquina mariae*
Maria's Acara

C *Bujurquina vittata*
Paraguay Acara

D *Laetacara curviceps*
Flag Acara

E *Laetacara dorsiger*
Dorsigerus

F *Cichlasoma portalegrense*
Port Acara

A 8 in. (20 cm). Guapori R. in Brazil. A rather delicate *Cichlasoma* species, it is however, not sensitive to water quality. Omnivorous, it will eat both dry and live foods such as aquatic worms and earthworms.

B 6 in. (15 cm). Upper reaches of the Amazon R, Peru, Colombia. Prefers slightly acidic, soft water. If the young are reared in alkaline water, they may become stunted and the body, misshapen. Live foods such as aquatic worms and earthworms are preferable. The eggs are laid on stones. When the fry hatch out, they will be immediately sucked into the parental oral cavity to be cared for. Egg cases will remain attached to the stone.

C 4¾ in. (12 cm). Parana R system. Prefers slightly acidic, soft water. Omnivorous, it likes live foods best. A mouthbrooder, it spawns on fallen leaves. Except during spawning season, this peaceful fish can be kept in a community tank with characins or other cichlids.

D 3¼ in. (8 cm). Amazon R. system. Prefers neutral to slightly acidic water. Well suited for community aquaria, it is mild tempered and not a bottom digger. An easy breeder, the ♀ lays 150-250 eggs on a stone or wood. Excellent parental care is extended over the eggs and fry. Although quite small, the newly hatched larvae are able to catch and eat brine shrimp.

E 3¼ in. (8 cm). Southern tributaries of the Amazon. Prefers neutral to slightly acidic, new water. An easy breeder, like the above, it lays about 300 eggs in a single spawning. The pair well cares for their fry, and it is said that they will not even drive them away when they next spawn.

F 10 in. (25 cm). Bolivia, southern Brazil. Although not fussy about water conditions and can even tolerate temperatures down to about 61°F (16°C), it does prefer new

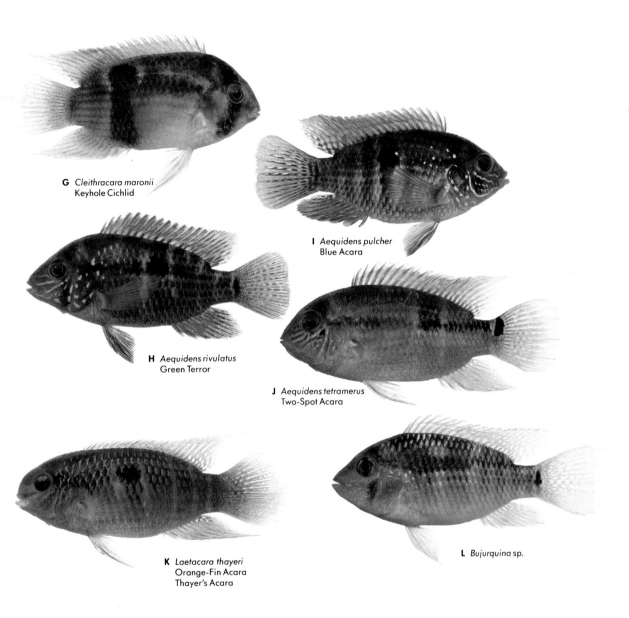

G *Cleithracara maronii*
Keyhole Cichlid

I *Aequidens pulcher*
Blue Acara

H *Aequidens rivulatus*
Green Terror

J *Aequidens tetramerus*
Two-Spot Acara

K *Laetacara thayeri*
Orange-Fin Acara
Thayer's Acara

L *Bujurquina* sp.

water. Care for this omnivorous fish is easy, but as it grows quite large, a good-sized tank is needed. For breeding, a temperature of around 75°F (24°C) is best.
G 6 in. (15 cm) max, in aquaria ♂ 4 in. (10 cm), ♀ 3 in. (7.5 cm). The Guianas. Prefers slightly acidic, soft water. A mild-mannered omnivorous fish that seldom digs in the tank bottom, it is well suited for community aquaria. Breeding is easy.
H 6 in. (15 cm). Colombia. Prefers slightly acidic, soft water. Periodic water replacement is important to keep this omnivorous fish in top physical condition as it does best in new water. Breeding is rather difficult.
I Reaches 6¾ in. (17 cm) in nature, 4¾-5 in. (12-13 cm) in aquaria. Colombia, Panama, Trinidad, Tobago, Venezuela. Rather tolerant of water quality, however it should be kept in new water as in used water it has a tendency to become infected with Ich. Omnivorous, its care and breeding are easy.

J 7-10 in. (18-25 cm). Guyana, northern and western Amazon Basin. Prefers slightly acidic, soft water. Although care of this rather large fish is said to be difficult, it is quite beautiful and attractive. A delayed mouthbrooder, juveniles are kept in the parent's oral cavity.
K 6 in. (15 cm). Southern Brazil, eastern Bolivia. Prefers neutral to slightly acid, soft water. A mild-tempered fish well suited for community aquaria, its care and breeding are easy.
L 2¾ in. (7 cm). Max. length unknown. Its care is easy. As both sexes are not available at the same time, breeding has not been attempted.

2 After ♀ lays the eggs, the ♂ ejaculates over them.

EARTHEATERS

Fishes of this five-genera lineage are widely distributed throughout S. America: *Geophagus* in the Amazon, Orinoco, Magdelena, Atrato basins, and the coastal rivers of the Guianas; a single species, *G. crassilabris,* extending as far north as Central Panama; *Gymnogeophagus* in the Rio Parana drainage, and coastal rivers of southern Brazil and Uruguay; *Satanoperca* and *Biotodoma* in the Amazon and Orinoco drain-ages and the coastal rivers of the Guianas; and *Retroculus,* highly modified eartheaters, lim-ited to the extensive rapid systems in the south-ern Amazon Basin and French Guiana. Most species are hardy and tolerant to variation in water chemistry, although all eartheaters are extremely sensitive to dissolved metabolic wastes. *Gymnogeophagus gymnogenys,* found in Argentina, is quite resistant to temperatures down to 54°F (12°C).

Eartheaters' habit of plunging their mouth deep into the substratum in search of food makes them incompatible with aquatic plants. A large tank, the bottom covered with fine sand, and outfitted with many shelters should be prepared for them. If kept in a small tank, however, quite a few should be kept together to prevent them from forming territo-ries. In general, they rarely attack even the same-sized fish of other species.

3 ♂ and ♀ poking at their eggs, sucking up newly hatched fry.

EARTHEATER SPAWNING BEHAVIOR

This behavior ranges from substratum spawners like *G. brasiliensis* which lay their eggs on flat surfaces and care for them in the open; to advanced mouthbrooders like *G. steindachneri* that take their eggs into the mouth just after laying them and mouthbrood them until an advanced juvenile stage; and the intermediate mode of primitive mouthbrooders such as *G. brachybranchus* and *Satanoperca leucostictus*.

A 1-2 Once the pair has carefully cleaned the spawning site with their mouths, the ♀ lays her eggs on this stone or other flat surface in a linear pattern. The ♂ then follows the same pattern and ejaculates over the eggs. After spawning is completed, the pair then spreads fine sand over the eggs.
3 Eggs hatch within 2-3 days. Here, the ♀ pokes at the eggs and sucks up the newly hatched fry.
4 As mainly the ♀ cares for the fry, the ♂ should be removed to prevent quarrels. During the next two weeks or so, the fry will move in and out of the oral cavity of the ♀.

4 Fry released from oral cavity.

A *Geophagus steindachneri.* Redhump Eartheater.   **1** ♀ (left) laying a batch of four eggs in a row, while ♂ waits.

Most cichlids dig a series of substrata depressions in advance, then, once the fry hatch, scoop them up into their mouth and transfer them from hole to hole. It is generally held that lengthening periods of holding the young within the buccal cavity led to mouthbrooding.

Gymnogeophagus balzanii lay eggs on stones, and then after about 25 hours, suck the larvae into their mouth cavity, leaving the egg cases behind. As the notochord formation in these larvae is incomplete, this behavior may represent the last stage in this species evolving into an advanced mouthbrooder that holds the eggs in the mouth from right after being laid.

A 1-2 The ♂ establishes a territory over a flat rock, and the ♀ enters it to begin spawning. She lays batches of 2-7 rather large eggs which she scoops into her mouth. This is repeated until a clutch totalling 20-40 eggs is being held. Unlike haplochromine cichlids, in which the ♀ sucks sperm from the spermiduct into her mouth, and then scoops in her eggs, the exact point of fertilization in *G. steindachneri* has not been observed and is therefore unknown.

2 ♀ (left) will then turn around and scoop the ova into her mouth.

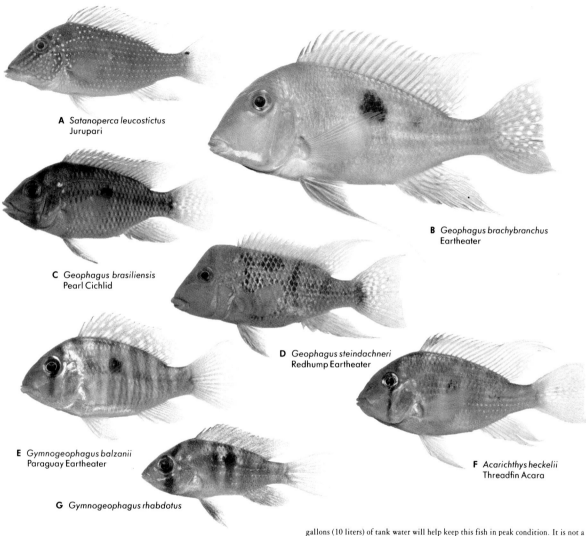

A *Satanoperca leucostictus*
Jurupari

B *Geophagus brachybranchus*
Eartheater

C *Geophagus brasiliensis*
Pearl Cichlid

D *Geophagus steindachneri*
Redhump Eartheater

E *Gymnogeophagus balzanii*
Paraguay Eartheater

F *Acarichthys heckelii*
Threadfin Acara

G *Gymnogeophagus rhabdotus*

A 10 in. (25 cm) max. in nature, 6-8 in. (15-20 cm) in aquaria. Northern Brazil, Guiana. Prefers neutral to slightly acidic water. This water should be kept at over 77°F (25°C) as it is sensitive to low temperatures. Care is easy for this peaceful community fish. A primitive mouthbrooder, it lays eggs on stones and mouthbroods the young after hatching for a relatively long period (two weeks). Feed the fry brine shrimp as they will periodically emerge from the mouth to forage. Due to its habit of repeatedly sucking up sand from the tank bottom, and then as it swims, spitting this sand out or having it pass out through the gill slits, this fish fully deserves the name "Eartheater."
B 10 in. (25 cm). The Guianas. Prefers slightly acidic, soft water. An easy to care for omnivore, it is quite attractive when in top shape when kept in favorable water conditions. It easily breeds like the above fish. However, a number of superficially similar species are native to the Amazon Basin, and several of these look-alike species are advanced mouthbrooders.
C 12 in. (30 cm) max., 8 in. (20 cm) in aquaria. Coastal rivers of SE Brazil. As it inhabits both fresh and brackish waters, the addition of a teaspoonful of salt per 2½

gallons (10 liters) of tank water will help keep this fish in peak condition. It is not a mouthbrooder.
D 4¾ in. (12 cm). Prefers neutral water. Peaceful when young, once the ♂ develops the characteristic head hump, it is highly territorial and pugnacious. For successful breeding, a single ♂ should be kept in a large tank with a number of shelters, and a few females should be introduced. *G. hondae* is a junior synonym.
E Reaches 4¾-6 in. (12-15 cm). La Plata R, Paraguay R. Prefers neutral to slightly acidic, soft water. This highly dimorphic eartheater is a primitive mouthbrooder. It prefers cooler water than most cichlids, and if kept too warm its care is rather difficult.
F 8 in. (20 cm). Brazil, Colombia, Venezuela, Guiana. A beautiful close relative of the acaras, this species closely resembles a *Geophagus* species. Care is like that of *Geophagus*. Spawning this harem breeding cave spawner is quite difficult under aquarium conditions.
G Reaches 4 in. (10 cm) in aquaria. Southern Brazil. This recently, rarely imported eartheater prefers cool, neutral water with a low nitrite content. Hostile to conspecifics, this substrate spawner should be kept in a large tank with many retreats.

APISTOGRAMMA & OTHER NEW WORLD DWARF CICHLIDS

Widely distributed throughout the jungle brooks of tropical and subtropical South America, over 50 species of the genus *Apistogramma* have been identified. Together with the other genera of New World dwarf cichlids, they are quite sensitive to water quality, especially so to a high nitrite content. Their preference is for slightly acidic, soft water (pH 5-6, 0-3°DH) kept at a relatively low temperature of 73-77°F (23-25°C). To keep the nitrite level down, the water should be periodically replaced and well aerated. The tank should also contain many areas for shelter such as driftwood and numerous plants.

All of these cichlids are relatively small, and do not uproot plants. They are highly appreciated as aquarium fish as they will coexist well in a community tank with characins.

SPAWNING BEHAVIOR

The pair will spawn on the underside of a rock, driftwood or inside a flower pot. 50-200 eggs will be laid which hatch out within 2-5 days, and become free swimming 4-6 days after hatching. Mainly the female cares for the eggs and fry. These larvae prefer live foods such as brine shrimp, daphnia, and cut up earthworms.

A 1 A cave spawner, the ♀ lays eggs inside a coconut shell while the ♂ waits to fertilize them in the same inverted manner.
2 Fry hover around the ♀. About 10 days after hatching, such behavior begins, and parental care will continue until the young are about one month old.

2 ♀ guarding young.

A *Apistogramma trifasciatum*. Blue Apistogramma. **1** Upside-down ♀ lays eggs inside a coconut shell; ♂ at left.

92

A *Crenicara filamentosa*. Checkerboard Cichlid. ♀ guarding her ova deposited on a plant leaf.

D *Crenicara* sp.

B An easily bred, long time aquarium favorite.

C 4 in. (10 cm). Western Amazon Basin. Prefers slightly acidic water. Care is easy. Previously, it was placed in the genus *Aequidens*.

B *Papiliochromis ramirezi*. Ram.

C *Crenicara punctulata*. Hercules Cichlid.

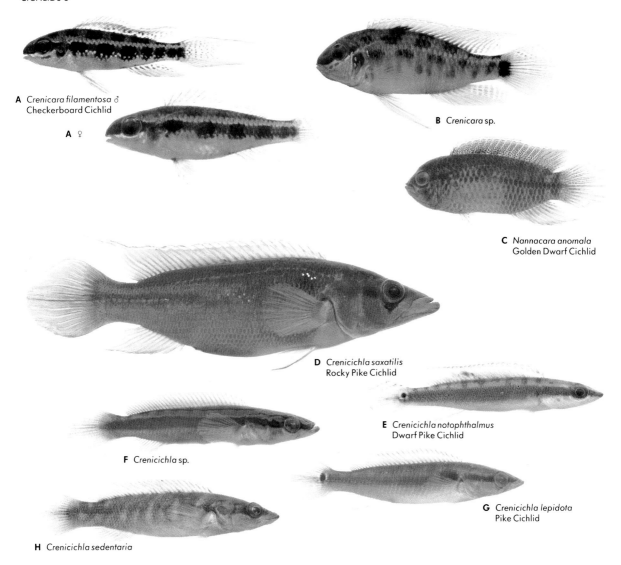

A *Crenicara filamentosa* ♂
Checkerboard Cichlid

A ♀

B *Crenicara* sp.

C *Nannacara anomala*
Golden Dwarf Cichlid

D *Crenicichla saxatilis*
Rocky Pike Cichlid

E *Crenicichla notophthalmus*
Dwarf Pike Cichlid

F *Crenicichla* sp.

G *Crenicichla lepidota*
Pike Cichlid

H *Crenicichla sedentaria*

A 3¼ in. (8 cm). Amazon R Basin. Prefers slightly acidic, soft water, and is quite sensitive to water pollution. A rather difficult omnivore to care for, it has a mild demeanor, so it may coexist with other fish if the tank is well planted. Breeding is also difficult, but not impossible.

B ♂ 4¾ in. (12 cm), ♀ 2¼ in. (6 cm). Middle reaches of the Amazon R including the Rio Negro basin. Prefers neutral to slightly acidic water.

C ♂ 3¼ in. (8 cm), ♀ 2 in. (5 cm). The Guianas. Prefers neutral to alkaline water. A peaceful fish, it does well in community aquaria. Spawning takes place inside a flower pot. Only the ♀ cares for the fry which hatch out after 2-3 days. They become free swimming when 4-5 days old.

D 10 in. (25 cm). Amazon R Basin, Grande R, Orinoco, Guiana. Tolerant of varied water conditions, this piscivore catches small fish, but will also eat dried shrimp.

E 4 in. (10 cm). Amazon R from Santarém to Manaus. Called the "Dwarf Pike," it is however, mild tempered compared to the larger, pugnacious cichlids, so it can be appreciated as a community fish. The ♀ can be identified by the dark blotch on the dorsal fin which is absent in the ♂.

F 10 in. (25 cm). Paraguay, Bolivia, Brazilian Mato Grosso State. Adult fish have a distinct black band running the full length of the reddish body.

G 10 in. (25 cm). Amazon R Basin, Guiana, Paraguay, Uruguay, Argentina. Like *C. saxatilis*, it is quite common, care is easy and it feeds on small fishes. A healthy pair, when available, will spawn 800-1,000 eggs in a single clutch.

H 6 in. (15 cm). Max. length unknown. Native to the western Amazon Basin. This species has a degenerate swim bladder and moves along the bottom in a hopping manner.

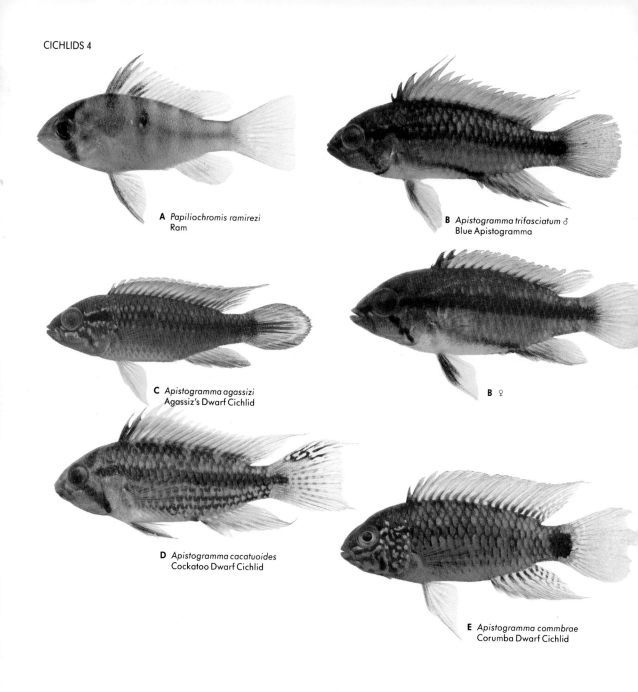

A *Papiliochromis ramirezi*
Ram

B *Apistogramma trifasciatum* ♂
Blue Apistogramma

C *Apistogramma agassizi*
Agassiz's Dwarf Cichlid

B ♀

D *Apistogramma cacatuoides*
Cockatoo Dwarf Cichlid

E *Apistogramma commbrae*
Corumba Dwarf Cichlid

F *Apistogramma inconspicua* ♂
Checkered Dwarf Cichlid

F ♀

G *Apistogramma borellii*
Yellow Dwarf Cichlid

H *Apistogramma pertensis*
Slender Dwarf Cichlid

I *Apistogramma eunotus*

J *Apistogramma rupununi*
Two-Spot Apisto

A 2 in. (5 cm). Upper and middle reaches of the Orinoco R in Venezuela and Colombia. Prefers slightly acidic, soft 79-82°F (26-28°C) water. A peaceful and popular community tank fish, its care is rather difficult. It spawns on stones or wood, laying about 100-400 eggs in a clutch. Both parents care for the spawn. An artificially selected fold form is widely available.

B ♂ 2¼ in. (6 cm), ♀ 1½ in. (4 cm). Paraguay R, Guaporé R. A hardy fish that is rather tolerant of water quality, it prefers slightly acidic, soft water. It spawns easily, laying 60-100 eggs on a flower pot or wood. Although parental care of the eggs is possible, it is probably better to separate the pair from their eggs the next day. The young will eat brine shrimp.

C 3 in. (7.5 cm). Amazon R Basin to Bolivia. Prefers neutral to slightly acidic, soft aged water. Care is rather difficult, but it does best when a few individuals are kept together in a large, well-aerated, planted tank to which a number of woody shelters have been added. Inside a flower pot or on wood it will lay a clutch of 50-100 eggs which will hatch out within 3-4 days. Feed the fry brine shrimp when they are about a week old and free swimming.

D 2¼ in. (6 cm). Extreme upper reaches of the Amazon R. Soft, slightly acidic water is preferred. A rather hardy fish that is easy to care for and breed. During the spawning season the ♂ becomes belligerent and will attack other fishes and even its mate. Accordingly, a large spawning tank should be prepared. About 50-150 eggs will be laid in an enclosed space. Parental care is exclusively the responsibility of the ♀.

E ♂ 2¼ in. (6 cm), ♀ 1¾ in. (4.5 cm). Upper reaches of Paraná R, Meta R. A well-planted tank with many shelters and filled with aged water is preferred. An acclimated fish will eat flake foods, but a ripe ♀ does best on live foods. It is easily bred.

F 2 in. (5 cm). Paraguay R down to Rio de la Plata. Caring for this mild-tempered species is very easy. A ♀ of about 1¼ in. (3 cm) is capable of spawning and will lay 60-100 eggs. This species is usually exported mixed in with such congeners as *A. borellii* and *A. trifasciatum.*

G 2¼ in. (6 cm). Paraguay R. Prefers neutral to slightly acidic, clear aged water. *A. reitzigi* is a junior synonym for this bright, metallic blue bodied fish, the ♂ of which has a tall, elongated dorsal and deep anal fin. It is easily bred. Recently, fish produced in Singapore have been exported to Japan and N. America.

H ♂ 2¼ in. (6 cm), ♀ 1¾ in. (4.5 cm). Middle reaches of the Amazon R from Santarém to Manaus. Prefers slightly acidic, soft water. A beautiful, easily raised and bred, nonbelligerent fish, it lays 50-100 eggs in a single spawning. Parents care for the eggs and young.

I 2 in. (5 cm). Solimões R (upper Amazon R – Manaus to Peru). Prefers slightly acidic, clear water. Blood worms plus other aquatic worms are its preferred food. Breeding is easy, and 50-100 eggs are laid in a spawning.

J 2¾ in. (7 cm). Potaro R & Rupununi R in Guyana. Prefers water low in nitrites. Its care and breeding are easy. One of the larger species of this genus, it is also known as the "Two-Spot Apisto." Similar in appearance to *A. steindachneri,* it lacks the lyre-shaped caudal fin of that species.

A *Pterophyllum altum*. Altum or Orinoco Angelfish. This wild angelfish can prove quite attractive when kept with discus and small characins.

ANGELFISH & ITS ARTIFICIAL STRAINS

Angelfish are among the most representative and popular of all tropical fish. Although the discus has increased in popularity, the angelfish still holds a large following because of the abundance of artificially produced strains and the ease with which it can be bred.

Four nominal species of angelfish are recognized at present: *Pterophyllum scalare, P. leopoldi, P. dumerilii* and *P. altum*. Both *P. dumerilii* and *P. leopoldi* are very similar in body shape and other characteristics to *P. scalare,* leading some authorities to suggest that they may

B *Pterophyllum scalare* var. Marble Angelfish.

C *Pterophyllum scalare* var. Blushing Angelfish.

D *Pterophyllum scalare* var. Golden Angelfish.

E *Pterophyllum scalare* var. Black Angelfish.

be synonyms of that species. Thus, only the taxonomic status of *P. altum* is certain, while the other three species need closer study.

Wild stocks are very sensitive to water conditions, making their care difficult, but the artificially produced strains have a mild demeanor and are easy to breed. As innumerable improved strains have been produced, there is a good chance for even an amateur to develop a new type of angelfish.

ANGELFISH SPAWNING BEHAVIOR

Angelfish exhibit typical cichlid spawning behavior. Among 5-8 fish, at least one pair will separate themselves from the others. Prepare another tank into which a flower pot, a spawning tube or broad-leaved plants such as Amazon Swords have been placed, and then introduce this pair into it. Once they begin cleaning a site, the pair will begin spawning in 1-2 days. The female creeps along the site laying down the ova in a linear fashion with the male following and fertilizing them in the same fashion. Sometimes the two will move in parallel. This is repeated a number of times until several hundred to a thousand eggs are laid. Hatching occurs within 2-4 days with the fry remaining attached to the site by a thread from their head. Once the yolk sac is depleted, the larvae become free swimming. At this point, the young should be fed brine shrimp. Throughout this period, the parents exercise strong care.

A 1 While the ♀ lays her eggs on an Amazon Sword-plant, the ♂ follows in parallel releasing sperm over the eggs to fertilize them.

2-3 Both parents take intensive care of the brood, circulating water over them by using their pectoral fins, and removing dead eggs so as to help prevent fungal growth. Once the fry begin swimming, the pair are kept busy scooping up errant young in their mouth and placing them back in the nest.

◀**A** *Pterophyllum scalare*. Angelfish.   **1** The spawn.   ◀**2** Water is circulated over newly hatched fry.   **3** Parent returns errant fry.

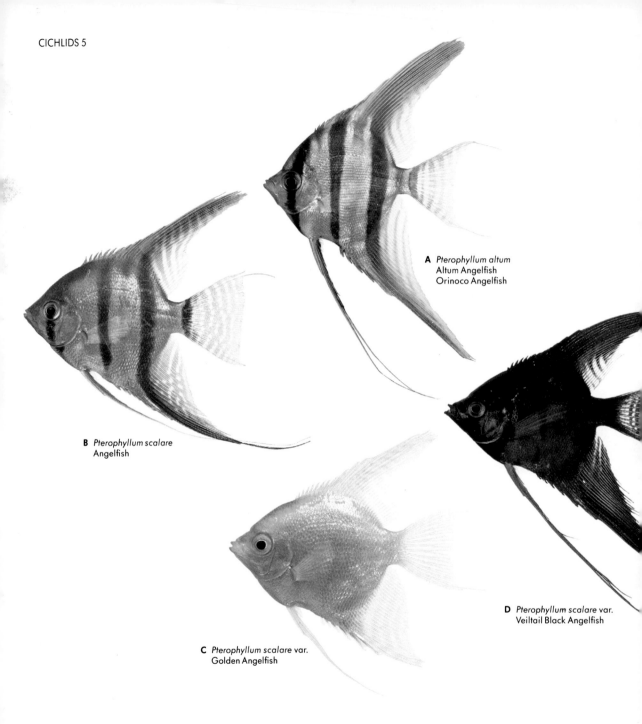

A *Pterophyllum altum*
Altum Angelfish
Orinoco Angelfish

B *Pterophyllum scalare*
Angelfish

C *Pterophyllum scalare* var.
Golden Angelfish

D *Pterophyllum scalare* var.
Veiltail Black Angelfish

A 6 in. (15 cm). Orinoco R in Venezuela. Prefers slightly acidic, soft (pH 6.8, 0°DH) 79°F (26°C) water. Being wilder than the cultured angelfishes, it is quite sensitive to water chemistry. About 300-400 eggs are laid on an Amazon Swordplant leaf, and will hatch out in 3 days. The fry will become free swimming at 10 days old, at which time they should be fed brine shrimp. Parental care is well exercised over the larvae.
B 6 in. (15 cm). Found in the grassy banks of the Amazon R or brooks that have

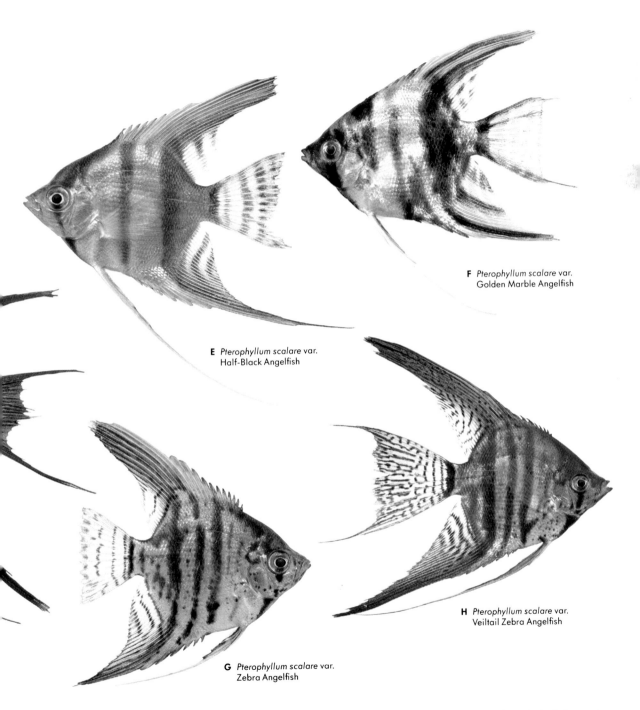

F *Pterophyllum scalare* var.
Golden Marble Angelfish

E *Pterophyllum scalare* var.
Half-Black Angelfish

H *Pterophyllum scalare* var.
Veiltail Zebra Angelfish

G *Pterophyllum scalare* var.
Zebra Angelfish

become ponds during the rainy season, it is hardy, easy to care for, and not fussy about water conditions. To induce pairing, 7-8 adult fish in a large tank should be heavily fed on earthworms or aquatic worms. Once a pair has formed, transfer them to a medium-sized aquarium that is furnished with Amazon Swords or a plastic tube for spawning. They will easily breed.
C-H are artificially improved strains.

A *Astronotus ocellatus* var. Red Oscar. Although its appearance is awesome, it's not so ferocious. A pair forms a stronger bond than other species.

HEROS & RELATED CICHLIDS

Most of the 60-plus species of this lineage were formerly included in the genus *Cichlasoma*. Widely distributed from southern N. America through Central America to S. America, these cichlids vary greatly in size, shape and temperament. The small Flag Cichlid and the Firemouth are quite peaceful, while many of the group's larger representatives are definitely belligerent and cannot be kept with other fish. So although attractive, members of this lineage are generally regarded as brawlers.

S. American species tend to prefer soft, slightly acidic water (espe-

cially the fry). Central American species prefer harder, neutral to moderately alkaline water. Frequent water replacement is however important, as all these fish are sensitive to nitrite build-up. Although their care is easy, they should be kept in a large aquarium equipped with a good outside filter. Most species are heavy diggers whose behavior will disrupt the workings of an undergravel filter. Omnivorous and heavy eaters, they require a balanced diet to prevent body deformation or a drop in fertility. Most members of this group are long lived and learn to recognize their owner.

B *Nandopsis octofasciatus.* Jack Dempsey. Named after the famous boxer, this is one of the most popular members of this group.

A *Nandopsis salvini*. Salvin's Cichlid. ♀ (below) spawns while the ♂ waits to fertilize the eggs.

BREEDING THE CICHLASOMA GROUP

The key to successful breeding of these cichlids is to have a healthy pair. To induce pairing, 5-6 adults should be kept in a single tank. Once a pair separates itself from the others, remove the other fish. A good pair will take devoted care of their eggs and young. It is well known that Jack Dempsey, Red Devil and Midas Cichlid fry eat a specially secreted mucus off the body of their parents. Salvin's Cichlid fry grow well in the company of their parents, but don't grow as fast if separated from their parents just after hatching. So maybe in this case too, the par-

B *Nandopsis managuensis*. Managuense. Guarding the eggs.

C *Neetroplus nematopus*. Eggs on the underside of a stone being guarded.

ents are supplying some unknown nutrient. Parental *Neetroplus nematopus,* Midas and Convict Cichlids will steal the young from other pairs and care for them along with their own young. In the wild, Nicaragua Cichlid males,

for some mysterious reason, assist pairs of the large and belligerent predator, *Nandopsis dovii,* to care for their fry.

B Managuense ♀ using her pectoral fins to circulate water over her eggs.
C During the period from spawning through parental care of the fry, the normal black on a grey striped pattern of *Neetroplus nematopus* reverses to white on black.

A *Herotilapia multispinosa*. Rainbow Cichlid. **1** Removing dead eggs.

2 Spawning continues for some time.

A 1 After spawning is completed, the pair pokes at the eggs and removes the infertile ones so as to keep the others from becoming fungused.
2 Eggs are laid and fertilized a few at a time until the full clutch is attached to the site.
3 Parents care for the fry long after they become free swimming.

3 Parent caring for its newly free-swimming fry. ▶

A *Cichla monoculus*. Tucunaré. This large cichlid, also known as the "Peacock Bass," can reach 40 in. (1 m) in length, and is thus a distinctive representative of Amazonian fishes.

A *Nandopsis octofasciatus*
Jack Dempsey

A (Young)

C *Theraps synspilus*
Quetzal Cichlid

B *Theraps nicaraguensis*
Nicaragua Cichlid

D *Amphilophus labiatus*

D *Amphilophus labiatus* var.
Red Devil

E *Nandopsis salvini*
Salvin's Cichlid

F *Hypselecara temporalis*
Chocolate Cichlid

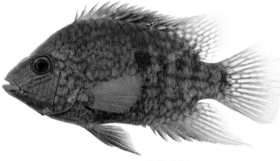

G *Herichthys carpintis*
Tampico Cichlid

H *Archocentrus nigrofasciatus*
Convict Cichlid

H *Archocentrus nigrofasciatus* var.
Pink Cichlid

A 8 in. (20 cm). Guatemala, Belize and SE Mexico. Not really fussy, but prefers neutral to slightly acidic water. Adult ♂ is quite pugnacious to the same and other species, but this appears to be a case of territoriality as it does not seriously attack others when placed in a very large tank. When a pair is healthy, it will easily spawn, laying 800 eggs in a clutch.

B 10 in. (25 cm). Great Lakes of Nicaragua, Atlantic slope of Costa Rica. Both sexes turn a brilliant orange during the spawning season. Breeding is rather difficult. Using the mouth, it digs a large hole in the sand under a flat stone where the eggs are laid. The eggs aren't adhesive. Parents take good care of the eggs and fry.

C 12 in. (30 cm). SE Mexico, Belize. Prefers neutral to slightly alkaline, fresh water. Hardy, it readily eats tubifex, blood worms, etc. as well as dry foods. While young, it peacefully coexists with other fish of about the same size, but as an adult, it becomes defensive during spawning season. Breeding is rather difficult.

D 10-12 in. (25-30 cm). Great Lakes of Nicaragua, Atlantic slope of Costa Rica. There are many color morphs including black, vermillion and mottled. One of the most aggressive cichlids, large individuals are quite pugnacious to conspecifics and other species. Breeding is easy if the pair is compatible. If not, they may kill each other.

E ♂ 7 in. (18 cm), ♀ 4 in. (10 cm). Honduras, Guatemala, Belize, SE Mexico. Prefers neutral to slightly alkaline, fresh water. A reclusive species, it usually remains hidden among aquatic flora or behind rocks. Extremely aggressive towards other cichlids in captivity. It is a beautiful fish with a strongly contrasting, variegated color pattern. Once a pair bonds, it spawns easily. The fry should be kept with the adults as they appear to furnish an early nutritional source, so that if the fry are separated, they will do poorly.

F Reaches 12 in. (30 cm) in nature, 8 in. (20 cm) in aquaria. Upper reaches of the Amazon R, Guiana. Sensitive to water quality. If neutral to slightly acidic new water is not maintained, its color quickly fades. It's hardy, and will readily devour any kind of food. Breeding is rather difficult.

G 10 in. (25 cm). Rio Panuco basin of northern Mexico. A large, beautiful fish that is pugnacious by nature, caution should be exercised when keeping its conspecifics or other species. Around spawning time, its ventral region from jaw to belly and the posterior body turn blackish, making it even more attractive.

H 4 in. (10 cm). Central America. Relatively small, it is still belligerent, so should be kept in a large tank. A bonded pair will spawn repeatedly and take good care of their eggs and larvae. Care and breeding are therefore easy. An oligomelanic, pink variant (below) is also available.

A *Mesonauta festivus*
Flag Cichlid

B *Thorichthys meeki*
Firemouth

C *Heros severus*
Severum

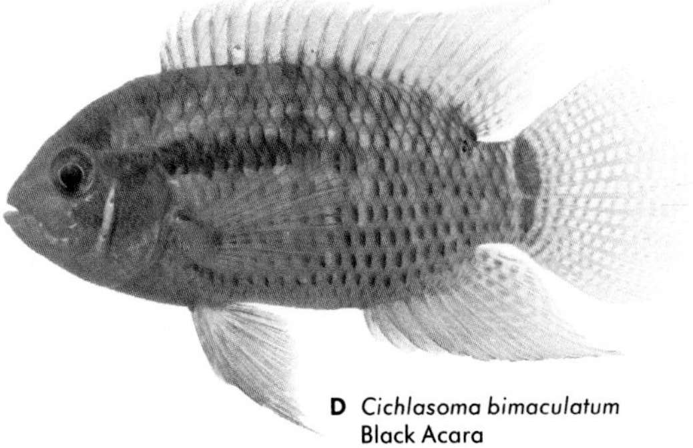

D *Cichlasoma bimaculatum*
Black Acara

C *Heros severus var.*
Gold Severum

A Reaches 6 in. (15 cm) in nature. Middle reaches of the Amazon R, the Guianas. Prefers neutral to slightly acidic water. Will eat both dry and live foods, but these should be supplemented with vegetable matter. A peaceful fish that does well in a community tank, it is somewhat skittish, so it shouldn't be kept with very active fish. It reaches maturity at about one year old, and will lay 500-1,000 eggs on wood, stone or aquatic plants.

B 6 in. (15 cm). From SE Mexico to Belize. Not fussy about water conditions, it is easy to care for. It will usually remain hidden behind stones as it is by nature, nervous. After spawning however, it becomes belligerent, menacing other fish with its extended red gill covers. Breeding is easy.

C Reaches 8 in. (20 cm) in nature, less in aquaria. Amazon R Basin and northern S. America. Hardy and easy to care for, it is tolerant of varied water conditions. A bonded pair will lay about 1,000 eggs and guard their young. The same is true for the "Golden Severum" variant shown at right.

D Max. 8 in. (20 cm) in nature, 6 in. (15 cm) in aquaria. The Guianas. One of "acaras" (see p. 80), it resembles the Port Acara, but can be distinguished by its greater number of anal fin spines.

E ♂ 20 in. (50 cm), ♀ 16 in. (40 cm). Atlantic slope of Central America from Honduras to southern Costa Rica. A large, beautiful fish that is mainly piscivorous, acclimated individuals will eat dry food. Breeding is rather easy, and the pair will lay

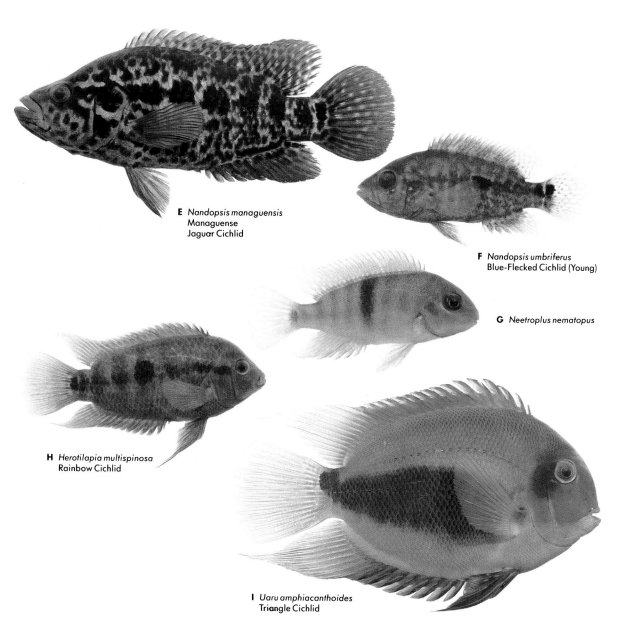

E *Nandopsis managuensis*
Managuense
Jaguar Cichlid

F *Nandopsis umbriferus*
Blue-Flecked Cichlid (Young)

G *Neetroplus nematopus*

H *Herotilapia multispinosa*
Rainbow Cichlid

I *Uaru amphiacanthoides*
Triangle Cichlid

more than 1,000 eggs. As the pair bond is not strong, swapping mates is possible.
F ♂ 24 in. (60 cm), ♀ 22 in. (55 cm). Central Panama to Magdalena R, Colombia. One of the largest representatives of the group. This fish is carnivorous, consuming small fish and shrimp, and is very pugnacious. It has been bred in aquaria.
G ♂ 5½ in. (14 cm), ♀ 3¼ in. (8 cm). Great Lakes of Nicaragua, Atlantic slope of Costa Rica. Hardy and easy to care for, it isn't fussy about water conditions. 50-80 eggs will be laid on the underside of stones, etc. and they will hatch out within 5-6 days. The fry will become free swimming when 7 days old.
H 6 in. (15 cm). Atlantic slope of Costa Rica and Nicaragua. Care of this omnivorous fish is easy as it can be kept in a community tank with other mild-mannered ones. A

pair will lay 200-400 eggs in a single spawning, and care for both eggs and fry.
I 10 in. (25 cm). Middle reaches of the Amazon R, Guyana. Sensitive to water quality that should be soft and slightly acidic. This strongly herbivorous cichlid is otherwise easy to care for, however. The irregular black body pattern seen on the young fades out. With good care a large triangular black patch takes its place in adults. Breeding is difficult. Parents care for the eggs which are laid on wood or stone. Like with the discus, mobile young gather around and eat a mucus secretion off the sides of their parents.

A *Astronotus ocellatus*
Oscar

A (Young)

A *Astronotus ocellatus* var.
Red Oscar

B *Cichla monoculus*
Tucunaré
Peacock Bass

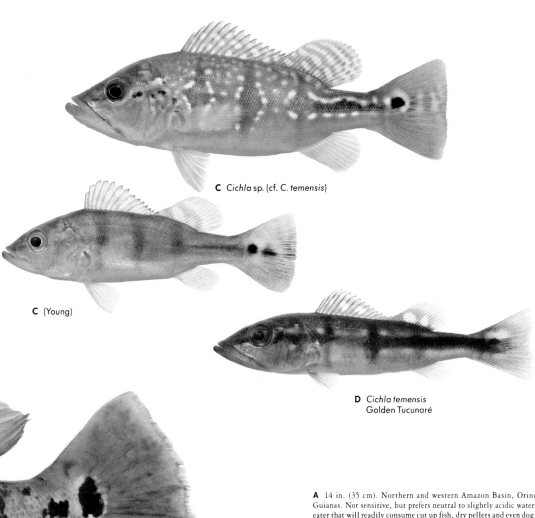

C *Cichla* sp. (cf. *C. temensis*)

C (Young)

D *Cichla temensis*
Golden Tucunaré

A 14 in. (35 cm). Northern and western Amazon Basin, Orinoco R basin, the Guianas. Not sensitive, but prefers neutral to slightly acidic water. It is a voracious eater that will readily consume cut up fish, dry pellets and even dog food to satisfy its appetite. As a young fish it will become accustomed to people, but adults are rather cautious. Usually rather docile, it can be kept with same-sized fish, but will become belligerent as spawning season nears. A bonded pair will in most cases exercise good parental care, but if they begin to eat the eggs, remove them. Better than 1,000 eggs will be laid. A little methylene blue should be added to the water and an aerator stone placed nearby. The Red Oscar (below) is an artificially selected form.

B-C Reaches 24-36 in. (60-90 cm) in nature. Northern and western Amazon. Related species are found throughout most of S. America where they are sought-after angling fish. All *Cichla* spp. are quite palatable. This species is known to anglers as an even stronger fighter than the Black Bass. Water chemistry is unimportant, but this species is very sensitive to nitrite concentration in its aquarium. Piscivorous and a voracious eater, it should be kept in a large aquarium and given a constant supply of live food. Its markings will vary from location to location. Spawning takes place in shallow water where the pair digs a hole in the muddy substratum and lays the eggs in it. Over 1,000 eggs are laid, and the parents care for them and the fry. When the fry are about a month old, the ♂ may chase the ♀ away, and care for them himself.

D Max. 16 in. (40 cm) in nature, 12 in. (30 cm) in aquaria. Discontinuous distribution in the Orinoco R, Negro R and the Amazon R Basin. Care is the same as *Cichla monoculus*. It is similar to it, but is easily distinguished by the three metallic stripes on the body.

A *Copadichromis* sp.

AFRICAN LAKE MALAWIAN CICHLIDS

Lake Malawi is a relatively young lake formed 1-2 million years ago. The ancestor stock cichlids invaded the lake from the rivers feeding it and from them, speciation occurred to fill the various biotopes. Over 200 species have been identified from this lake, and there may be at least as many yet undescribed. Moreover, most of these cichlids are endemic, and all but two tilapia species are maternal mouthbrooders. This ichthyofauna makes the lake quite unique.

The dominant group of cichlids found in Lake Malawi are the haplochromines with over 120 species grouped in forty-eight genera. All these highly specialized feeders are maternal mouthbrooders. The female

118

B *Placidochromis electra*. Deep-Water Haplo.

picks up the eggs as soon as she lays them. Fertilization occurs in her buccal cavity. Their eating habits vary greatly. This assemblage of species includes snail eaters, leaf eaters, zooplankton feeders (utaka) and robust piscivores. Among these 48 genera, are the Mbuna, a group of specialized algae-feeders that inhabit the rocky shores of the lake, the peacock cichlids of the genus *Aulonocara* and the large predators of the genus *Serranochromis*. Most are easy to care for and breed. This is one of the main reasons Lake Malawi cichlids are favored by aquarists. Another is surely the brilliant colors of the breeding males.

119

A *Aulonocara baenschi.* Yellow Peacock Cichlid. ♂ releases sperm when the ♀ pecks at the egg dummies on his anal fin.

B *Aulonocara stuartgranti.* ♂ inducing ♀ (only partially visible) to spawn.

C *Aulonocara jacobfreibergi.* Jacobfreibergi.

D *Aulonocara hansbaenschi.* African Peacock Cichlid.

Mouthbrooders & Egg Dummy Spots

There are several variants of the highly specialized spawning behavior known as mouthbrooding. Such behavior probably emerged with the holding of the eggs by both parents, and then diverged into male and female mouthbrooding habits. Among these behavioral modes, the female mouthbrooding type seems to be the most widespread and effective.

The faster the eggs are taken into the mouth, the better the chance of preventing a predator from taking any of them. Also, fertilization timing is important. Males of some mouthbrooder species have specialized oval-shaped color spots on the anal fin. After the female has laid her eggs and scooped them up into her mouth, the male will spread open his anal fin. She will see these egg spots and suck at them thinking they are eggs she has forgotten. At that moment, the male ejaculates sperm packets which the female sucks in, fertilizing the mouthbrooded eggs. For this reason, these spots are known as "egg spots" or "egg dummies."

Some Malawian haplochromine species lack these egg spots, but the spawning procedure remains the same as described with the eggs being fertilized inside the oral cavity. Females of these species mouth the male's vent directly. This behavior without the need for egg spots is believed to be the more advanced type.

A *Haplochromis* sp. (cf. *H. riponianus*). **1** ♀ (left) dives at the ♂'s egg spots.

A 1 After the ♀ scoops the eggs into her mouth, the ♂ displays his egg spots. Believing these are remaining eggs, she sucks at them, taking in sperm that the ♂ has just released. At this moment, the eggs are fertilized within the buccal cavity.
2 Within 2 weeks, the yolk sac will be absorbed and the fry will forage for themselves outside the oral cavity. They will move in and out of the mouth for the next 4-6 days, returning immediately if danger is imminent.
3 Extended lower jaw shows that the oral cavity is filled with fry.

B *Haplochromis burtoni*. Anal fin egg spots.

2 ♀ *H.* sp. (cf. *H. riponianus*) causing fry to return.

3 *H.* sp. (cf. *H. riponianus*) mouthbrooding ♀ with extended lower jaw.

A *Sciaenochromis ahli.* Electric Blue Haplo. Has a truly splendidly beautiful metallic blue body color.

B *Nimbochromis venustus.*

C *Fossorochromis rostratus.* Rostratus.

D *Copadichromis borleyi.*

E *Nimbochromis polystigma.* Polystigma.

F *Nimbochromis livingstonii.* Livingstoni.

A *Cyrtocara moorii*
Blue Lumphead
Blue Dolphin Cichlid

B *Sciaenochromis ahli* ♂
Electric Blue Haplo

B ♀

C *Dimidiochromis compressiceps*

D *Otopharynx lithobates*
Red-Top Aristochromis

A 8 in. (20 cm). It lives in the sandy bottom of L Malawi, and usually schools with *Lethrinops* species and *Fossorochromis rostratus*. Both sexes have the same body shape. Care and breeding are easy.

B ♂ 6¼ in. (16 cm), ♀ 4 in. (10 cm). L Malawi. Prefers hard, alkaline water. Quite sensitive to water pollution, frequent water replacement is required. Care and breeding are difficult. A sexually stimulated ♂ will induce the ♀ to spawn by getting her attention with quick movements of his whitish tinged, deep blue body.

C 8 in. (20 cm). Inhabits the *Vallisneria* thickets of L Malawi. Prefers rather hard,

alkaline new water. Although it is rather nonbelligerent and can be kept with other fish, it is piscivorous, ambushing small fish from behind aquatic plants. It is a popular, frequently bred fish.

D ♂ 6 in. (15 cm), ♀ 4¾ in. (12 cm). L Malawi. Prefers hard, alkaline water. Care and breeding of this beautiful fish are easy. It is sold under the name "Red-Top Aristochromis," but is without doubt a member of the genus *Otopharynx*.

E 8 in. (20 cm). Lives in the sandy bottom of L Malawi. Piscivorous, its coloring is said to mimic a decaying fish, so that when it plays dead on the sandy bottom, other

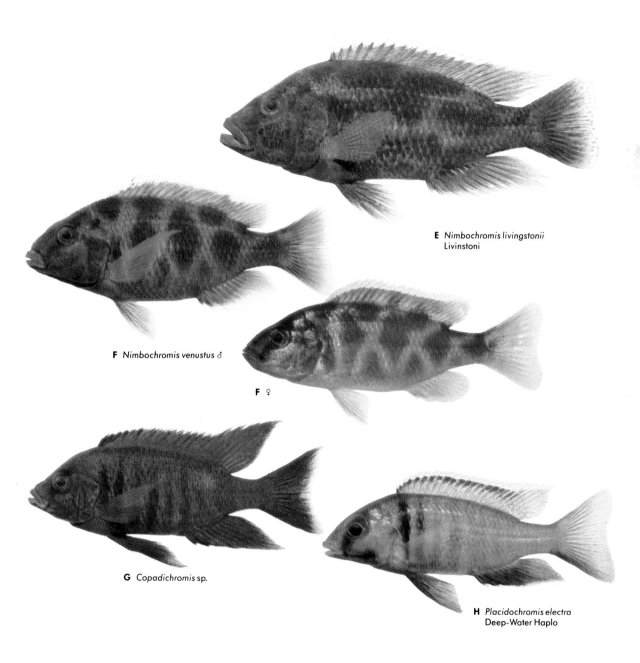

E *Nimbochromis livingstonii*
Livinstoni

F *Nimbochromis venustus* ♂

F ♀

G *Copadichromis* sp.

H *Placidochromis electra*
Deep-Water Haplo

fish will come along to pick at it. At this point, this unsuspecting fish becomes the bait, and is quickly snatched up. In aquaria, it is hardy, easy to care for, and will eat dry food. The ♀ has brighter coloration.

F Reaches 12 in. (30 cm) in nature, 10 in. (25 cm) in aquaria. L Malawi. Prefers hard, alkaline water. This large, yet nonaggressive, species is hardy and easy to care for. When the ♂ becomes sexually stimulated, he turns a very attractive, brilliant gold.

G ♂ 6 in. (15 cm), ♀ 4 in. (10 cm). L Malawi. One of the utaka group that eats zooplankton moving over the sandy bottom in the wild. Individuals acclimated to

aquaria will eat almost anything. It will spawn as a territorial group on the sandy bottom, but getting it to breed is difficult.

H 8 in. (20 cm). L Malawi. Prefers hard, alkaline water. A very beautiful, easily cared for, even-tempered fish, it is ideal for the beginning aquarist. Breeding it is easy as a ♀ over 3¼ in. (8 cm) will readily spawn.

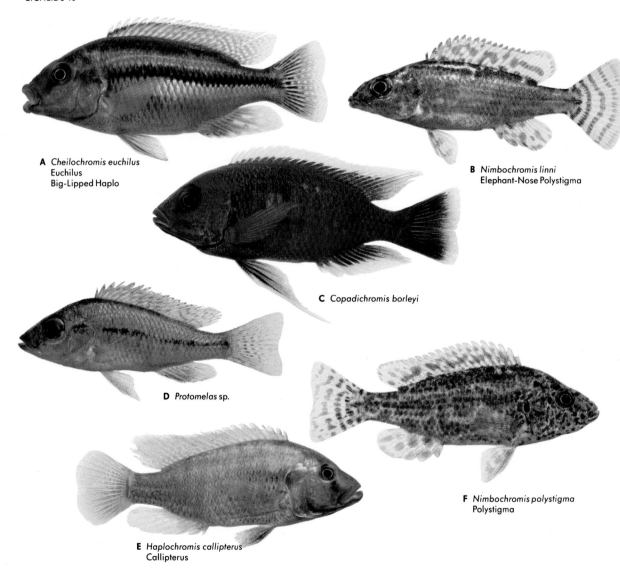

A *Cheilochromis euchilus*
Euchilus
Big-Lipped Haplo

B *Nimbochromis linni*
Elephant-Nose Polystigma

C *Copadichromis borleyi*

D *Protomelas sp.*

F *Nimbochromis polystigma*
Polystigma

E *Haplochromis callipterus*
Callipterus

A Reaches 13 in. (33 cm) in nature. Inhabits the shallow, rocky shore of L Malawi. In the wild it eats small insects, etc,, but in aquaria it will take aquatic worms and even dried shrimp. Care as well as breeding are rather difficult. It matures at over 4 in. (10 cm), spawning 20-30 large eggs per clutch. Larvae emerge from the oral cavity after 3-4 weeks.

B 14 in. (35 cm). L Malawi. Prefers hard, alkaline water. A large, yet nonbelligerent fish, it does well with its congeners. In nature, it is a specialized eater of the fry of other fish, waiting quietly among rocks with just its snout projecting out. Unsuspecting larvae are thus sucked up as they pass by. It lays about 200 eggs per spawn, and the fry emerge from incubation in the buccal cavity after 3 weeks.

C 8 in. (20 cm). A zooplankton feeder that lives on the sandy bottom of L Malawi, it

prefers hard, alkaline water and is sensitive to water pollution. Care and breeding are difficult. The adult ♂ has elongated pelvic fins and a very striking body coloration suffused with yellow. Its eggs are orange colored.

D ♂ 4¾ in. (12 cm). ♀ 3¼ in. (8 cm). It inhabits the rocky shore of L Malawi, and prefers hard, alkaline water. A relatively small fish, it is easy to keep. The light blue nuptial coloration of the ♂ has its own attractiveness, quite different from that of the deep blue Peacock. Fish reach maturity at about 2¾ in. (7 cm) long.

E 6 in. (15 cm). Though exported from L Malawi, this small *Haplochromis* is not endemic to the lake, and ranges over much of southern Africa. It is rather easy to keep, but prefers hard, alkaline water. The yellow-green coloration of a ♂ intensifies when he becomes sexually stimulated.

G *Eclectochromis milomo*
VC-10 Haplo

H *Maravichromis sphaerodon*

J *Copadichromis* sp.
Ivory-Head Utaka

I *Protomelas triaenodon*

K *Fossorochromis rostratus*
Rostratus

F 8 in. (20 cm). L Malawi. Prefers hard, alkaline water. Care in aquaria is rather difficult. Like *N. livingstonii* and *N. venustus*, it is a piscivore, favoring live food, especially small fish and aquatic worms, but when acclimated to aquaria, may accept dry food. Requires a large (≧90 gallon) tank to prosper.

G 10½ in. (27 cm). Monkey Bay of L Malawi. Prefers hard, alkaline water. It swims above the sandy bottom, sticking its head into the substratum to feed. In a sexually stimulated ♂, the body markings which persist from infancy, disappear beneath a blue suffusion. Care is quite hard.

H 6¼ in. (16 cm). Southern L Malawi. Prefers hard, alkaline water. In appearance, it is similar to, but has a shorter head than, *C. heterotaenia*. Care is difficult. This species is prone to "Malawi Bloat," a distended belly caused by a systemic bacterial infection.

I Reaches 4¾-5½ in. (12-14 cm). L Malawi. Although similar to the *Protomelas* sp. shown on p. 128, its black longitudinal midline reaches all the way to the gill cover. A rather rare species, it is relatively easy to maintain and breed.

J 5½ in. (14 cm). L Malawi. This undescribed species, easily identified by the white band which extends from the mouth to the dorsal fin, is one of the zooplankton-feeding utaka group. Its feeding behavior is facilitated by its specialized extensile mouth for sucking.

K 10 in. (25 cm). L Malawi. It eats small fish or benthic invertebrates. Although a large haplochromine and needs a large aquarium, it is however, nonbelligerent and does well as a community fish. In the wild it dives into the sand when threatened, and so a like behavior is seen in aquaria when it is chased with a net. Breeding is not easy.

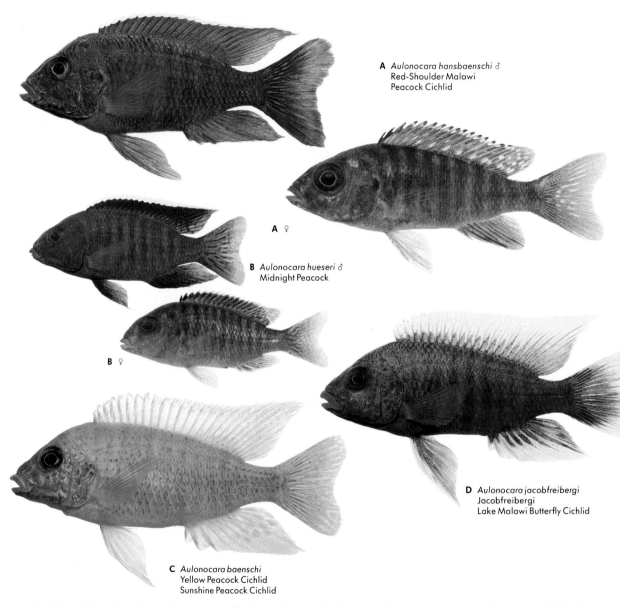

A *Aulonocara hansbaenschi* ♂
Red-Shoulder Malawi
Peacock Cichlid

A ♀

B *Aulonocara hueseri* ♂
Midnight Peacock

B ♀

D *Aulonocara jacobfreibergi*
Jacobfreibergi
Lake Malawi Butterfly Cichlid

C *Aulonocara baenschi*
Yellow Peacock Cichlid
Sunshine Peacock Cichlid

A 6 in. (15 cm). L Malawi. Prefers hard, alkaline water. In the wild, it lives mainly on aquatic insects, while in aquaria, it will accept live foods such as blood worms, but may also eat dry food. Hardy, easy to keep and breed, this fish's coloration is quite exquisite, especially during spawning season. A mouthbrooded clutch of 20-60 eggs are incubated for a period of 21 days at 82-86°F (28-30°C).

B 4¾ in. (12 cm). L Malawi. This species was initially confused with *A. auditor,* a closely related congener. The generally used vernacular name Midnight Peacock has since been applied to several other undescribed congeners. Although quite attractive and mild tempered, this fish is difficult to keep. Breeding is possible, but producing F$_2$ is difficult.

C ♂ 6 in. (15 cm), ♀ 3¼ in. (8 cm). Found around Maleri Islands in L Malawi, it may be a color morph of *A. nyassae,* and to further confuse the issue, there is a fish with the same common name that comes from the rocky Chindoka shore near Chipoka, but it has an all yellow body *without* the blue on the head. Both care and breeding are easy.

D 4¾ in. (12 cm). L Malawi. Prefers hard, alkaline (pH 7.6-8.0) water. Care and breeding are rather easy, but the ♂ will become combative as the spawning season nears. Several color variants have been imported. These may reflect adaptations to different biotopes.

E 8 in. (20 cm). L Malawi. Prefers hard, alkaline new water. This omnivorous fish is famous for its feeding behavior of crushing shells in its jaws, but its upkeep is difficult.

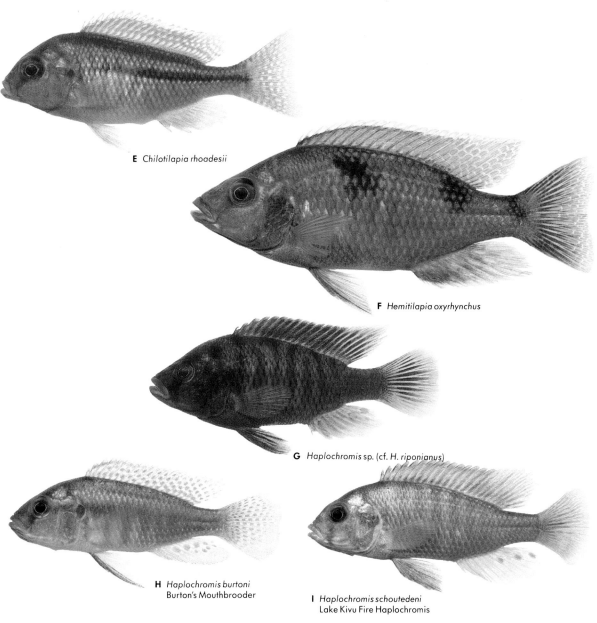

E *Chilotilapia rhoadesii*

F *Hemitilapia oxyrhynchus*

G *Haplochromis* sp. (cf. *H. riponianus*)

H *Haplochromis burtoni*
Burton's Mouthbrooder

I *Haplochromis schoutedeni*
Lake Kivu Fire Haplochromis

Unlike most L Malawian fishes that have a dark blue body ground color, this one is a light sky blue.
F 8 in. (20 cm). Living within the sandy bottom *Vallisneria* beds along the L Malawi shore, it sucks the algae, microorganisms, etc off these plants. Likewise omnivorous in aquaria, it is rather difficult to breed.
G ♂ 4¾ in. (12 cm), ♀ 3¼ in. (8 cm). Inhabits both sandy and rocky shoreline bottoms of L Victoria. Hardy and easy to care for, it eats aquatic insects and molluscs in the wild, but will readily eat anything in aquaria. This fish is an easy breeder, the ♀ mouthbrooding 30-50 eggs, and the fry emerging after about two weeks at 82-86°F (28-30°C).

H 4¾ in. (12 cm). Found in shallow coastal waters throughout southeastern and western Africa, it is not at all fussy about water conditions. Keeping it in hard, alkaline water is however recommended. Care and breeding of this species which closely resembles the L Malawian *A. calliptera* are easy. As it breeds freely under pond conditions in Florida, healthy individuals are readily available.
I Specimen shown 2¾ in. (7 cm), max. unknown. Found inhabiting the pebbled, sandy bottom of the east side of L Victoria, it prefers hard, alkaline water. Readily eating even dry food, this fish is rather easy to maintain.

131

A *Pseudotropheus lombardoi.* Kennyi. **1** ♂ & ♀ exhibit clear sexual dichromatism as in the case of this orange-yellow ♂.

2 Immature fish.

THE MBUNA GROUP

A highly specialized group of haplochromine genera that lives among the rocky biotope of Lake Malawi has been given the name "Mbuna," a Chitonga word meaning "rockfish." All members of this group are very similar in body shape, feed off the algae growing on the rocks, and are mouthbrooders. To date, ten genera of mbuna have been identified, and among them, each species has become rather specialized to make its living in a slightly different manner. Examples of this include feeding adaptations such as the inferior mouth with linear dentition of *Labeotropheus* that allows it to eat algae off rocks while in a horizontal swimming position, and the pointed mouth and tweezer-like front teeth of *Labidochromis* that allows it to pick out aquatic invertebrates from the algal mat.

B *Cynotilapia afra*. Red-Dorsal Afra.

C *Labeotropheus trewavasae*. Red-Top Trewavasae.

D *Pseudotropheus* sp. (cf. *P. macrophthalmus*). Red-Headed Macrophthalmus.

E *Melanochromis auratus*. Auratus.

As the mbuna are opportunistic feeders even in nature, they quickly become accustomed to aquarium living and will then eat any type of food; live blood worms, tubifex, and even dry food. This regrettably negates the ability of observing these different specialized feeding behaviors in a home aquarium. Cichlids are known for this sort of behavioral flexibility, and the mbuna are no exception.

On the other hand, the mbuna are extremely sensitive to nitrites and dissolved metabolic wastes, so frequent water replacement is recommended to keep it as close to new as possible. The water should be kept at 74-81°F (23.5-27.5°C), moderately hard (10-18°DH), alkaline (pH 7.7-8.8) and the bottom of the tank covered with coral sand to act as an alkaline buffer. All mbuna are polygamous, so for successful breeding, more than one female should be kept with a male, but care should be exercised as a male of most species, once mature, is highly territorial (defending an area ranging from 2-9 ft², dependent on mbuna species) and combative to others, especially conspecific or of similar coloration.

A *Pseudotropheus livingstonii.* Livingstonii.　**1** Eggs in mouth, ♀ (right) dives at ♂'s egg spots.

2 ♀ mouthbrooding eggs.

A 1 The ♂'s anal fin has one or two dummy egg spots. After the ♀ is holding her clutch of 20-30 large eggs in her mouth, she'll dive at these spots and pick up sperm to fertilize the ova.
2 A ♀ holding eggs in her oral cavity. She will incubate the larvae for about 3 weeks, and then vigorously care for the emergent fry for another 4-6 days.

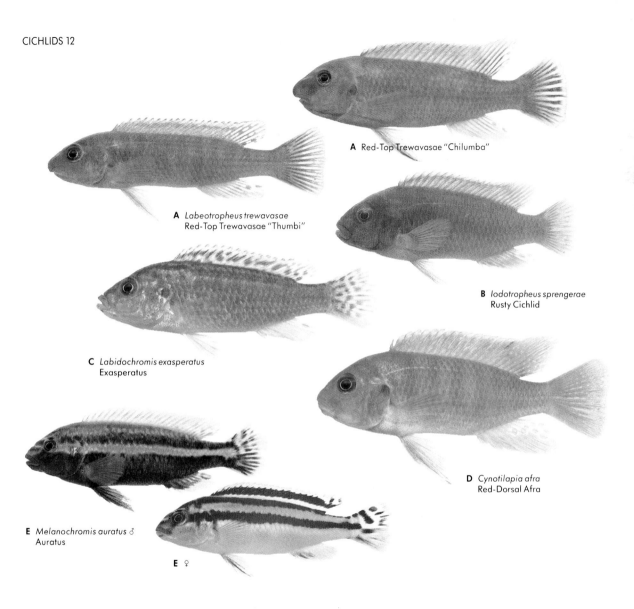

A Red-Top Trewavasae "Chilumba"

A *Labeotropheus trewavasae*
Red-Top Trewavasae "Thumbi"

B *Iodotropheus sprengerae*
Rusty Cichlid

C *Labidochromis exasperatus*
Exasperatus

D *Cynotilapia afra*
Red-Dorsal Afra

E *Melanochromis auratus* ♂
Auratus

E ♀

A 4 in. (10 cm). Inhabiting the rocky coast of L Malawi, it's an "aufwuchs" feeder (eating off filamentous algal layers and associated minute organisms), and prefers hard, alkaline water. With its inferior mouth, it is able to scrape off this algal growth from the rocks while maintaining a horizontal swimming position. In aquaria, live foods will readily be eaten, but the lack of ample vegetable matter is said to cause the fish's coloration to fade. Also, ample rocky caves and other hiding places should be provided. Like its cogeners, there is geographical variation in its sexual dichromatism; "Thumbi" (left) and "Chilumba" (right) are named for the islands around which they are found.

B 4 in. (10 cm). L Malawi. Like the above, inhabits the rocky coastal waters, feeds off of algal growths and associated invertebrates, and prefers hard, alkaline water. Plenty of rocky caves should be provided. Although aggressive to a conspecific ♂, it will co-exist with other species. Breeding is easy. Only about 10 eggs will be laid; mouth-brooded fry emerging after 3 weeks.

C 4 in. (10 cm). Rocky coast of L Malawi. Feeds exclusively on aquatic insects by using its long, narrow mouth. This, *L. freibergi* and *Labidochromis* sp. "Lion's Cove Yellow" are the species of the genus commercially bred in Florida. They all need a large tank in which only a few fish should be placed.

D 4 in. (10 cm). Around Likoma Island in L Malawi. Closely resembling *P. zebra* (see **D** next page), it is distinguishable by its dentition. Feeding on zooplankton in nature, in aquaria it quickly becomes accustomed to eating flake food. Solitary care in a large tank is recommended as it's rather aggressive.

E 4¾ in. (12 cm). Rocky coast of L Malawi. Prefers hard, alkaline water. Quite hardy, it will eat anything. When a ♂ reaches about 2 in. (5 cm), nuptial coloring, alternating black and yellow bands, will appear, and he will strongly defend his territory, so the tank should have numerous shelters.

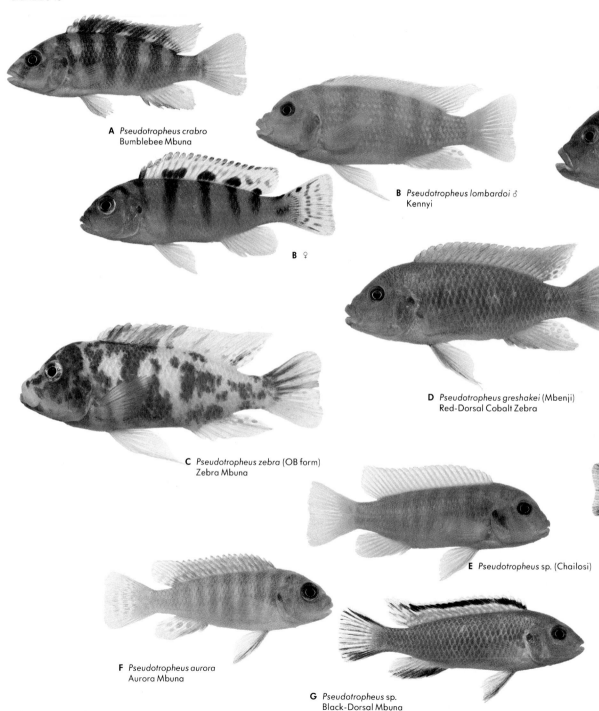

A *Pseudotropheus crabro*
Bumblebee Mbuna

B *Pseudotropheus lombardoi* ♂
Kennyi

B ♀

D *Pseudotropheus greshakei* (Mbenji)
Red-Dorsal Cobalt Zebra

C *Pseudotropheus zebra* (OB form)
Zebra Mbuna

E *Pseudotropheus* sp. (Chailosi)

F *Pseudotropheus aurora*
Aurora Mbuna

G *Pseudotropheus* sp.
Black-Dorsal Mbuna

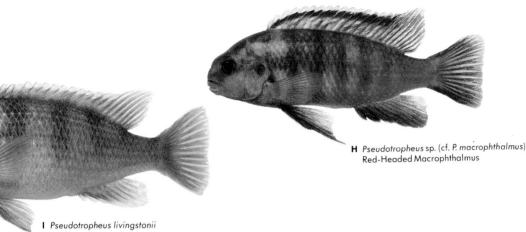

H *Pseudotropheus* sp. (cf. *P. macrophthalmus*)
Red-Headed Macrophthalmus

I *Pseudotropheus livingstonii*
Livingstonii

J *Pseudotropheus elegans*

K *Pseudotropheus* sp.

L *Pseudotropheus heteropictus*

A 4 in. (10 cm). Rocky coastal waters of L Malawi. Prefers hard, alkaline water. In nature, it feeds mainly on fish lice. It is recommended that this fish be kept in a large tank with a number of cogeners, but numerous rocky caves should be available as it tends to be pugnacious.

B 4¾ in. (12 cm). Found around Mbenji Island in L Malawi. Prefers hard, alkaline water. Care is easy as it will eat anything. Although it can be kept with haplochromines, a mature ♂ will tend to be belligerent. Sexual dimorphism is evident as the ♂ develops a brilliant golden nuptial coloration while the ♀ does not change. Breeding is easy, the fry emerging after a 3-week incubation.

C 4¾ in. (12 cm). Rocky coast of L Malawi. Prefers hard, alkaline water, and frequent water replacement is recommended. Hardy and omnivorous, this species has many color morphs. Females with this piebald pattern are abundant, but males such as shown here, may also be found. As all forms of *P. zebra* hybridize freely, it is recommended that the geographical color morphs be type bred only.

D Around Mbenji Island in L Malawi. In the wild, an algae eater, in aquaria it prefers blood worms and other animal foods. The fish shown here is a ♂; while the ♀ has an orange body. Formerly thought to be a localized color form of *P. zebra*.

E 4 in. (10 cm). Lake Malawi. Care is easy. Originally imported as a geographical color form of *P. zebra*, this mbuna is now recognized as an undescribed species. The fish shown is a ♀.

F 4 in. (10 cm). Found inhabiting the sandy plus scattered rock bottom of L Malawi around Likoma Island and Mdemba Bay. Mainly an algae feeder, care and breeding of this peaceful mbuna are quite easy. At most, only 10 fish should be kept in a large tank. The ♂ is blue and yellow, but the ♀ is brownish.

G 4 in. (10 cm). Rocky coast of L Malawi. This hardy, rather small mbuna is peaceful and will eat most anything including flake foods, thus making it highly suitable for novice aquarists wishing to try their hand at keeping this group of cichlids. A ♀ mouthbrooder that typically spawns 30-60 eggs.

H 4¾ in. (12 cm). Found around Likoma Island in L Malawi, this beautiful member of the widely distributed *P. macropthalmus* complex is readily available commercially. Care is easy.

I ♂ 5 in. (13 cm), ♀ 3¼ in. (8 cm). Unlike other mbuna which live among the coastal underwater rocks of L Malawi, this species lives inside *Lanistes* sp. shells on the lake bottom near the coast. This omnivore prefers hard, alkaline water, but its care and breeding are easy.

J 5 in. (13 cm). Found around Chilumba Island, among other localities in L Malawi. A rather large-sized mbuna, it prefers living in the wide open sandy bottom of the lake. Accordingly, the tank shouldn't be planted as the fish will dig into the sandy substrate. Somewhat belligerent, caution should be exercised in keeping it with other mbuna. Maintenance and breeding are easy.

K 4 in. (10 cm). Nkhata Bay in Lake Malawi. The ♂ of this rather mild-tempered mbuna has 7-9 yellowish vertical stripes on a brilliant blue body, while the ♀ has a grayish tint. Sometimes erroneously identified as *Pseudotropheus minutus*.

L 3¼ in. (8 cm). Found around Thumbi Island, among other areas of L Malawi, this species is similar to *P. zebra*, but has a deeper body. The fish shown here is a ♀; while the ♂ is a brilliant blue. Care is easy.

A rockscaped aquarium without plants as shown here is the ideal layout for a L Tanganyikan cichlid community tank as it approximates the fishes' native habitat.

Lake Tanganyika.

LAKE TANGANYIKAN CICHLIDS

The many lakes and rivers that lie within the Great Rift Lake Valley, running north to south in eastern Africa, have proved to be important sites for cichlid evolution. Among these, Lake Tanganyikan cichlids appear to be a remarkable example of evolved specialization and speciation.

Lake Tanganyika, believed to have been formed some 7-10 million years ago, is 440 miles (700 km) long and 50 miles (80 km) at its widest point. Its deepest point is 4,820 ft (1,470 m), but normally fish live down to a depth of about 300-650 ft (100-200 m) from the water's surface. The transparent waters of this lake are 75-84°F (24-29°C), alkaline – pH 7.7-8.8, and slightly hard – 7-11°DH. An understanding

of these conditions is important when designing a proper maintenance strategy for cichlids of this lake.

At present, over 150 species of some 51 genera have been described, but the western and southern shores of the lake have not been well investigated, so there may yet be numerous undescribed species in these waters. In contrast to the cichlids of nearby Lakes Malawi and Victoria, which are mainly maternal mouthbrooders, the species of Lake Tanganyika include both mouthbrooders and substratum spawners. The latter category is known to include some species with very specialized spawning and social behavior. Similarly, Lake Tanganyikan cichlids, as exemplified by the genus *Lamprologus,* display a remarkable variation in body shape related to their feeding habits and biotopes. This contrasts with the haplochromines of Lake Tanganyika which have different mouths adapted to their feeding habits, but little difference in body shape, and the cichlids of Lake Malawi which except for *H. compressiceps,* all have a similar body shape.

With few exceptions, most of the cichlids of Lake Tanganyika can be kept in relatively small aquaria. *L. brichardi* and the *Julidochromis* species require a medium-sized tank for care and breeding once they have paired. Generally, various species can be housed in a large community tank that will serve as a source of many hours of observable pleasure.

Tanganyikan Substrata Spawners

The substratum spawning cichlids which inhabit the rocky inshore waters of Lake Tanganyika include the genera *Lamprologus, Julidochromis, Telmatochromis* and *Chalinochromis*. A pair will dig a depression in the sandy bottom or among rocks, establish their territory around it, spawn therein and care for both the eggs and larvae. Since this territory is naturally confined to narrow spaces within the rocky area, a complex social structure among conspecifics and cogeners is established. Although Lake Tanganyikan bottom-spawners, for example lamprologines, will defend their territory and guard their young within these confines, they appear to be less aggressive and have a weaker parent-young bond than the South American cichlids.

In the case of *L. brichardi,* immature individuals, so-called "helpers," stay within the parental territory and help the pair defend it and their most recently spawned young against other fishes. While *L. savoryi* lays less than ten in a single clutch, its cogener *L. tetracanthus* lays several hundred. On the other hand, members of *Julidochromis* spawn again and again, irrespective of earlier young remaining in the territory, so usually there are many sizes of fry mixed in. There are many similarities and differences in reproductive behavior between Lake Tanganyikan and South American cichlids when they are kept in aquaria.

A 1 ♀ of *L. savoryi* laying eggs in an upside-down position.
2 Parental care is exercised over the pair's eggs and young.

A Juvenile.

A *Lamprologus savoryi.* Savoryi. **1** ♀ laying eggs on the underside of a rocky ledge.

◆ **2** Parents guarding eggs.

B *Lamprologus brichardi.* Brichardi with its young.

A *Lamprologus tetracanthus.* Tetracanthus. **1** Eggs can be seen on the rock behind the fish.

2 A mouthful of pebbles is taken in and then spit out.

3 Just-hatched fry being guarded.

B *Lamprologus calliurus.* Lamprologus Magarae. **1** As ♀ dives in to check eggs, ♂ waits nearby.

2 Cut snail shell shows ♀ checking eggs.

SNAIL SHELL SPAWNERS

Some bottom spawners that are shelter spawners live in and lay their eggs in the empty shells of such snails as *Neothauma*. Nine endemic lamprologine species to date are known to exhibit this behavior, including *L. brevis, meeli,* and *multifasciatus*. The males of these species are either monogamous or polygamous. In the latter case, he will visit more than one female's shell and fertilize the eggs. Only the female cares for the eggs.

A 1 Tetracanthus guarding its large egg clutch.
2 A digger, the ♀ is shown with her mouth full of pebbles.
3 Parent guarding its brood.
B 1 While the ♂ watches, the ♀ *L. calliurus* (Magarae) uses her fins to circulate water over the eggs in the snail shell.
2 A cut shell shows the ♀ at the mouth, moving water over her eggs (faint yellow yolks are visible).

143

A *Lamprologus longior.* Lemon Cichlid. Called so because of its yellow body coloration.

B *Lamprologus meeli.*

C *Lamprologus compressiceps.* Compressiceps.

D *Lamprologus caudopunctatus.*

E *Lamprologus brevis.*

F *Lamprologus moorii.*

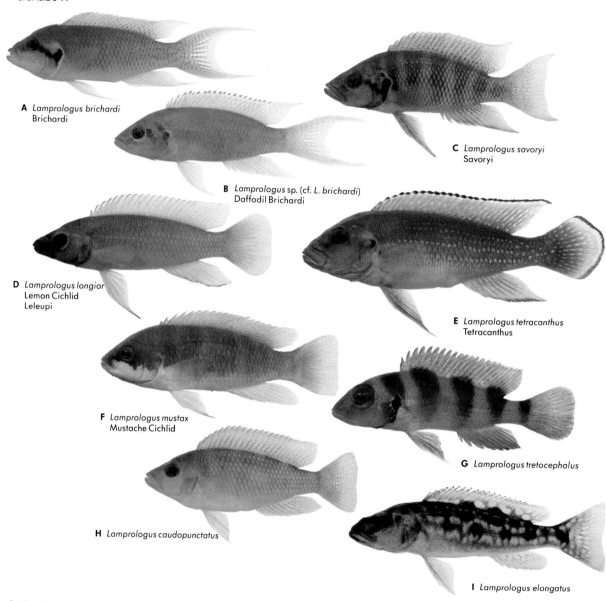

A *Lamprologus brichardi*
Brichardi

B *Lamprologus* sp. (cf. *L. brichardi*)
Daffodil Brichardi

C *Lamprologus savoryi*
Savoryi

D *Lamprologus longior*
Lemon Cichlid
Leleupi

E *Lamprologus tetracanthus*
Tetracanthus

F *Lamprologus mustax*
Mustache Cichlid

G *Lamprologus tretocephalus*

H *Lamprologus caudopunctatus*

I *Lamprologus elongatus*

A 3¼ in. (8.5 cm). L Tanganyika. An elegant fish, one of its English common names, "Fairy Cichlid," derives from its ethereal appearance. Its reproductive pattern is characterized by the presence of "helpers" in a pair's breeding territory.

B 3¼ in. (8.5 cm). L Tanganyika. Imported from Germany, its shape and behavior are similar to the above species. The common name derives from its yellow fin coloration.

C 3½ in. (9 cm). L Tanganyika. Rarely exported and seldom bred, this secretive, but aggressive species, prefers hard, alkaline water, and needs caves for refuge.

D 3½ in. (9 cm). L Tanganyika. Prefers hard, alkaline water. To bring out this fish's pure yellow body coloration, the tank bottom should be covered with fine, light-colored sand.

E 8 in. (20 cm). Sandy bottom of L Tanganyika. This fish eats insects, small fish, crustaceans and molluscs. Keeping it is quite easy.

F 3 in. (7.5 cm). L Tanganyika.

G 4¼ in. (11 cm). L Tanganyika. Similar to *L. sexfasciatus,* but this species has one less vertical stripe.

H 2¼ in. (6 cm). L Tanganyika. This highly social plankton feeder is easy to breed. Older fry remain within their parents' territory and assist in the defense of their younger siblings, just like those of *L. brichardi.*

I 8 in. (20 cm). L Tanganyika. Usually it is found about 3-6 ft (1-2 m) above the lake bottom and close to rocky areas.

J 4 in. (10 cm). Rocky areas in southern L Tanganyika. Young fish are a light yellow, becoming a dark brown as they grow and mature.

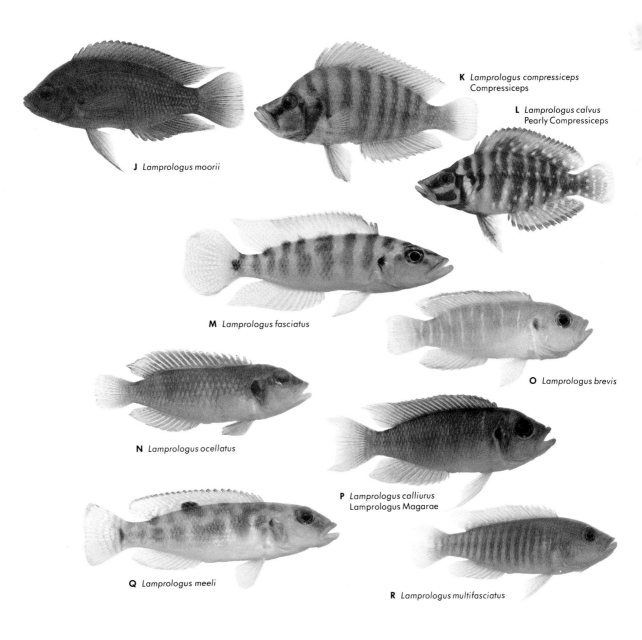

K *Lamprologus compressiceps*
Compressiceps

L *Lamprologus calvus*
Pearly Compressiceps

J *Lamprologus moorii*

M *Lamprologus fasciatus*

O *Lamprologus brevis*

N *Lamprologus ocellatus*

P *Lamprologus calliurus*
Lamprologus Magarae

Q *Lamprologus meeli*

R *Lamprologus multifasciatus*

K 5 in. (13 cm). L Tanganyika. A mild-mannered fish that does well with others, there are several geographical color morphs available. Breeding is quite difficult and has only rarely been accomplished.

L 5 in. (13 cm). L Tanganyika. Similar to the above species.

M 5 in. (13 cm). This predator is widely distributed among the sandy and rocky bottoms of southern L Tanganyika.

N 2 in. (5 cm). L Tanganyika. A pretty lamprologine that lives in snail shells, each fish, ♂ or ♀, lives in its own shell and sets up a territory around it. Spawning often takes place within the ♀'s shell. The highly territorial parents tend to be aggressive even to their own young, so it is best that as soon as the fry emerge from the shell, they be separated from their parents.

O 2 in. (5 cm). Another shell dweller, it will eat most anything and is easy to keep. Breeding in an aquarium has not yet been accomplished.

P 2 in. (5 cm). L Tanganyika. Known as "Lamprologus Magarae," this fish is another small-sized shell dweller.

Q ♂ 2¾ in. (7 cm), ♀ 2 in. (5 cm). L Tanganyika. This species also spawns in a snail shell, but some males are monogamous, while others are polygamous.

R 1½ in. (3.5 cm). L Tanganyika. This is the smallest shell-dwelling species in this genus.

A *Julidochromis dickfeldi*. Dickfeldi or Blue Julie. Guarding behavior includes occasionally mouthing the eggs.

LAKE TANGANYIKAN SUBSTRATA SPAWNER BREEDING TECHNIQUE

The dominant mating system in these sub-stratum-spawning cichlids is monogamy. Thus the breeder's first task is to come up with a compatible, healthy pair. To accomplish this, 5-6 subadult fish should be grown in the rock-scaped spawning tank which should have a number of refuges. The size of this aquarium will vary according to species. A 15 or 20 gallon one will suffice for *Julidochromis* species or *L. brichardi*, while a 30 or 40 gallon one is needed for *L. tetracanthus* or *L. elongatus*.

As the fish grow, some individuals will be driven away from the other members of the group. These tend to stay in a corner of the tank or to hang just below the surface of the water.

These fish should be moved to another aquarium. This should be repeated until only a male and female remain. These two should be a mated pair. Spawning this pair of Lake Tanganyikan cichlids will not come easily or quickly. Rather than spawning as soon as the pair is formed, they will often wait a few months, or sometimes as much as a year. Once the pair proves compatible, however, they should be moved to a larger tank to grow further.

Julidochromis species tend to spawn deep inside rocky caves, so the first spawning is frequently overlooked. When the young suddenly emerge from between the rocks, it becomes obvious that a breeding event has been missed.

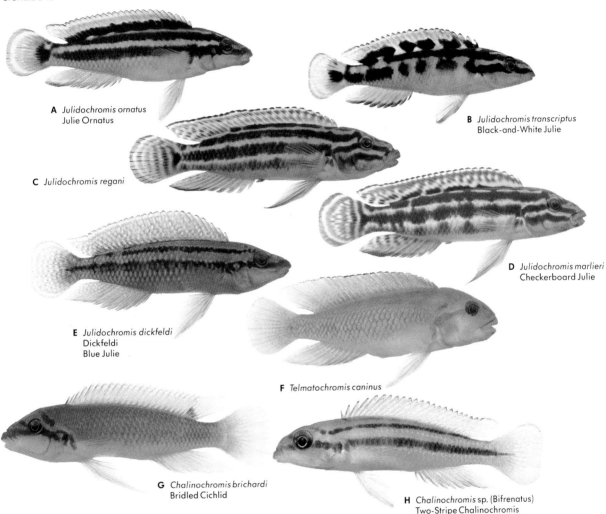

A *Julidochromis ornatus*
Julie Ornatus

B *Julidochromis transcriptus*
Black-and-White Julie

C *Julidochromis regani*

D *Julidochromis marlieri*
Checkerboard Julie

E *Julidochromis dickfeldi*
Dickfeldi
Blue Julie

F *Telmatochromis caninus*

G *Chalinochromis brichardi*
Bridled Cichlid

H *Chalinochromis* sp. (Bifrenatus)
Two-Stripe Chalinochromis

A 4 in. (10 cm). Lives 6-13 ft (2-4 m) deep along the rocky coastal waters of north-western L Tanganyika. It prefers hard, alkaline water. As it is sensitive to sudden changes in tank conditions, only partial water changes should be effected. A pair in top condition can be kept in a small tank, and will spawn continuously, clutches of 10-40 eggs, one after another.

B 2¼ in. (6 cm). Found in the rocky coastal area of the northwestern extreme of L Tanganyika, it feeds on small insects, crustaceans and algae, but quickly adapts in aquaria to eating flake food. The tank should be rockscaped, the bottom covered with fine silica or coral sand, and filled with hard, alkaline water.

C Reaches 6 in. (15 cm) in nature. Throughout L Tanganyika. Care is easy, and breeding possible. There are a few geographically separate pattern variants such as the southern "Zambia" type shown here, and the northern type off Bujumbura, Burundi, that has wider, beautiful black longitudinal bands.

D 5 in. (13 cm). Found throughout L Tanganyika. Several geographic variants are known. Easily raised, breeding is also easy once a pair has formed. As this species and *J. regani* will easily pair and hybridize, they should not be raised together.

E 4 in. (10 cm). Living 6-20 ft (2-6 m) deep along the southwestern rocky coast of L

Tanganyika, it eats small insects, molluscs and crustaceans. Prefers hard, alkaline water. As this species actively guards a very large territory, it may kill weaker individuals if the tank isn't big enough. However, this fish will spawn in a small aquarium after pairing, laying about 40 eggs.

F 4¾ in. (12 cm). L Tanganyika. Aggressive towards other individuals of its own species, this fish will coexist well with other cichlid species. Adults usually remain hidden in caves. It will eat anything. Spawning within rocky formations, the pair will take good care of their clutch of eggs and young, usually numbering 50-100.

G 4¾ in. (12 cm). Discontinuously distributed in southern and northern L Tanganyika about 6-33 ft (2-10 m) deep along the rocky coast. Its mild demeanor allows it to peacefully coexist with other L Tanganyikan cichlid genera. Feeding mainly on live foods, after much effort it may become accustomed to dry ones.

H 4 in. (10 cm). Northwestern L Tanganyika. Known by the cheironym "Chalinochromis bifrenatus," this species was previously known as "Malagarsi." The two distinct black bands running horizontally the length of its body distinguish it from *C. brichardi*. Rather mild tempered, it will easily pair and spawn in an amply rockscaped aquarium.

A *Cyphotilapia frontosa.* Frontosa.

LAKE TANGANYIKAN MOUTHBROODERS

Among the genera of Lake Tanganyikan mouthbrooding cichlids are *Cyphotilapia, Tropheus* and *Lobochilotes.* Spawning modes range from the most primitive to the most advanced, specialized ones. The mode in *Lobochilotes,* a close relative of *Haplochromis,* whereby a few hundred small eggs are mouthbrooded is considered to be rather primitive. On the other hand, the most advanced mode is exhibited by *Tropheus* which lays only several to 10 large (¼ in. or 7 mm in diameter) eggs which have a good-sized yolk. Among the cichlids, this genus has the longest oral incubation period of nearly 30 days at 82-86°F (28-30°C) before the young emerge. When they emerge, the larvae are already ½-⅝ in. (12-15 mm) long. Also, even though the fry are capable of being fully independent, for another week they will still seek refuge in their mother's mouth if danger approaches. While mouthbrooding the eggs and young, the parents take in food, and it is believed that the fry also eat inside this oral cavity during the long incubation period.

1 View showing humphead of adult. ▶

A *Tropheus moorii*. The so-called Firecracker Moorii, one of a number of known color variants.

B *Tropheus duboisi*. Duboisi. **1** Juvenile fish.

2 Adult fish.

C *Spathodus erythrodon*. Pair in prespawning courtship.

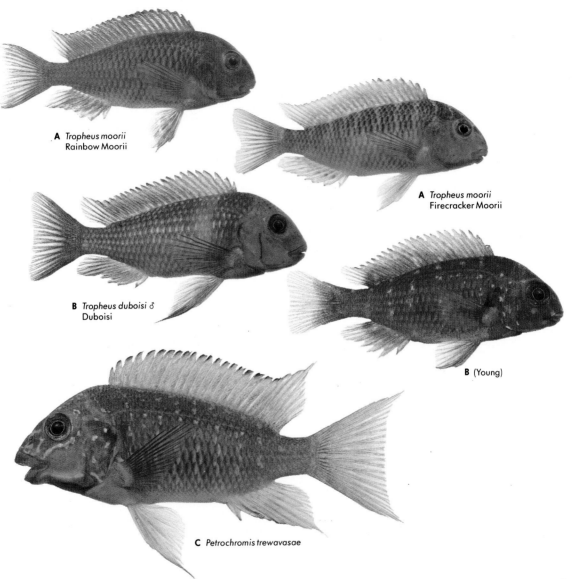

A *Tropheus moorii*
Rainbow Moorii

A *Tropheus moorii*
Firecracker Moorii

B *Tropheus duboisi* ♂
Duboisi

B (Young)

C *Petrochromis trewavasae*

A 5½ in. (14 cm). Lives 6-10 ft (2-3 m) deep on the bottom of the rocky coast of L Tanganyika. Eating algae off of rocks, each group remains rather separate, staying over one patch of rocks. Since individuals of these populations don't stray over the sandy bottom area, groups of this species tend to develop in geographical isolation. Accordingly, about 30 geographical color variants have been identified, two of which are shown here. The top left fish was caught at Moliro, while the right one was collected at Sonsitt. This number will probably rise in the future, and some groups may even be recognized later as distinct species. Very sensitive to sudden changes in water conditions, great care should be taken when replacing water. This species will eat most anything, but requires a diet rich in fresh vegetable foods to prosper. Strongly territorial, it requires a large tank with many rocky refuges. Keeping it with other species is to be avoided, and to minimize the chance of the ♂ attacking its mate, a harem of 4-5

♀ should be provided. The eggs are large (¼ in. or 7 mm in diameter), and the ♀ will mouthbrood 8-12 per spawn.

B 4 in. (10 cm). Lives 10-50 ft (3-15 m) deep in L Tanganyika, deeper than *T. moorii*. The markings are quite different in the young and adults (as shown here). Very aggressive to others of its own species, it needs a large aquarium with numerous shelters. Mouthbrooding lasts about 30 days after spawning, and the young will still seek cover in the oral cavity for more than another week after emergence. Food should be supplied, as the parents eat during the oral incubation period.

C 12 in. (30 cm). Its jaws have rasp-like dentition adapted for scraping algae off rocks. A mouthbrooder, it spawns while circling above a rock. Its eggs are large and few in number. Five species have been described in this genus, but there are a number as yet unidentified.

D *Cyphotilapia frontosa*
Frontosa

E *Lobochilotes labiatus*

F *Eretmodus cyanostictus*
Striped Goby Cichlid

G *Tanganicodus irsacae*

H *Spathodus erythrodon*

D 14 in. (35 cm). Found 15-160 ft (5-50 m) deep in L Tanganyikan rocky areas. Adults live in the deeper zones, while the fry live closer to the surface. Mild-tempered, this species is easy to care for. In nature, it eats mainly crustaceans. It lays a few to several tens of 5/16 in. (8 mm) eggs which are mouthbrooded for about four weeks.

E Reaches 16 in. (40 cm) in nature. Adults live 130 ft (40 m) or deeper in the rocky coastal waters of L Tanganyika. It eats crustaceans and molluscs. A mouthbrooder, it holds several hundred eggs in a single clutch.

F 2¾-3¼ in. (7-8 cm). Found on the fine gravel beds along the shore of L Tanganyika. It is a small, pretty fish that skips over the tank bottom in a movement that's quite beyond description. This fish can be easily kept with midwater-swimming species, and will do well on only dry food. A biparental mouthbrooder, its clutches number about 25 eggs. Each sex carries the developing young for half of the 21-day incubation period.

G 2¼ in. (6 cm). Living near the shore of L Tanganyika, this fish eats algae, diatoms, insect larvae and crustaceans. In aquaria, it is peaceful, easy to care for and takes any type of food. A monogamous biparental mouthbrooder like the preceding species, it will do well with midwater-swimming fishes.

H 3¼ in. (8 cm). Lives 100-160 ft (30-50 m) below the surface along the L Tanganyikan coast. A pair should be housed in a large aquarium, in which also *Julidochromis* and *Lamprologus* species can be kept. They should be fed a varied diet of most any fish foods. About 20 eggs are laid in a spawning, and mouthbrooding of the eggs is shared by the pair.

AFRICAN RIVERINE CICHLIDS

There are many cichlids living in the large and small rivers of Africa which have developed behavioral and anatomical specialization quite different from those of their African lacustrine cousins.

The cichlids of eastern Africa have developed mainly in the lakes of this region, with only a few riverine species inhabiting the savannas. On the other hand, there are many rivers in western and central Africa, notable among them, the immense Zaire River, and many cichlids can be found inhabiting their various biotopes.

In the main, these riverine cichlids are found in the clear river waters of the tropical rain forests, and these waters are mostly slightly acidic and soft. While most of the lacustrine cichlids of eastern Africa are mouthbrooders, the western African cichlids are primarily substratum spawners, and the behavior of the few mouthbrooders manifests numerous primitive features.

Among the riverine cichlid genera that have already become popular are *Pelvicachromis, Nanochromis* and *Hemichromis*. Most of the species of *Tilapia* are rarely exported as ornamental fish. Generally, most of these riverine cichlids are easy to care for and breed in a large aquarium, with methods being basically the same as those for similar South American cichlids.

A 1 *Anomalochromis* sp. (cf. *A. thomasi*). Dwarf Jewel Fish from Liberia.

2 ♂ fertilizing previously laid eggs.

B *Hemichromis guttatus*. Red Jewel Fish. Water being circulated over the eggs.

A 1 Pair carefully cleans the spawning site.
2 After the ♀ lays her eggs, the ♂ follows in like manner, but releasing sperm to fertilize the eggs. This spawning pair is of Liberian provenance. As this type will not interbreed with those from Sierra Leone, even in a no-chance situation, they may represent a distinct species.
3 About 300 eggs are laid in a single spawning, and hatch out in about 2 days. At that time, the fry will be moved to a depression dug in advance.
4 Note typical form from Sierra Leone lacks red eyes and the lines of black dots on the dorsum.
B The ♀ Red Jewel Fish circulates water over her eggs.

156

♀ with extended ovipositor as eggs are being laid.

4 *Anomalochromis thomasi.* Parent of Sierra Leone type guards its young.

A *Oreochromis mossambicus* var. Albino Mozambique Mouthbrooder. Two males in combat.

B *Tilapia rendalli.* Young being guarded by both parents.

A *Pelvicachromis pulcher.* Kribensis. Pair guarding their free-swimming larvae.

B *Pseudocrenilabrus multicolor.* Dwarf Egyptian Mouthbrooder.   **1** Larvae just released from their mother's mouth.

2 Eggs seen through the skin of the lower jaw.

3 ♀ mouthbrooding fry.

A *Steatocranus casuarius.* Buffalohead Cichlid. Bottom-dwelling cichlids from the Zaire R have this characteristic humphead.

B *Tilapia joka.*

C *Tilapia buttikoferi.* Hornet Tilapia.

D *Pelvicachromis humilis.*

E *Lamprologus mocquardii.*

F *Nanochromis parilius.* Nudiceps.

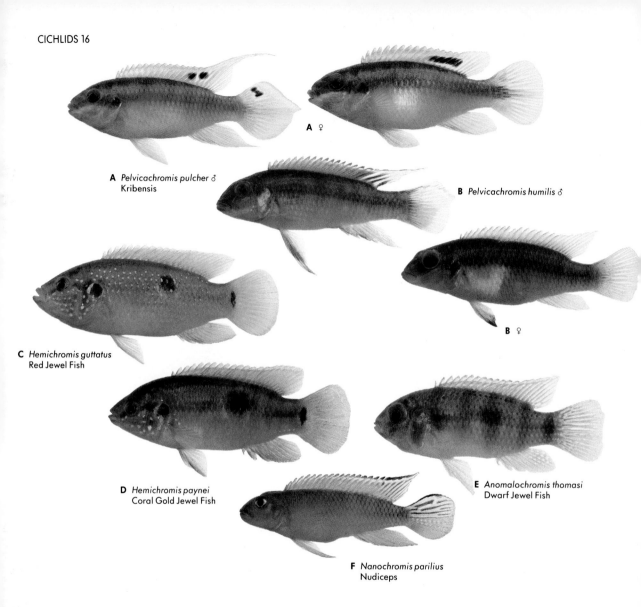

A *Pelvicachromis pulcher* ♂
Kribensis

A ♀

B *Pelvicachromis humilis* ♂

C *Hemichromis guttatus*
Red Jewel Fish

B ♀

D *Hemichromis paynei*
Coral Gold Jewel Fish

E *Anomalochromis thomasi*
Dwarf Jewel Fish

F *Nanochromis parilius*
Nudiceps

A ♂ 4 in. (10 cm), ♀ 2¾ in. (7 cm). Coastal rivers of southern Nigeria. In its native habitat it lives in acidic (pH 4.8), soft (below 1°DH) water. Not fussy about water conditions, its care is easy. As this species is somewhat timid, it is recommended that it be kept in a community tank with midwater swimmers. About 50-100 eggs are laid inside a flower pot or on the underside of a stone.
B 4 in. (10 cm). Southeastern Guinea and Sierra Leone. It lives in slightly acidic (below pH 6), soft (below 1°DH) water. Care is hard, and breeding, rare, but control of water quality is the most important point.
C 4¾ in. (12 cm). Western Africa. Not sensitive to water conditions, it prefers slightly acidic, soft water. Feeding it live food is best, but otherwise its care is easy, being able to live in a community tank as long as the tank is big enough. The pair will take good care of their eggs and larvae, making them very suitable for observing cichlid breeding behavior.

D 4 in. (10 cm). Guinea, Sierra Leone, Liberia of western Africa. It lives with *H. bimaculatus* in brooks crossing the savanna, and in rivers within rain forests.
E 2¾ in. (7 cm). Sierra Leone, Liberia (?). Living in the acidic soft waters of brooks flowing through rain forests and shrubbery, this mild-tempered fish is easy to care for. It doesn't eat aquatic flora or dig up the substratum, plus it does well in a community tank. For breeding, the most important point is maintenance of water quality. Good parental care is provided to both the eggs and larvae. The Liberian population might represent a distinct species.
F ♂ 2¾ in. (7 cm), ♀ 2 in. (5 cm). Lower reaches of the Zaire R. Prefers slightly acidic, soft water. Quite pugnacious by nature, it defends a large territory, so a large tank with many shelters is recommended. 60-100 eggs are laid on the underside of a stone and guarded only by the ♀. Larvae are able to eat brine shrimp.
G 8 in. (20 cm). Rivers of coastal western Africa. The common name comes from the

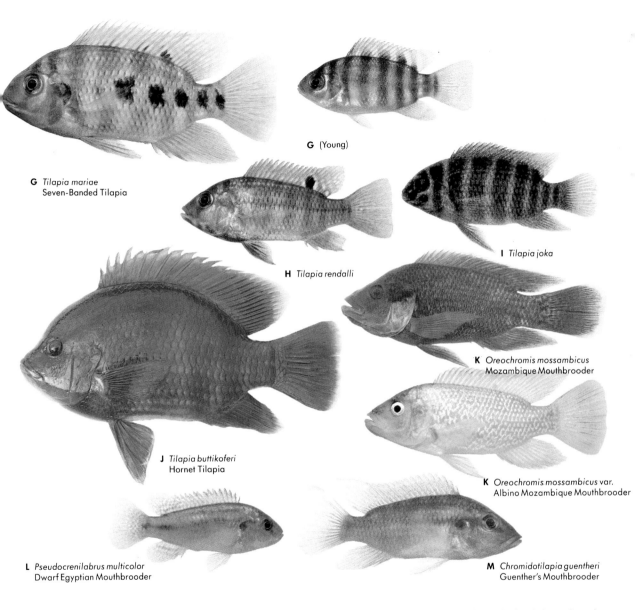

G (Young)

G *Tilapia mariae*
Seven-Banded Tilapia

I *Tilapia joka*

H *Tilapia rendalli*

J *Tilapia buttikoferi*
Hornet Tilapia

K *Oreochromis mossambicus*
Mozambique Mouthbrooder

K *Oreochromis mossambicus* var.
Albino Mozambique Mouthbrooder

L *Pseudocrenilabrus multicolor*
Dwarf Egyptian Mouthbrooder

M *Chromidotilapia guentheri*
Guenther's Mouthbrooder

6 or 7 vertical stripes on its yellowish body when young. It reaches maturity at about 4 in. (10 cm) long. Care is easy. Peaceful, except during the breeding season, it lays 200-500 eggs on a stone in a single spawning. Good parental care is exercised.

H 6 in. (15 cm). Eastern Africa. This tilapine with a beautiful red belly is an ideal aquarium fish as its care is easy and it soon becomes accustomed to its owner. Feeding is no problem either as it will eat both live and dry foods. An easy breeder, it is sometimes sold as *T. melanopleura*.

I 4 in. (10 cm). Sierra Leone in western Africa. This small, pretty tilapiine with white stripes on a black ground is difficult to culture.

J 10 in. (25 cm). Liberia to Guinea-Bissau in western Africa. A beautiful, large-sized fish that will eat anything, it is hardy and easy to keep. Its stripes, although distinct, vary in width depending on stress factors. If the pair is healthy, breeding is easy.

K In its native waters of eastern Africa, it grows to 16-20 in. (40-50 cm). From these

waters it has been transplanted worldwide to subtropical and tropical areas. Care and breeding are easy, making it ideal for observation of breeding and parental care behavior, but it's not really best for aquaria.

L 2 in. (5 cm). Lower reaches of the Nile R. Water quality is unimportant. Small in size, it has a sober demeanor and is easy to care for.

M 4-4¼ in. (10-12 cm). Ivory Coast to Cameroon in western Africa. Tolerant of varied water conditions, its care is easy. Blood worms and other aquatic worms are preferred as food, but it will become accustomed to eating flake foods. The pair spawns on a stone, the ♂ keeping the eggs in his oral cavity after fertilization, and the ♀ assisting after the fry become free swimming, about 6 days after hatching. Parental care continues for a few weeks.

165

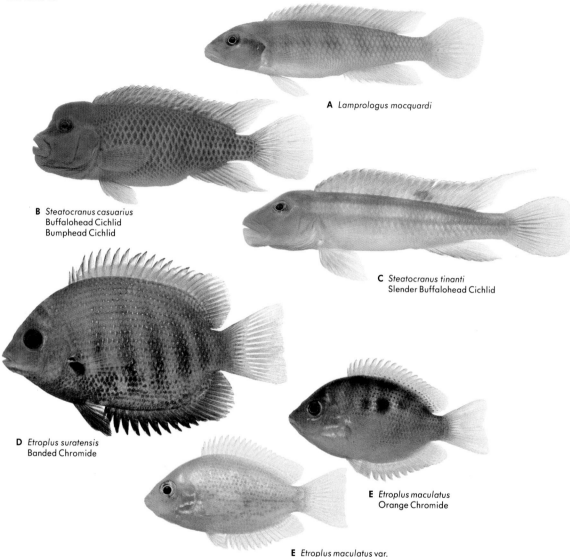

A *Lamprologus mocquardi*

B *Steatocranus casuarius*
Buffalohead Cichlid
Bumphead Cichlid

C *Steatocranus tinanti*
Slender Buffalohead Cichlid

D *Etroplus suratensis*
Banded Chromide

E *Etroplus maculatus*
Orange Chromide

E *Etroplus maculatus var.*

A 4¾ in. (12 cm). Upper and middle reaches of the Ubangi branch of the Zaire R. Prefers neutral to alkaline, soft water. Care is easy as it will eat most anything. A large aquarium is necessary, however, as it aggressively guards a large territory during the breeding season.
B 4 in. (10 cm). Zaire R. Lives in slow-moving waters such as in clefts in rocks. It prefers neutral to alkaline water with a low degree of hardness. Any type of food will be readily eaten. This very peaceful fish is easily spawned even in a small tank. 30-100 eggs will be spawned inside a flower pot or spawning tube, with parents taking good care of their young.
C 5 in. (13 cm). Found around Kinshasa and Pomareibo on the lower reaches of the Zaire R. Prefers neutral, soft water. Since they live in rapidly flowing waters, it is recommended that the tank water be kept circulating well. It prefers to feed on aquatic

worms such as blood worms and tubifex. When a compatible pair forms, breeding is easy. A large ♀ lays more than 100 eggs.
D Reaches 12 in. (30 cm) in nature. Sri Lanka. Since it inhabits brackish waters, it is recommended that a moderate amount of salt be added to the aquarium water. It may be easier to keep it with salt water fishes than freshwater tropicals.
E 4 in. (10 cm). India, Sri Lanka. Found in rivers from fresh to brackish water regions. Like with the above species, the addition of one teaspoonful of salt per 2½ gallons (10 liters) of water will make the fish more comfortable. Timid by nature, often hiding in caves, it will not exhibit its natural beauty until it becomes accustomed to the aquarium. The fish shown at the lower left is an artificially selected golden oligomelanic form.

NANDIDS, CHAMELEON PERCHES AND TRIPLETAILS

5

FAMILY	**LOBOTIDAE (Tripletails)**
Genus	*Datnioides*
FAMILY	**NANDIDAE (Leaffishes)**
SUBFAMILY	NANDINAE
Genera	*Monocirrhus*
	Nandus
	Polycentrus
	Pristolepis
FAMILY	**BADIDAE**
	(Chameleonfishes)
Genus	*Badis*

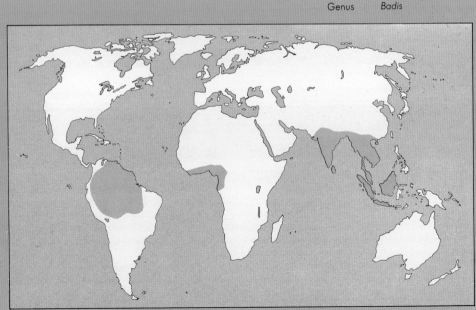

A *Datnioides* sp. (cf. *D. microlepis*). Siamese Tiger Fish. There are two variants—narrow or wide vertical black banding. This is the narrow type found in the Mekong R.

LIFE NOTES & SPAWNING BEHAVIOR

Nandids are distributed throughout SE Asia, northern South America and a small part of central western Africa. This family of fishes has features which are considered ancient, and therefore, the leaffishes are called "living fossils" by some authorities. During prehistoric times, the ancestral form is believed to have widely flourished across an ancient continent that split apart, accounting for the family's current discontinuous distribution.

Most nandids are piscivorous, ambushing prey (up to ¾ their body size) from behind underwater foliage or twigs, and sucking it in by using their comparatively large, protrusible mouth. On the other hand, they are rather shy, and if many rocky or grassy refuges are provided in the aquarium, they will frequently move between them. Healthy fish are easy to breed, and will do so with the opposite sex of about the same size. Acclimated fish can be fed earthworms and mealworms.

On the basis of recent morphological and behavioral studies, the two chameleon fish species were separated from the nandids and placed

B *Monocirrhus polyacanthus*. Leaffish ♀. **1** Resembles a withered leaf.   **2** Protrusible mouth pose.

C *Nandus nandus*. Nandus. Usually exceeding 8 in. (20 cm) in length, young of about 2 in. (5 cm) are sometimes imported.

A *Badis badis*. Dwarf Chameleon Fish. **1** In spawning embrace, ♂ entwines ♀.

in their own family, the Badidae. They are much less predatory than nandids, and thus better fishes in a community situation. While they prefer live food, chameleon perches will accept frozen foods readily.

Tripletails, although placed in a separate family, the Lobotidae, are superficially nandid-like predators, easily capable of swallowing prey up to ⅔ of their length. This predominantly marine group is represented in the fresh and brackish waters of SE Asia by the genus *Datnioides*. Juveniles of these robust predators are strikingly marked and make excellent pet fish. However, prospective owners should keep in mind that these fish can grow to over 24 in. (60 cm) in length.

Various forms of spawning behavior have been observed among the leaffishes. Nandids carefully clean the underside of leaves or stones prior to spawning 200-400 eggs on this surface. Once spawning is completed,

the female should be removed. The male, however, should be left with the eggs as he will care for the brood once it hatches out in about 3-4 days. Larvae will hang onto the hatching site until they become free swimming at about 5 days, and will then be able to catch and eat brine shrimp. They will reach adult size within one month. It is important to have a supply of fish larvae on hand at this time for use in order to avoid sudden death of the one-month-old Leaffish. *Polycentrus* parents spawn on the underside of rocks. The male takes care of the 300-1,000 egg clutch. Be cautious, for even though juveniles feed on brine shrimp, they are cannibalistic to smaller broodmates.

With the Dwarf Chameleon Fish, the ripe female seeks out the territorial male in the prepared site. The male enwraps the female (like with gouramis), the eggs are pushed out, sink to the bottom, and attach

2 Eggs released and fertilized. As the pair spawns, the eggs are spewn out, fertilized and then settle to the bottom.

to the gravel. Just after hatching, the larvae hang to the bottom of overhanging stones. Both eggs and larvae are guarded by the male. Once the young become free swimming, however, the male should be separated from the brood.

Nothing is known of the reproductive pattern of the two *Datnioides* species commonly available through commercial channels.

A 1-2 Dwarf Chameleon Fish spawning sequence shows ♂ embracing ♀ to force eggs out, at which instant sperm is ejaculated to fertilize the eggs.
3 Male tends larvae as they hang from the underside of the rock.

3 Brood care by ♂ Dwarf Chameleon Fish.

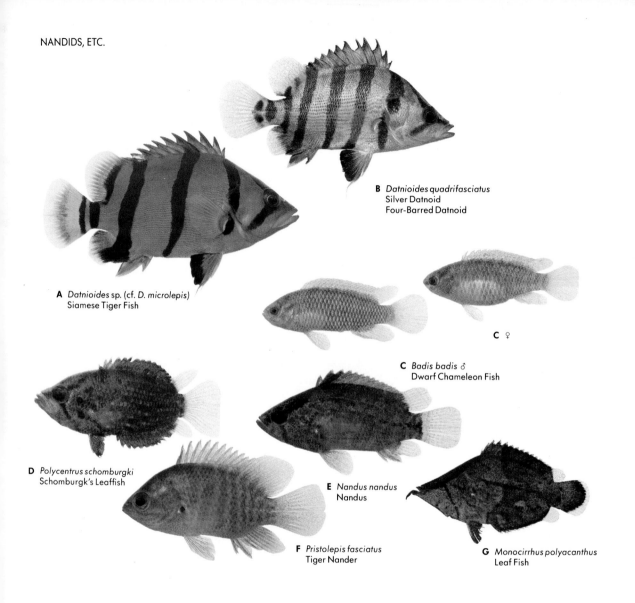

B *Datnioides quadrifasciatus*
Silver Datnoid
Four-Barred Datnoid

A *Datnioides* sp. (cf. *D. microlepis*)
Siamese Tiger Fish

C ♀

C *Badis badis* ♂
Dwarf Chameleon Fish

D *Polycentrus schomburgki*
Schomburgk's Leaffish

E *Nandus nandus*
Nandus

F *Pristolepis fasciatus*
Tiger Nander

G *Monocirrhus polyacanthus*
Leaf Fish

A 16-24 in. (40-60 cm). Thailand, Sumatra, Borneo. Prefers neutral to slightly acidic water. Although it can peacefully coexist with larger or same-size fish, keeping it with smaller fish should be avoided. Variation in the width of the black banding is known, the wider banded type found in the Chao Phraya R, and the narrower in the Mekong R.

B 18 in. (45 cm) in nature. Thailand, India, Burma, Australia. Prefers neutral to slightly acid water. A mild-tempered fish, but like the above, it is known to attack smaller fish. As to food, it prefers small fish to brine shrimp. Spawning behavior is unknown.

C 2¼ in. (6 cm). India. Tolerant to alkalinity, it prefers neutral to slightly acidic water. Worms are recommended over dry foods. A mild-tempered fish, it tends to stay hidden in a refuge. It is recommended that it be kept with small, mid-water characins.

D 4 in. (10 cm). Coastal rivers of the Guianas. Prefers soft, slightly acidic water. Mild tempered while young, the adult male becomes pugnacious during the spawning

season. It spawns on stone surfaces, with the male caring for the eggs (hatch in 48 hours) and the brood. The larvae eat brine shrimp.

E 8 in. (20 cm). Thailand, Burma, India. Found in grassy swamps, stagnant and brackish waters, it prefers alkaline water. Best foods include small fish and crustaceans which they can ambush from behind refuges. The addition of a small amount of salt to the water may bring it into better physical condition. Spawning in an aquarium has not been recorded.

F 3¼ in. (8 cm). Thailand, Burma. Very common in Thailand, it lives in grassy swamps and stagnant water habitats. Live foods are preferred.

G 4 in. (10 cm). Guiana and Amazon River Basin. Its body shape and coloration cause it to resemble a withered leaf, and so is considered a classic case of mimicry. Prefers soft, slightly acidic water, plus dislikes strong aeration. It eats small fish which it vacuums in rapidly. The male tends the eggs and the brood, but breeding is difficult.

ANABANTOIDS
AND PIKEHEADS

6

FAMILY	**ANABANTIDAE**
	(Climbing Gouramies)
Genera	*Anabas*
	Ctenopoma
FAMILY	**BELONTIIDAE**
	(Gouramies & allies)
Genera	*Belontia*
	Betta
	Colisa
	Macropodus
	Malpulutta
	Sphaerichthys
	Trichogaster
	Trichopsis
FAMILY	**HELOSTOMATIDAE**
	(Kissing Gouramies)
Genus	*Helostoma*
FAMILY	**OSPHRONEMIDAE**
	(Giant Gouramies)
Genus	*Osphronemus*
FAMILY	**LUCIOCEPHALIDAE**
	(Pikeheads)
Genus	*Luciocephalus*

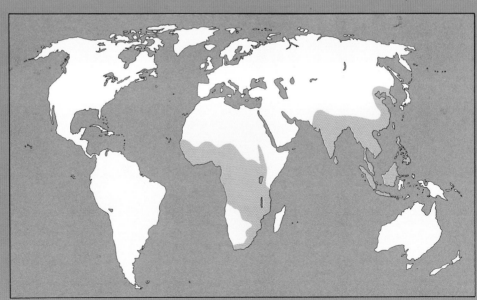

From the very beginning of the tropical fish hobby, bettas have been among the most popular aquarium residents. Many color and fin variations exist in *Betta splendens,* the result of artificial selection by dedicated breeders. The photos on these and the next two pages of fish from stocks cultured in Thailand, Singapore and Taiwan show how spectacular their appearance can be. In Thailand, their original habitat, where fighting fish bouts and wagering are still popular, the wild type is preferred over the more showy, selectively bred types. A wild type fish will have a price tag from two to ten times that of selectively bred one. Yet even fish collected in the wild show great variation. Stocks cultured in Southeast Asia are still not genetically stable, so many variants can be found within the brood of selected pair of parents.

In recent years, betta breeding has become popular among serious U.S. hobbyists, and many new, beautiful variations have been fixed by these breeders. Such types include the "Super White" with solid white body and fins, the "Black" and the "Double-Tail."

Breeding bettas is relatively easy as the male makes a bubble nest by blowing bubbles around a floating leaf base, and then induces the female to spawn under it. As the eggs are spewn out, fertilized and begin to sink, the male sucks them into his mouth and spits them into the nest. He then continues to care for the nest, eggs and larvae. Approximately half of the *Betta* species known are mouthbrooders. These include *B. picta, B. taeniata,* and *B. imbellis.*

A *Betta imbellis.* Peaceful Betta. A mild-tempered species.

B *Betta* sp. Undescribed species, similar to above. Caught near Phuket, Thailand.

C *Betta splendens* var. Super-White Betta. A graceful type developed by an avid American aquarist.

D *Betta splendens* var. Well known as the "Siamese Fighting Fish," a bout can continue until one of the males is fatally injured.

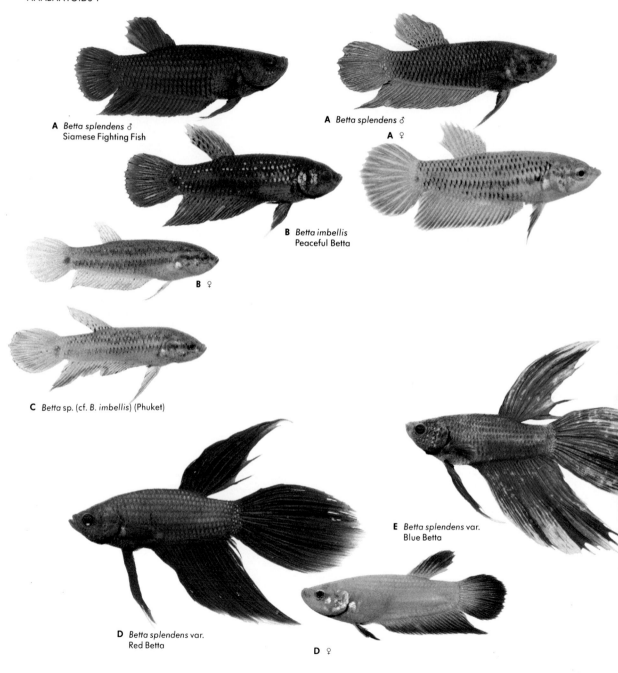

A *Betta splendens* ♂
Siamese Fighting Fish

A *Betta splendens* ♂

A ♀

B *Betta imbellis*
Peaceful Betta

B ♀

C *Betta* sp. (cf. *B. imbellis*) (Phuket)

E *Betta splendens* var.
Blue Betta

D *Betta splendens* var.
Red Betta

D ♀

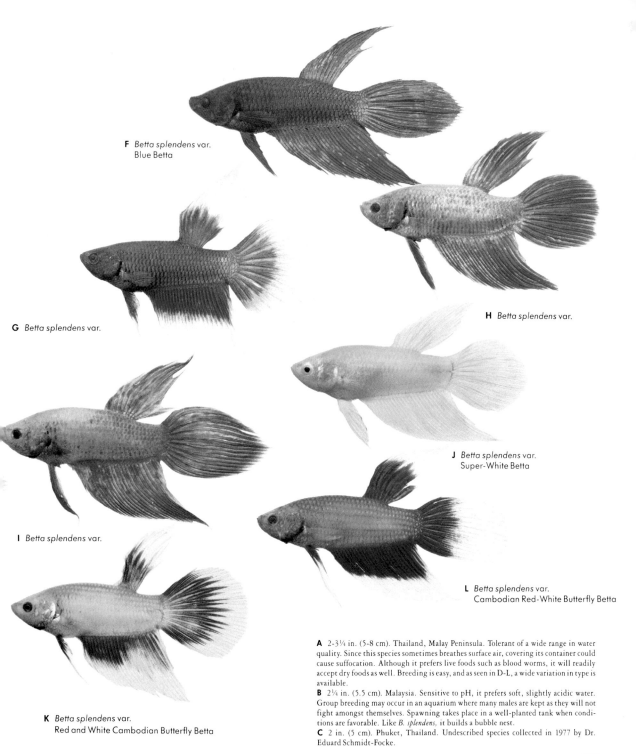

F *Betta splendens* var. Blue Betta

G *Betta splendens* var.

H *Betta splendens* var.

J *Betta splendens* var. Super-White Betta

I *Betta splendens* var.

L *Betta splendens* var. Cambodian Red-White Butterfly Betta

K *Betta splendens* var. Red and White Cambodian Butterfly Betta

A 2-3¼ in. (5-8 cm). Thailand, Malay Peninsula. Tolerant of a wide range in water quality. Since this species sometimes breathes surface air, covering its container could cause suffocation. Although it prefers live foods such as blood worms, it will readily accept dry foods as well. Breeding is easy, and as seen in D-L, a wide variation in type is available.

B 2¼ in. (5.5 cm). Malaysia. Sensitive to pH, it prefers soft, slightly acidic water. Group breeding may occur in an aquarium where many males are kept as they will not fight amongst themselves. Spawning takes place in a well-planted tank when conditions are favorable. Like *B. splendens,* it builds a bubble nest.

C 2 in. (5 cm). Phuket, Thailand. Undescribed species collected in 1977 by Dr. Eduard Schmidt-Focke.

177

A *Colisa lalia*. Sunset Gourami. Displaying ♂ under the pair's bubble nest.

ANABANTID FAMILY – LABYRINTH FISH

This group includes fishes of the four families of the Suborder Anabantoidei. Some ichthyologists also include the Family Luciocephalidae within this group. While some anabantoids such as *B. splendens* are quite pugnacious, other species are mild mannered. Gouramis are among the most graceful and well appreciated of aquarium fishes.

Labyrinth fishes are distributed throughout SE Asia (12 genera grouped in 4 families) and Africa (2 genera in 1 family). They can be found in such habitats as streams, swamps, bogs, irrigation ditches and intermittent waters. Fishes in this group have a more-or-less well developed accessory respiratory organ under their operculum (gill cover) which allows them to breathe surface air. This adaptation allows them to live in high-temperature water with a low oxygen content. The common name of this group is derived from this convoluted organ.

A A pair of Sunset Gouramis using their modified pelvic fins as feelers, while the male also displays.
B 1 A pair of Chocolate Gouramis.
2 ♀ holding eggs in her oral cavity. This is a difficult fish to breed in captivity.
3 Juvenile just out of the oral cavity.
C A pair of Dwarf Gourami in a spawning embrace just as the eggs are being expelled and fertilized.
D Pygmy Gourami fixing the bubble nest which is attached to the underside of an aquatic plant leaf. ♂ cares for the eggs.

B *Sphaerichthys osphromenoides.* Chocolate Gourami. **1** Nuptial coloration, ♂ (rt.) has red abdomen.　　**3** Juvenile right out of mouth.

C *Colisa lalia.* Dwarf Gourami. Nuptial embrace with eggs rising.　　**D** *Trichopsis pumilus.* Pygmy Gourami. ♂ caring for eggs.

ANABANTID SPAWNING BEHAVIOR

Some anabantoids have developed a peculiar spawning behavior to adapt to the rather harsh environmental circumstances of the habitats mentioned previously.

Below the water surface, gouramis, paradise fishes and many bettas make bubble nests in which the eggs are incubated and the young brooded to prevent suffocation. Climbing Perch, many African bushfishes and the Kissing Gourami, on the other hand, do not build a bubble nest or care for their eggs or young. About 500-1,000 eggs, which are transparent and float at the surface, are spewn out in a single spawning. The Croaking Gourami places its eggs in a bubble nest built on the underside of wide aquatic plant leaves, rather than at the surface. The name "gourami" comes from *Osphronemus goramy,* a species famous for building large nests (somewhat like a bird) out of aquatic grasses. As this fish grows quite large (can exceed 20 in. or 50 cm) even in an aquarium, and becomes definitely belligerent, it is best to avoid keeping it with other species. It does, however, easily become accustomed to humans.

BREEDING THE PEARL GOURAMI

The fish may be bred in a 15-gallon (56-liter) aquarium which contains both floating and rooted plants such as Water Sprite or Water Fern. No aeration or filtration is required, and the temperature should be kept at around 82°F (28°C). Although this species is considered rather mild mannered, mature males might attack immature or sexually unreceptive females. When both sexes have matured, however, and the female's abdomen has swelled noticeably, a pair should be separated out from the others. This pair should be kept together even if the male attacks the female at first.

Once the male has completed building the bubble nest, he begins displaying in front of the female. The ripe female then responds by poking at the body of the male. After this response, the male wraps his body around the female's, and in this spawning embrace, 1,000-3,000 eggs are released and fertilized. These eggs rise into the bubble nest, and will hatch out in about 24 hours. About three days after that, the larvae will become free swimming. At this point, they should be fed infusoria or pulverized egg yolk. Because growth varies greatly among the brood, sorting by size is important to avoid cannibalism. Juveniles should reach about ¾-1¼ in. (2-3 cm) in about two months.

A *Trichogaster leeri.* Pearl Gourami. **1** ♂ (left) lures ♀.

2 After inhaling surface air, the ♂ releases adhesive bubbles.

A 1 As courtship begins, the ♂ Pearl Gourami (left) spreads his fins in a beautiful display under the bubble nest to induce the ♀ to respond by poking at his body.
2 The ♂ inhales surface air, and then back underneath the water surface, exhales, producing bubbles of air surrounded by mouth secretions. These form the bubble nest which can reach some 3-4 in. (8-10 cm) in diameter.
3 Typical of anabantid spawning behavior, the ♂ wraps his body around that of the ripe ♀.
4 ♂ enwrapping ♀. After the ♀ is induced to enter the bubble nest, she assumes a position that makes it easy for her mate to wrap around her. Egg release during spawning lasts but 1-3 seconds.
5 This photo shows the instant of egg release from the ♀'s urogenital pore. Just afterwards, the ♂ takes the eggs in his mouth and then places them in the bubble nest.
6 The ♂ cares for the brood until they become self-feeding. He expends much effort in repairing the nest, returning stray larvae to the nest and guarding them from other fish that enter his territory.

3 ♂ (top) begins nuptial embrace, entwining ♀.

x

180

4 ♀ assumes pose under bubble nest and ♂ fully enwraps her.

5 Eggs at instant of release.

6 ♂ caring for brood.

A *Colisa labiosa*. Thick-Lipped Gourami. This mid-sized species can reach up to 4 in. (10 cm) in length. The coloration of a ripe ♂ is quite beautiful.

B *Colisa sota* var. Golden Honey Gourami.

D *Osphronemus goramy*. Giant or True Gourami.

A *Colisa sota*
Honey Gourami

B *Colisa lalia*
Dwarf Gourami

C *Colisa lalia* var.
Neon Gourami

D *Colisa lalia* var.
Sunset Gourami

E *Colisa labiosa* var. ♂
Thick-Lipped Gourami

E ♀

A 1½ in. (4 cm). Northeastern India. Although tolerant of a wide pH range, neutral to slightly acidic water will produce fish with the most brilliant color, especially the ♂ when he's ready for spawning. Despite the pair's relatively small size, the ♂ guards quite an expansive territory, so a large aquarium is preferable. Breeding them is easy.
B 2 in. (5 cm). Bengal and Assam in India. Prefers neutral to slightly acidic water. Though it will readily eat any foods, live ones should be included. It builds a thick bubble nest using the tips of aquatic grasses as a base. 50-200 eggs are laid in a single spawning, and these will hatch out in 1-2 days. Infusoria and mashed egg yolk is given as the fry's first food, followed by brine shrimp about 4-5 days later. As the young's growth rate varies greatly, frequent sorting is important to avoid cannibalism.
C Neon Gourami strain.
D Sunset Gourami strain produced around 1980 in Singapore.
E 3¼ in. (8 cm). India, Burma. Tolerant to pH variation, it is quite hardy, readily eating any food, but preferring live ones. As it coexists well with other species, it is a good community tank fish. Breeding is easy with 100-200 eggs being laid in a single spawning.

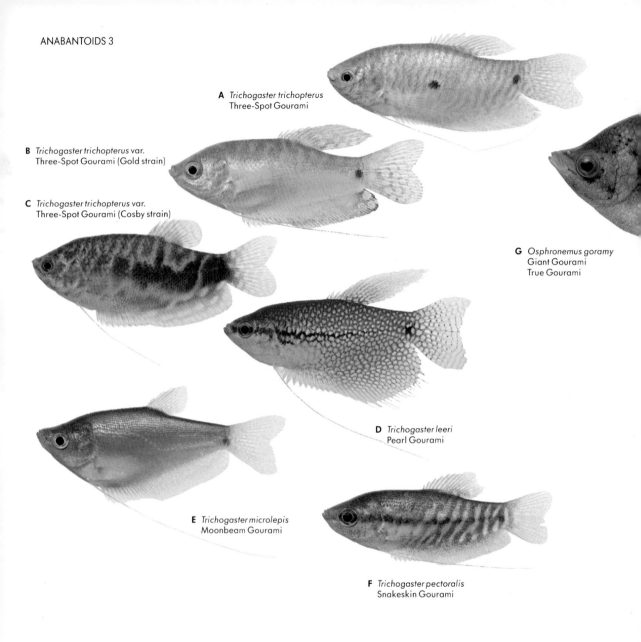

A *Trichogaster trichopterus*
Three-Spot Gourami

B *Trichogaster trichopterus* var.
Three-Spot Gourami (Gold strain)

C *Trichogaster trichopterus* var.
Three-Spot Gourami (Cosby strain)

G *Osphronemus goramy*
Giant Gourami
True Gourami

D *Trichogaster leeri*
Pearl Gourami

E *Trichogaster microlepis*
Moonbeam Gourami

F *Trichogaster pectoralis*
Snakeskin Gourami

A 6 in. (15 cm) in nature, smaller in aquaria. Thailand, Malay Peninsula, Borneo. Found in brooks and ponds, it is quite hardy and well suited for beginning aquarists. Breeding it is quite easy. A large, heavily planted breeding tank is necessary however, as the larger ♂ becomes pugnacious and sometimes kills the ♀ during this period. If she is attacked very frequently, it is best to separate her until she matures more fully. In a single spawning, 500-1,000 eggs are laid. These hatch out in the bubble nest within 1-2 days. Infusoria and pulverized yolk are the preferred first food as the larvae begin feeding immediately as they become free swimming.
B A yellow variant of the Marble Gourami strain.
C Popular variant of the Three-Spot Gourami.
D 4 in. (10 cm). Thailand, Malaysia, Sumatra, Borneo. Tolerant of pH variation, it is

a mild-tempered, mid-water species that readily eats dry or live food.
E 4¾ in. (12 cm). Thailand. Although not so sensitive to pH, it prefers slightly acidic, soft water. Rather mild-mannered, when compared to the Pearl Gourami it is quite skittish, often cowering in a tank corner. A tank with shallow water, numerous floating plants and a grassy refuge for the ♀ are essentials for breeding. As juveniles are sensitive to sudden changes in pH and frequently die after water is replaced, good filtration is very important. Water shouldn't be replaced until the young reach ½-¾ in. (1-2 cm).
F 12 in. (30 cm) in nature. Southern Vietnam, Malay Peninsula. Prefers slightly acidic, soft water. Its body coloration is very attractive. All types of food are readily eaten. The fish matures at about 4¾ in. (12 cm), and breeds quite easily.

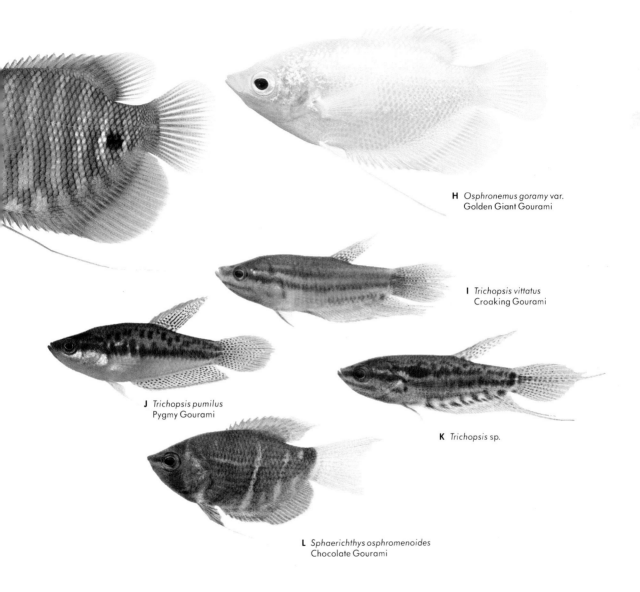

H *Osphronemus goramy* var.
Golden Giant Gourami

I *Trichopsis vittatus*
Croaking Gourami

J *Trichopsis pumilus*
Pygmy Gourami

K *Trichopsis* sp.

L *Sphaerichthys osphromenoides*
Chocolate Gourami

G 24 in. (60 cm). Its original habitat was Sumatra and Java, but it is now found throughout SE Asia as a food fish. Widely tolerant to pH, it can be found even in brackish waters. Hardy and easy to breed, it becomes quite large. This species builds a nest somewhat like birds, but out of aquatic grasses. Larger fish are extremely herbivorous.

H They have recently begun breeding this strain in SE Asia for export.

I 2¼ in. (6 cm). Thailand, Indonesia, Vietnam, Malay Peninsula. Found in grassy ponds and channels, it is tolerant of pH variation. Although omnivorous, it does prefer live food. Usually it spawns only in the early spring, but tank breeding is rather difficult. During spawning, both sexes are known to emit croaking sounds as over 200 eggs are laid.

J 1½ in. (3.5 cm). Southern Vietnam, Thailand, Indonesia. Rather sensitive to pH, slightly acidic, soft water kept at a high 81-82°F (27-28°C) is preferred. This omnivorous species builds a bubble nest on the underside of an aquatic plant leaf. During spawning, the pair is known to emit croaking sounds.

K 2¼ in. (6 cm). Thailand. Similar to the Croaking Gourami, its body pattern differs somewhat. A mild-tempered species that is easy to breed, it builds a bubble nest on aquatic plants. Rarely exported.

L 2¼ in. (6 cm). Sumatra, Malay Peninsula. Prefers acidic, soft water of 81-86°F (27-30°C). This mouthbrooder has quite elegant coloration and delightful behavior. Difficult to rear and breed, it is said that the addition of a small amount of artificial sea water may induce spawning.

A *Anabas testudineus.* Climbing Perch. By using its labyrinth organ, this fish can breathe out of water.

ANABAS & ITS LABYRINTH ORGAN

The Climbing Perch may have developed its unusual behavior after wiggling free from the beak of a piscivorous bird and falling onto a fallen palm leaf, then accidentally finding it could move on land. It is well known to climb onto wet land or grass, especially on rainy days, in search of food. As long as its body remains wet, this fish can remain alive out of water for many hours by using its special accessory respiratory organ found within the gill cavity. This superbranchial or labyrinth organ is composed of modified lamellae of the upper part of the outermost gill arch. A highly vascular layer, this organ resembles a rose. Air is taken in through the mouth to the labyrinth organ where gas exchange takes place. During spawning, the pair will frequently rise to water surface to breathe by taking in gulps of air. Sometimes, they will suffocate to death if they can't get to the surface to take in atmospheric oxygen.

In addition to the anabantids, a labyrinth organ can also be found in electric eels, walking catfishes, snakeheads and the Pikehead.

B *Ctenopoma acutirostre.* Leopard or Panther Bushfish. Members of this anabantid genus can be found widely distributed throughout Africa.

C *Luciocephalus pulcher.* Pikehead.

D *Ctenopoma maculata.*

A *Helostoma temminckii* var. Kissing Gourami.   **1** A large species growing to over 12 in. (30 cm). Young fish of about 3¼ in. (8 cm) are frequently sold in pet shops.

2 Famed kissing behavior.

B *Macropodus opercularis* var. Albino Paradise Fish.

C *Macropodus opercularis*. Paradise Fish.

D *Belontia signata*. Combtail Gourami or Paradise Fish.

VARIOUS SE ASIAN ANABANTOIDS

In addition to the previously mentioned bettas and gouramis, there are many other closely related anabantoids which are quite interesting and easily obtainable as tropical aquarium fishes.

The Kissing Gourami, well known as the "Kissing Fish," has long been considered an affectionate fish because of this behavior. Recent advances in behavioral studies have revealed that to the contrary, this display is really a type of ritualized aggression. This behavior is first observed in young of about 2¼ in. (6 cm), and does not result in fatal injuries.

Well known among "fighting fishes" are the Paradise Fish and the Combtail Paradise Fish which will sometimes enter into serious combat. Conversely, other species of *Macropodus* as well as the belontid *Malpulutta kretseri* are considered quite peaceful.

There are many interesting and attractive anabantoid species native to SE Asia and tropical Africa.

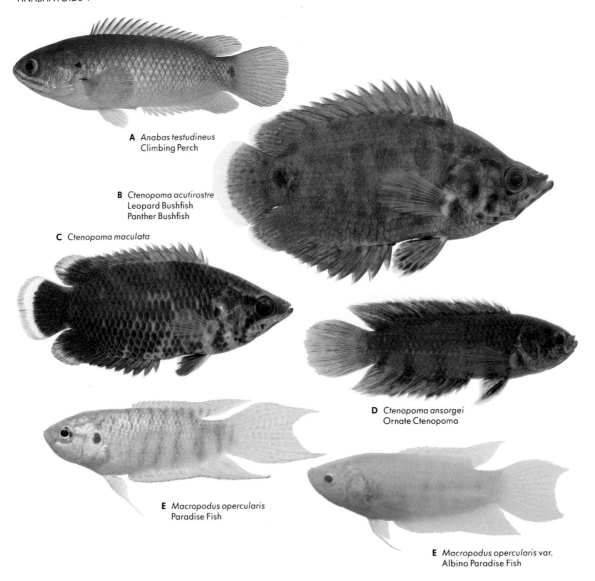

A *Anabas testudineus*
Climbing Perch

B *Ctenopoma acutirostre*
Leopard Bushfish
Panther Bushfish

C *Ctenopoma maculata*

D *Ctenopoma ansorgei*
Ornate Ctenopoma

E *Macropodus opercularis*
Paradise Fish

E *Macropodus opercularis var.*
Albino Paradise Fish

A 10 in. (25 cm) in nature, smaller in aquaria. India to Indonesia and southern China. Tolerant to pH variation, this omnivorous fish prefers live aquatic worms such as tubifex, while larger individuals will eat small fish. The tank should be covered to avoid the fish "climbing" out.
B 4¾ in. (12 cm). Lower Zaire R. Prefers soft water. It only eats live food and larger individuals devour small fish. Although it is a tranquil mid-water swimmer, both sexes are quite pugnacious, making pairing quite difficult. Breeding in captivity has to date been unsuccessful.
C 4 in. (10 cm). Lower Zaire R. Tolerant to water quality, it does prefer a water temperature of about 82°F (28°C). Live aquatic worms or small fish are the preferred foods. Breeding is quite easy, the pair spawning close to the tank bottom. Similar to

bettas, the ♂ embraces the ♀. Young hatch out in 2-3 days.
D 2¾ in. (7 cm). West African reaches of the Zaire R. Prefers neutral to slightly acidic water of about 82°F (28°C). Live worms such as tubifex or small fish are the foods of choice. A mild-tempered fish that can normally coexist with other species larger than itself, it does become pugnacious during breeding season. Said to be a nocturnal spawner, it builds a bubble nest. The young require small live foods.
E 4 in. (10 cm). Southern Vietnam, China, Taiwan, Korea, Okinawa. Tolerant of low temperatures down to 59°F (15°C), this fish is omnivorous. Pugnacious at times, the ♂ should be kept alone as the ♀ may be attacked at times other than the spawning season. When the ♀ is mature, a pair should be moved to separate tank. Breeding them is quite easy.

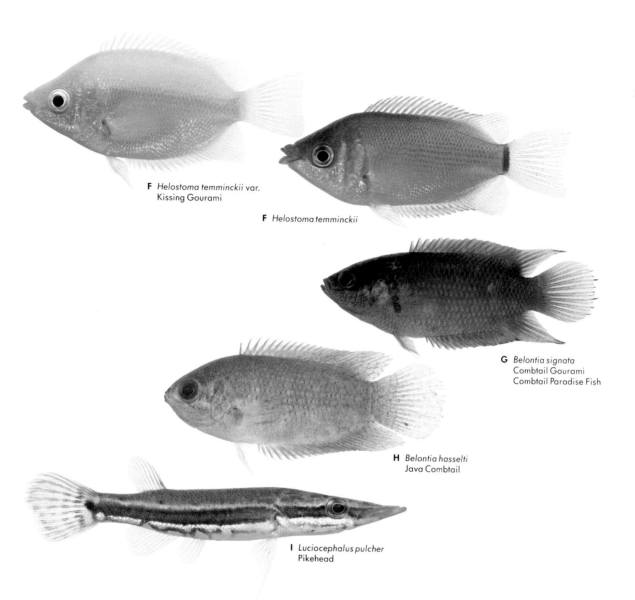

F *Helostoma temminckii* var.
Kissing Gourami

F *Helostoma temminckii*

G *Belontia signata*
Combtail Gourami
Combtail Paradise Fish

H *Belontia hasselti*
Java Combtail

I *Luciocephalus pulcher*
Pikehead

F 8-12 in. (20-30 cm). Thailand, Malay Peninsula, Sumatra, Java, Borneo. Water quality is unimportant. Omnivorous, its minute file-like dentition make it an ideal algae eater. A large number of floating eggs are spawned, but no bubble nest is built, nor are the eggs cared for. Wild form shown at right.

G 5 in. (13 cm). Sri Lanka. Tolerant to any water quality, it can coexist with much larger fish. Live worms or small fish are the preferred foods. A healthy pair is easily successfully spawned, the ♂ building a simple bubble nest and then inducing the ♀ to spawn under it. As the fry are relatively large, just after hatching they can eat brine shrimp.

H 4 in. (10 cm). Java, Borneo, Sumatra. This not so popular anabantid is more mild tempered than its congener above. It spawns under a bubble nest.

I 7 in. (18 cm). Malay Peninsula, Sumatra, Bangka, Billiton. Not an anabantoid, but it possesses an accessory respiratory organ. It is piscivorous, catching small fish in its distensible mouth. A mouthbrooder that spawns after it reaches 4 in. (10 cm) in length, breeding is quite difficult. Frequently, it dies suddenly for no apparent reason.

Guppy farm in Singapore. Many improved types of guppies are produced under ideal conditions—large farms, plentiful water and live food, and extensive sunshine.

SE ASIAN FISH FARMS

Culling Red Tuxedo Guppies.

Many of the tropical fishes sold in N. America, Europe and Japan are imported from SE Asia. Singapore's governmental support of the tropical fish culturing industry, including actively assisting fish breeders financially, plus helping to concentrate and integrate the scattered fish farms and shippers is well known. Such facilities found along both sides of "Fish Farm Road" have a history going back a few decades. These farms specialize in production of guppies, angelfish and a few other types of tropicals. A guppy farm (such as the one shown here) has some 800 concrete ponds ranging in size from 40-160 ft² (4-15m²) each. One can find stocks of Tuxedo, King Cobra, Mosaic and even some new types of guppies being bred and improved. Under the tropical sun, these fish exhibit excellent, brilliant coloration.

LIVEBEARERS 7

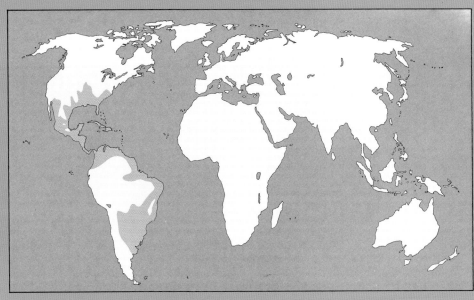

GUPPIES

The brooks, ponds, swamps and brackish waters near the mouths of the rivers north of the Amazon across to Trinidad and Barbados were the original habitat of the Guppy. Nowadays it is widespread across tropical and subtropical areas where it was introduced for mosquito control, having escaped from culturing ponds or been discarded from home aquaria.

Even among wild stocks there is a wide variation especially in ♂ coloration and finnage shape. The present rich choice in varieties is the result of repeated artificial selection and hybridization. When the offspring are of poor configuration and less colorful than beautiful parents, this may be caused by nature's tendency to revert to the wild type being stronger than the hereditary factors of artificially selected stock. Careful selection and repeated outcrosses to better parent stocks should help retention of the desired beautiful characteristics. Breeding pure lines separately, sexing and dividing the young early (prior to full differentiation of the gonopodium), setting up an intentional breeding program, and maintaining optimal environmental conditions are all requirements for a successful breeding program.

Breeding guppies close to the wild stock is easy even under unfavorable conditions, but the production of show quality fish from pure lines of artificially improved stocks is quite a bit harder. Important to such culture is the maintenance of neutral, moderately hard water, along with periodic water replacement and addition of a pinch of salt.

A Varied improved type guppies in a single tank. Guppies selectively produced by serious breeders exhibit a graceful body shape, a slender caudal peduncle, a widely expansive tail, and regal swimming movements.

A *Poecilia reticulatus* var. Guppy.

A *Poecilia reticulatus* var. Japanese Mosaic Guppy.

B *Poecilia reticulatus* var. Japanese Glass Mosaic Guppy.

C *Poecilia reticulatus* var. Japanese Albino King Cobra Guppy.

D *Poecilia reticulatus* var. Japanese King Cobra Guppy.

JAPANESE GUPPIES

Guppy breeding first became popular in North America in the 1930's, and in Japan around 1955. Today, a number of guppy contests which include many fixed varieties are held annually in both countries and in Europe. Even so, there are still a number of varieties which produce offspring with many intermediate or mosaic characters, making their classification in shows quite difficult. Among the most popular lines exhibited are:

Glass Type: Preference is to tail finnage that sports a striated pattern appearing like fine glass fibers.

Mosaic Type: The tail markings form a strong mosaic pattern.

King Cobra Type: First produced in the U.S., the snakeskin-like patterns extend across the entire body and tail.

Tuxedo Type: An improved long-tailed type from Germany and other countries, the rear half of the body is either black or red.

Miscellaneous: Other types including the Flamingo and Leopard guppies.

E *Poecilia reticulatus* var. Singapore Guppies. ♂ (left) chasing a ♀.

F Baby guppy at the instant of birth.

G *Poecilia reticulatus* var. Japanese Albino Scissortail King Cobra Guppy.

OVOVIVIPARITY

Most livebearing fishes are ovoviviparous, that is, the ova inside the female are fertilized and develop internally and the young are born alive. Accordingly, the male has a modified anal fin called the gonopodium which serves as the intromittent organ for transfer of the sperm packet into the female. This fin appears quite normal in the young, but begins to modify in males as they mature. As female poeciliids are known to be able to store these sperm packets, several broods can be born from a single copulation. Unborn poeciliid young utilize nutrients stored in their yolk sac, unlike mammalian viviparity where nutrients are passed through a placenta, until they hatch and emerge from the mother's genital pore. A modified form of full viviparity is known in goodeid, jenynsiid and embiotocid fishes.

E ♂ (left) chasing ♀. Note the modified anal fin of the ♂ being swung to its front. This copulatory organ used for sperm transfer is known as the gonopodium. Gravid females with a dark belly are known to avoid the male's advances, while ones with a light belly as shown here, will not.
F ♀ giving birth. The young emerge curled up, but start straightening out as they descend towards the tank bottom. Very soon thereafter, the brood forms a shoal near the water surface and begin their search for food.

A *Poecilia reticulatus* ♂
Guppy

A ♀

B *Poecilia reticulatus* var.
Half-Black Swallowtail Guppy

B

F *Poecilia reticulatus* var.
Japanese Albino Glass Veiltail Guppy

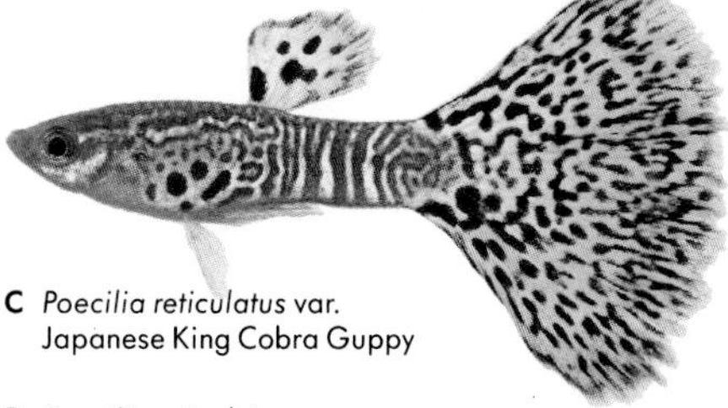

E *Poecilia reticulatus* var.
Japanese Fancy Deltatail Guppy

C *Poecilia reticulatus* var.
Japanese King Cobra Guppy

D *Poecilia reticulatus* var.
Japanese Albino
Scissortail King Cobra Guppy

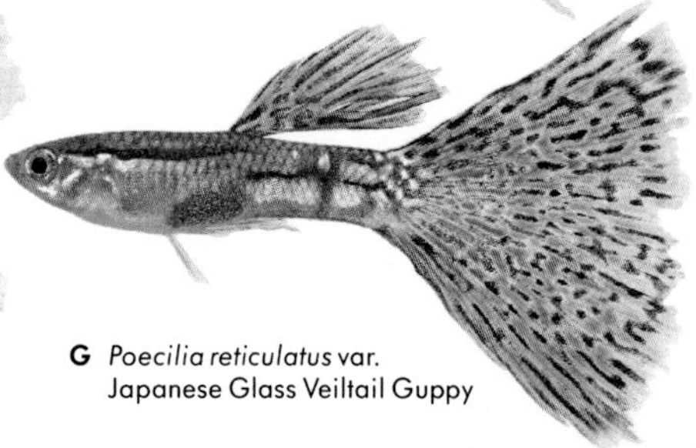

G *Poecilia reticulatus* var.
Japanese Glass Veiltail Guppy

H *Poecilia reticulatus* var.
Blue Deltatail Guppy

J *Poecilia reticulatus* var.
Half-Black Guppy

I *Poecilia reticulatus* var.
Half-Black Red Veiltail Guppy

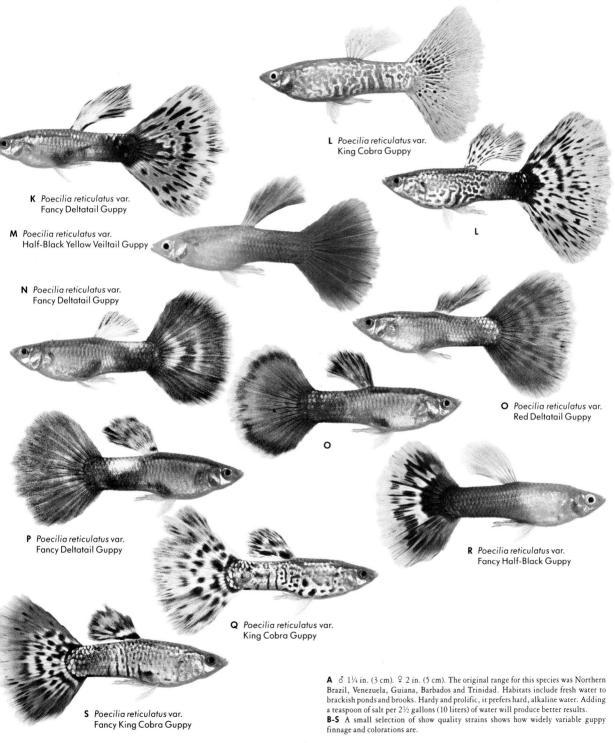

K *Poecilia reticulatus* var.
Fancy Deltatail Guppy

M *Poecilia reticulatus* var.
Half-Black Yellow Veiltail Guppy

N *Poecilia reticulatus* var.
Fancy Deltatail Guppy

L *Poecilia reticulatus* var.
King Cobra Guppy

L

O *Poecilia reticulatus* var.
Red Deltatail Guppy

O

P *Poecilia reticulatus* var.
Fancy Deltatail Guppy

R *Poecilia reticulatus* var.
Fancy Half-Black Guppy

Q *Poecilia reticulatus* var.
King Cobra Guppy

S *Poecilia reticulatus* var.
Fancy King Cobra Guppy

A ♂ 1¼ in. (3 cm). ♀ 2 in. (5 cm). The original range for this species was Northern
Brazil, Venezuela, Guiana, Barbados and Trinidad. Habitats include fresh water to
brackish ponds and brooks. Hardy and prolific, it prefers hard, alkaline water. Adding
a teaspoon of salt per 2½ gallons (10 liters) of water will produce better results.
B-S A small selection of show quality strains shows how widely variable guppy
finnage and colorations are.

199

A *Xiphophorus helleri* var. Neon Swordtail. **1** Moment of birth. ♀ releases a brood of 30-150, 1-4 at a time.

2 Fry emerging from the genital pore.

3 Fry just after release. It will begin feeding momentarily.

SEX REVERSAL IN SWORDTAILS

Swordtails are well known to undergo sex reversal; mature females commonly becoming males, but never vice versa.

Differentiation into males can occur at roughly three different times: 2-3 and 4-5 months after birth, plus in older females who have exhausted their supply of primary oocytes. In the last case, the resultant males have a less pronounced "sword" and somewhat different coloration from ordinary ones.

Although males differentiating at other times are productive, the ones doing so at 4-5 months tend to be the most prolific and suitable for breeding. In some strains of swordtails, over 30% of older females differentiate into males.

A 1 ♀ swordtails usually drop fry in groups of 3. She swims up and down the tank, dropping fry every 1-5 minutes. Parturition may last over one month, with 50-150 young being born over this period.
2 Swordtail young at emergence. It emerges head first, the body slightly bent.
3 Just after release, the fry drops to the bottom, but momentarily becomes free swimming and actively seeks out food.

B *Poecilia velifera* var. Golden Yucatan Sailfin Molly. The large dorsal fin is extended like a fan during displays and challenges.

A *Xiphophorus maculatus* var. Half Red Platy. These small, mild-tempered tropical fish are ideal for beginners.

B *Xiphophorus helleri* var. Red Tuxedo Lyretail Swordtail.

C *Belonesox belizanus.* Pike Top Minnow.

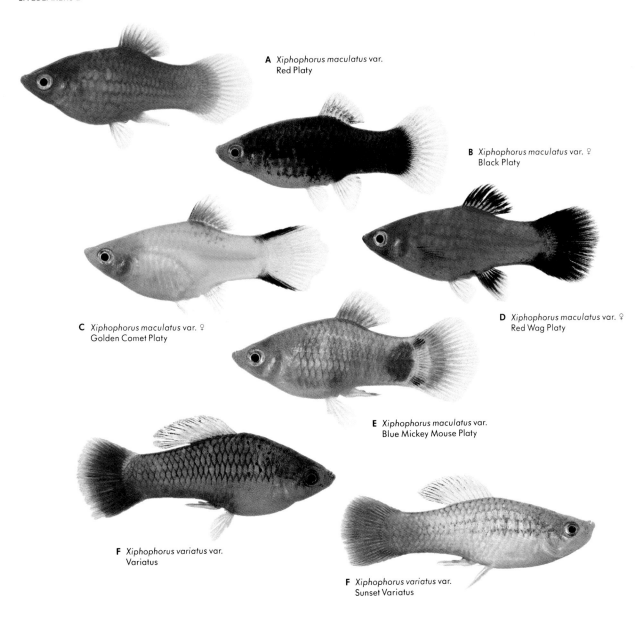

A *Xiphophorus maculatus* var.
Red Platy

B *Xiphophorus maculatus* var. ♀
Black Platy

C *Xiphophorus maculatus* var. ♀
Golden Comet Platy

D *Xiphophorus maculatus* var. ♀
Red Wag Platy

E *Xiphophorus maculatus* var.
Blue Mickey Mouse Platy

F *Xiphophorus variatus* var.
Variatus

F *Xiphophorus variatus* var.
Sunset Variatus

A–E ♂ 1½ in. (4 cm). ♀ 2¼ in. (6 cm). Southeastern Mexico, Guatemala, Belize. Mainly found in swamps and brooks, it prefers hard, alkaline water. It is a mild-mannered, pretty fish that is easy to breed. Although many varieties are available, due to mixed breeding, a great deal of them are poorer quality than the original stocks. As adults generally do not eat the fry, they will easily breed among themselves in a well planted aquarium. 10-50 young in a single brood, they should be fed brine shrimp just after they're released.

F ♂ 1½ in. (4 cm). ♀ 2 in. (5 cm). Northeastern Mexico. Found in brooks, it prefers slightly hard, alkaline water. A very beautiful species with many color variations being produced. About 100 fry are dropped during an extended parturition period. The young require attentive care.

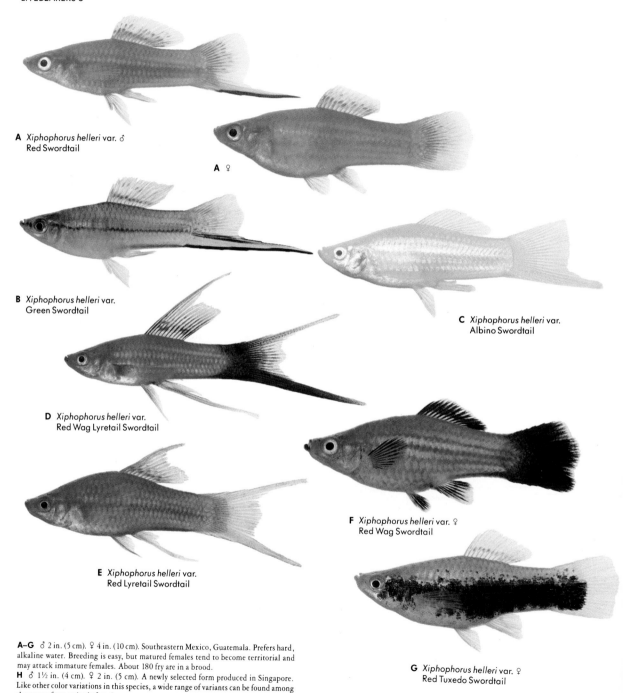

A *Xiphophorus helleri* var. ♂
Red Swordtail

A ♀

B *Xiphophorus helleri* var.
Green Swordtail

C *Xiphophorus helleri* var.
Albino Swordtail

D *Xiphophorus helleri* var.
Red Wag Lyretail Swordtail

F *Xiphophorus helleri* var. ♀
Red Wag Swordtail

E *Xiphophorus helleri* var.
Red Lyretail Swordtail

G *Xiphophorus helleri* var. ♀
Red Tuxedo Swordtail

A–G ♂ 2 in. (5 cm). ♀ 4 in. (10 cm). Southeastern Mexico, Guatemala. Prefers hard, alkaline water. Breeding is easy, but matured females tend to become territorial and may attack immature females. About 180 fry are in a brood.
H ♂ 1½ in. (4 cm). ♀ 2 in. (5 cm). A newly selected form produced in Singapore. Like other color variations in this species, a wide range of variants can be found among the young from a single female.
I 4¾ in. (12 cm). Yucatan Peninsula, Mexico. Found in fresh to brackish waters, it

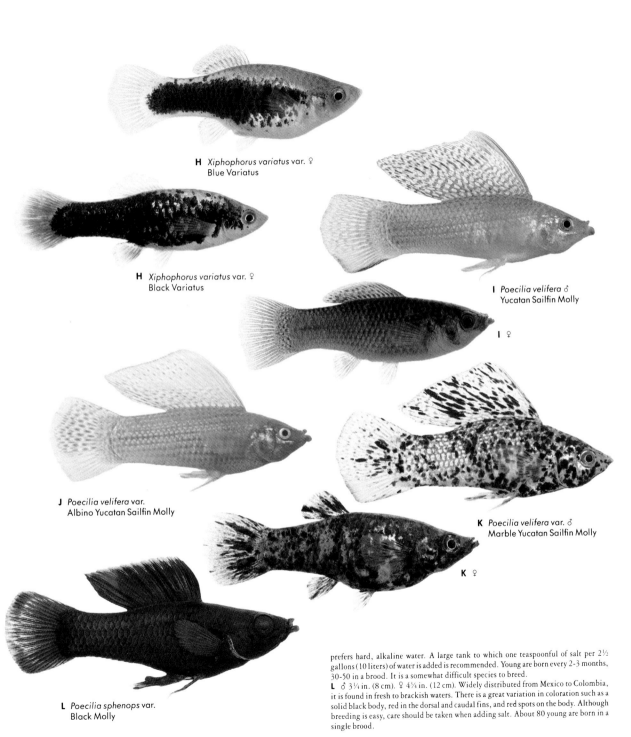

H *Xiphophorus variatus* var. ♀
Blue Variatus

H *Xiphophorus variatus* var. ♀
Black Variatus

I *Poecilia velifera* ♂
Yucatan Sailfin Molly

I ♀

J *Poecilia velifera* var.
Albino Yucatan Sailfin Molly

K *Poecilia velifera* var. ♂
Marble Yucatan Sailfin Molly

K ♀

L *Poecilia sphenops* var.
Black Molly

prefers hard, alkaline water. A large tank to which one teaspoonful of salt per 2½ gallons (10 liters) of water is added is recommended. Young are born every 2-3 months, 30-50 in a brood. It is a somewhat difficult species to breed.
L ♂ 3¼ in. (8 cm). ♀ 4¾ in. (12 cm). Widely distributed from Mexico to Colombia, it is found in fresh to brackish waters. There is a great variation in coloration such as a solid black body, red in the dorsal and caudal fins, and red spots on the body. Although breeding is easy, care should be taken when adding salt. About 80 young are born in a single brood.

205

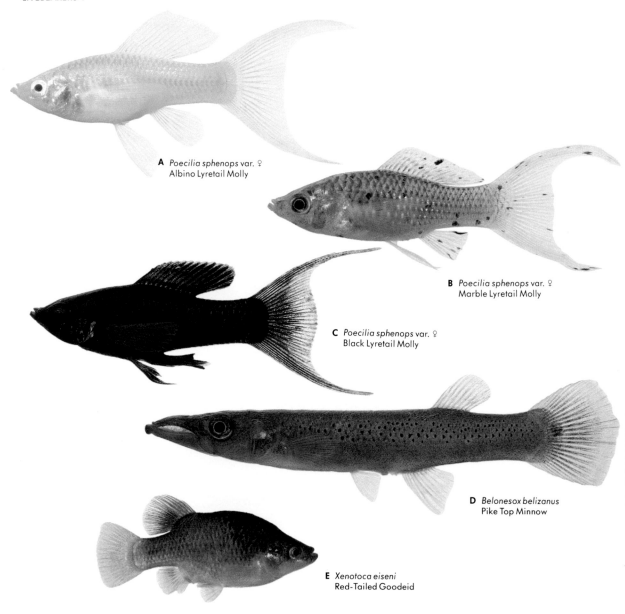

A *Poecilia sphenops* var. ♀
Albino Lyretail Molly

B *Poecilia sphenops* var. ♀
Marble Lyretail Molly

C *Poecilia sphenops* var. ♀
Black Lyretail Molly

D *Belonesox belizanus*
Pike Top Minnow

E *Xenotoca eiseni*
Red-Tailed Goodeid

A–C 2-4 in. (5-10 cm). As the molly is easily hybridized, quite a number of color variations are available to the hobbyist. There are however, three generally recognized sailfin molly species, *Poecilia velifera* (Yucatan Peninsula), *P. latipinna* (Florida to Belize), and *P. petensis* (limited to L Petén, Guatemala, plus a few shortfinned species of which *P. sphenops* (Mexico to Costa Rica) is the most often available commercially.

D ♂ 4 in. (10 cm), ♀ 8 in. (20 cm). Atlantic slope of Central America from southeastern Mexico to Nicaragua. It is found in abundance in brackish waters, and prefers hard, alkaline water. Even though it is piscivorous, eating small fish, it is definitely a picky eater, and quite skittish. Solo habitation in a well planted aquarium is best. About 100 fry are born per brood, but the parents will eat their young. Unless very well fed, the growing young will also cannibalize each other.

E 4 in. (10 cm). Highlands of Mexico. This species is very tolerant to water quality, and easy to breed, but somewhat aggressive to other fishes. Unlike the poeciliids which are ovoviviparous with embryos having no direct blood circulation with the mother, goodeids are viviparous (similar to mammals) having a placenta-like blood circulation with the mother. 20-50 fry are born in a single brood.

FAMILY	**APLOCHEILIDAE** (Rivulines)	FAMILY	**CYPRINODONTIDAE** (Killifishes)
SUBFAMILY	APLOCHEILINAE (Old World Rivulines)	SUBFAMILY	CYPRINODONTINAE
		Genus	*Jordanella*
Genera	*Aphyosemion*	SUBFAMILY	APLOCHEILICHTHYINAE
	Aplocheilus	Genera	*Aplocheilichthys*
	Epiplatys		*Procatopus*
	Nothobranchius		
	Pachypanchax	FAMILY	**ADRIANICHTHYIDAE**
	Pseudepiplatys	SUBFAMILY	ORYSIINAE (Medaka or Ricefishes)
SUBFAMILY	RIVULINAE (New World Rivulines)		
		Genus	*Oryzias*
Genera	*Cynolebias*		
	Cynopoecilus		
	Pterolebias		
	Rivulys		
	Simpsonichthys		

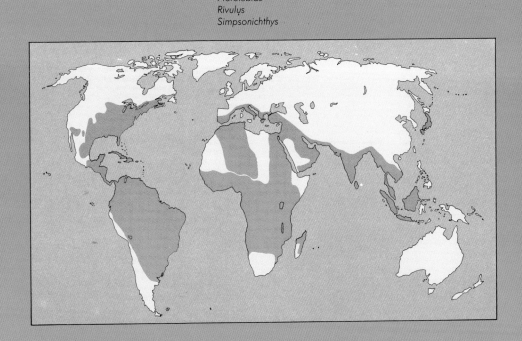

A *Nothobranchius guentheri.* Guenther's Notho. **1** ♂ (above) inducing ♀ to spawn.

KILLIFISH

Killifish is the general name given to the oviparous cyprinodonts inhabiting tropical and subtropical habitats. Among these, those found in the African and New World tropics with definite dry and rainy seasons, are among the most interesting in terms of spawning behavior and fecundity, as well as exhibiting quite attractive coloration. They are roughly divided into two major groups on the basis of their spawning behavior.

The "annuals" bury their demersal eggs in sand or peat moss, while the "non-annuals" lay their adhesive eggs on aquatic plants. Some even exhibit both types of spawning behavior depending upon environmental conditions.

Included among the non-annuals are the fishes of the genera *Aplocheilus, Epiplatys* and *Rivulus.* The superficially similar but unrelated medaka of the Subfamily Oryziinae also breed in the same manner as "non-annual" killies. Among the annuals are the genera *Nothobranchius* and *Cynolebias. Aphyosemion* exhibits both types of behavior depending on species and circumstances.

Many killifish become pugnacious as they mature. To prevent damaging fights between males, it is best to separate pairs out to small individual aquaria. They generally prefer slightly acidic, soft, well-conditioned aged water.

KILLIFISH BREEDING & CARE

Breeding Annuals

To prepare the small spawning tank, first thoroughly boil enough peat moss to cover the bottom. Place the sterilized peat moss in the tank, and once it has settled, introduce a ripe pair for breeding. If they are in top condition, they should begin spawning within that day. They will lay a few eggs very day. After about 2-4 weeks, remove the peat moss and carefully strain it until a slight degree of dampness is

2 Pair in the act of spawning.

3 Eyed eggs just prior to hatching.

reached. Put this in a vinyl bag, and store it at about 77°F (25°C). After about 1-6 months (depending on species), place the moss back into a small, well-aged tank of water, and then most of the eggs will hatch out within a few minutes to one day afterwards.

Breeding Non-annuals
Under favorable conditions, a good pair will spawn naturally among the flora of a well-planted aquarium. From the breeding pair's perspective, such natural spawning is most preferable. However, many species have a habit of eating their eggs. To avoid this, a nylon wool spawning mop is placed in the tank with the

pair, and removed when spawning is completed. The eggs will hatch out within 10-20 days.

A1 A characteristic courtship display just prior to spawning.
2 Pair spawning. The ♂ holds the ♀ with his dorsal fin.
3 Eggs just prior to hatching. After lying dormant in the damp peat for 1-2 months, the stimulus of being returned to water causes the eggs to soon hatch.

A *Nothobranchius* sp. An undescribed species given the code name TZ-83.

B *Nothobranchius rachovii*. Rachow's Notho.

C *Nothobranchius cyaneus*. (Warfa).

D *Nothobranchius patrizii*.

E *Nothobranchius palmquisti*. (Mrima).

F *Nothobranchius furzeri*.

G *Nothobranchius eggersi*.

A *Aphyosemion multicolor.* (Ijebu-Ode). Males in threat display.

B *Aphyosemion bivittatum.* (Iwere).

C *Aphyosemion volcanum.* (Meme).

D *Aphyosemion volcanum.* (Bolifumba).

213

A *Aphyosemion australe* (Orange). The popular Orange Lyretail.

B *Aphyosemion mirabile.* (Takuai). This species has numerous, beautiful fine spots.

C *Aphyosemion scheeli.*

D *Aphyosemion deltaense.*

E *Aphyosemion gardneri.* (Nsukka).

F *Aphyosemion puerzli.*

G *Aphyosemion striatum.* Five-Lined Killie. A "water gem" with an emerald green shine.

215

A *Pachipanchax playfairi*. Playfair's Panchax. **1** ♂ displaying in front of the ♀.

PLAYFAIR'S PANCHAX

2 A pair spawning among willow moss.

Among the African rivulins, the distinct coloration of *Aphyosemion* and *Nothobranchius* makes them among the most popular with aquarists. Their pure blues, reds, yellows and other colors make them appear as "water gems."

One of the Old World rivulines of the subfamily Aplocheilinae, this fish originates from eastern Africa. Its subtle red spots and dark borders on an olive base color may make this killifish more favored by experienced hobbyists. Under some lighting conditions, it may even exhibit a metallic sheen.

During the spawning season, this subtle fish adds a delightful contrasting flashing movement. The male could be said to be a "brilliant understated beauty."

B *Cynolebias alexandri.* Entre Rios Pearl Fish.

C *Epiplatys dageti.* Red-Chinned Panchax.

D *Pseudepiplatys annulatus.* Clown Killie.

E *Simpsonichthys boitonei.* Brazilian Lyretail.

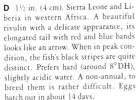

D 1½ in. (4 cm). Sierra Leone and Liberia in western Africa. A beautiful rivulin with a delicate appearance, its elongated tail with red and blue bands looks like an arrow. When in peak condition, the fish's black stripes are quite distinct. Prefers hard (around 8°DH), slightly acidic water. A non-annual, to breed them is rather difficult. Eggs hatch out in about 14 days.

F 2¼ in. (6 cm). Venezuela. A fairly well known annual killifish, it requires the same care as *Cynolebias* and *Pterolebias,* but breeding is rather more difficult. Eggs are spawned in peat moss, and require a six month dormant period.

F *Cynolebias dolichopterus.* Sabrefin Killie.

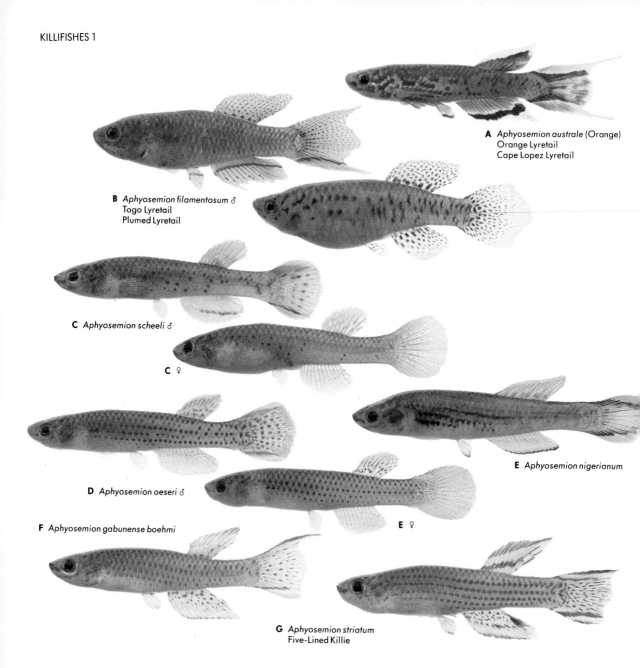

A *Aphyosemion australe* (Orange)
Orange Lyretail
Cape Lopez Lyretail

B *Aphyosemion filamentosum* ♂
Togo Lyretail
Plumed Lyretail

C *Aphyosemion scheeli* ♂

C ♀

D *Aphyosemion oeseri* ♂

E *Aphyosemion nigerianum*

F *Aphyosemion gabunense boehmi*

E ♀

G *Aphyosemion striatum*
Five-Lined Killie

A 2¼ in. (6 cm). Gabon. Non-annual. The wild stock is brownish, but morphs include a golden or orange one shown here. Breeding is easy, with eggs requiring about 21 days to hatch.

B 2¼ in. (6 cm). Southern Nigeria, western Cameroon. Annual. After it spawns in peat moss, the peat should be strained and stored. The eggs will hatch out after a 45-day dormant period when the peat is returned to water.

C 2¾ in. (7 cm). Nigeria. Non-annual. Suitable for beginners, care and breeding of this fish are easy. It spawns on water plants, with eggs hatching after 14 days.

D 1¾ in. (4.5 cm). Near Santa Isabel, Fernando Po in the Gulf of Guinea. Non-annual. Hatching required about 14 days.

E 2¼ in. (6 cm). Easy to raise. Spawns readily on aquatic plants.

F 2¼ in. (6 cm). Gabon. Non-annual. Within this species, there are many beautiful subspecies.

G 2¼ in. (6 cm). Gabon. Non-annual. Breeding this fish is a worthy challenge as it isn't easy.

H 2¼ in. (6 cm). Cameroon. Non-annual. Of this species, this variation with

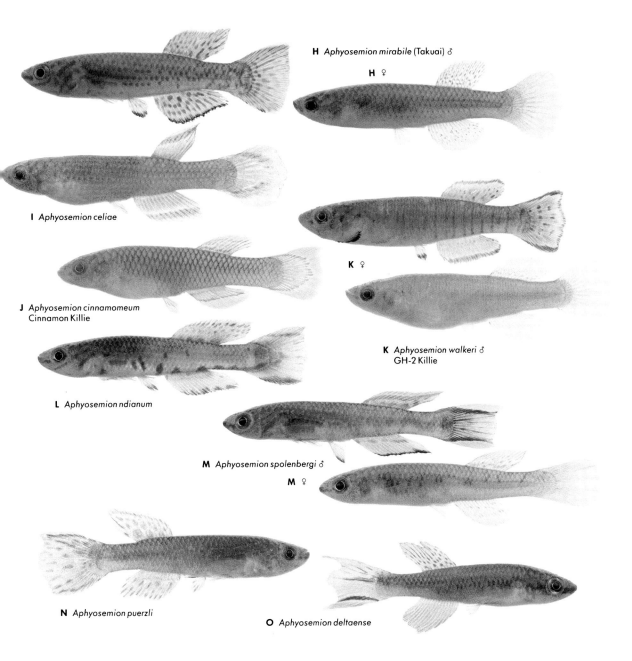

H *Aphyosemion mirabile* (Takuai) ♂

H ♀

I *Aphyosemion celiae*

K ♀

J *Aphyosemion cinnamomeum*
Cinnamon Killie

L *Aphyosemion ndianum*

K *Aphyosemion walkeri* ♂
GH-2 Killie

M *Aphyosemion spolenbergi* ♂

M ♀

N *Aphyosemion puerzli*

O *Aphyosemion deltaense*

numerous beautiful spots is the easiest to breed.
I 2 in. (5 cm). Around Kumba, western and southern Cameroon. Annual. Quite a hardy fish, this species can even be placed in a community tank.
J 2 in. (5 cm). Mountain range of western Cameroon. Annual. Best suited for experienced aquarists, this fish is quite delicate and liable to disease. Eggs hatch after a 30-day dormancy period.
K 2¼ in. (6 cm). Ghana, Ivory Coast. Non-annual.
L 2¼ in. (6 cm). Ndian R. in western Cameroon. Annual. Spawns in peat moss or

sand, with eggs needing to remain dormant about a month.
M 3¼ in. (8 cm). Cameroon. Non-annual. As care and breeding are rather hard, this fish is best suited for an experienced aquarist.
N 4 in. (10 cm). Cameroon. Annual. A large species, it is especially attractive due to its distinct red and blue markings.
O 4¾ in. (12 cm). Western Nigeria. This large species belongs to the *A. gulare* complex. One of the largest bottom-spawning killifish, it has a well defined w-shaped tail. Hatching, which is not easy, requires about 2 months.

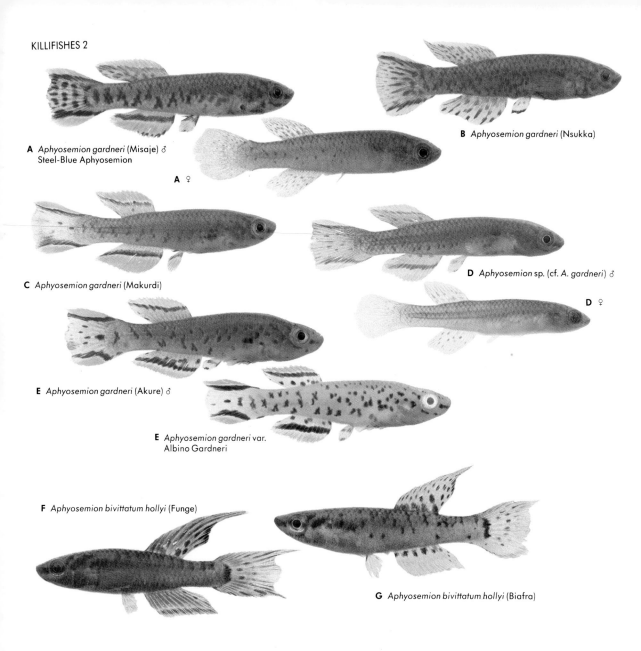

A *Aphyosemion gardneri* (Misaje) ♂
Steel-Blue Aphyosemion

A ♀

B *Aphyosemion gardneri* (Nsukka)

C *Aphyosemion gardneri* (Makurdi)

D *Aphyosemion* sp. (cf. *A. gardneri*) ♂

D ♀

E *Aphyosemion gardneri* (Akure) ♂

E *Aphyosemion gardneri* var.
Albino Gardneri

F *Aphyosemion bivittatum hollyi* (Funge)

G *Aphyosemion bivittatum hollyi* (Biafra)

A 2¼ in. (6 cm). All the various forms of this species are colorful, plus easy to raise and breed. A non-annual, it spawns on aquatic plants, with eggs hatching after 18 days. Even so, the eggs will tolerate an up to one year dormant period. This hardy variant was first described in 1973.
B 2¼ in. (6 cm). Nsukka in eastern Nigeria. Hardy and easy to breed, a pair in top condition will lay a clutch of about ten eggs daily.
C 2¼ in. (6 cm). Along the Makurdi in Nigeria. Distinguishable from the other forms by its wider yellow border on the dorsal and anal fins. Easily bred and cared for, eggs hatch within 14-21 days.

D 2¼ in. (7 cm). Resembling the Akure variant, its point of origin is unknown.
E 2¼ in. (7 cm). Akure, Nigeria. The most popular of the *A. gardneri* complex, this type is also the easiest to raise and breed. An albino mutant as seen below was found and fixed by an American aquarist. Eggs hatch after 14-21 days.
F 2 in. (5 cm). Funge, Nigeria. Similar to the Biafra type, but differs in that it has a bluish head and tail. It is easily cared for and bred.
G 2 in. (5 cm). Biafra, Nigeria. With fewer spots on the flanks, it has more subtle appearance overall than other variants. Care and breeding are easy. Eggs are laid on aquatic plants, and hatch after about 14 days.

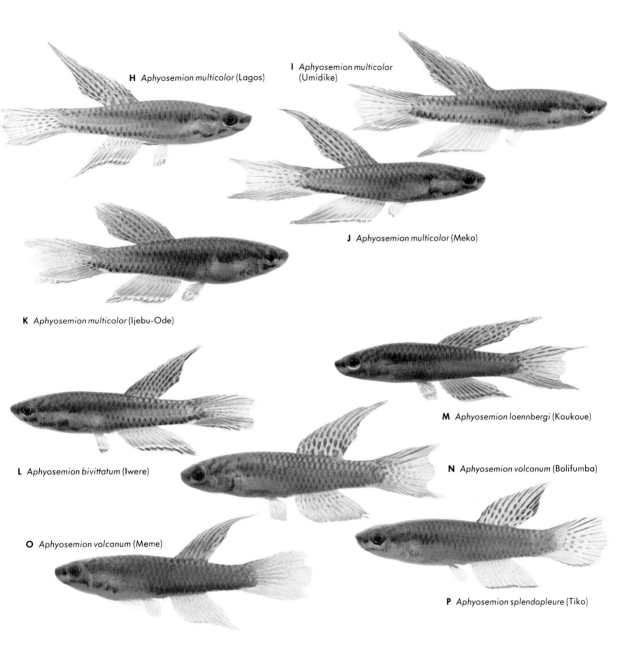

H *Aphyosemion multicolor* (Lagos)

I *Aphyosemion multicolor* (Umidike)

J *Aphyosemion multicolor* (Meko)

K *Aphyosemion multicolor* (Ijebu-Ode)

L *Aphyosemion bivittatum* (Iwere)

M *Aphyosemion loennbergi* (Koukoue)

N *Aphyosemion volcanum* (Bolifumba)

O *Aphyosemion volcanum* (Meme)

P *Aphyosemion splendopleure* (Tiko)

H 2 in. (5 cm). Lagos, Nigeria. Having a delicate charm, it is distinguished from other populations by the blue margin of the dorsal and pectoral fins.
I 2 in. (5 cm). Umidike, Nigeria. Quite different in coloration from other populations of this species, it is also quite sensitive to water pollution, making daily water control vital.
J 2¼ in. (5.5 cm). Meko, Nigeria. Quite colorful, it is hardy and easy to raise.
K 2¼ in. (5.5 cm). Ijebu-Ode, Nigeria. Although it resembles the bluish Meko population, it has larger finnage.
L Max. 2 in. (5 cm). Non-annual from Iwere, Nigeria.

M 2¼ in. (6 cm). Koukoue, Cameroon. Its two dark stripes running horizontally across the orange body color give this fish a graceful appearance. Easy to care for, it breeds readily.
N 2 in. (5 cm). Bolifumba, Cameroon. Its specific name comes from the fact that its habitat is a volcanic area. Quite prolific, it's easy to care for.
O 2 in. (5 cm). Meme, Cameroon. Easy to raise and breed, this population exhibits a subtle, yet delicate coloration.
P 2 in. (5 cm). Tiko, Cameroon. A smallish species with fantastic coloration, it is hardy and easy to breed.

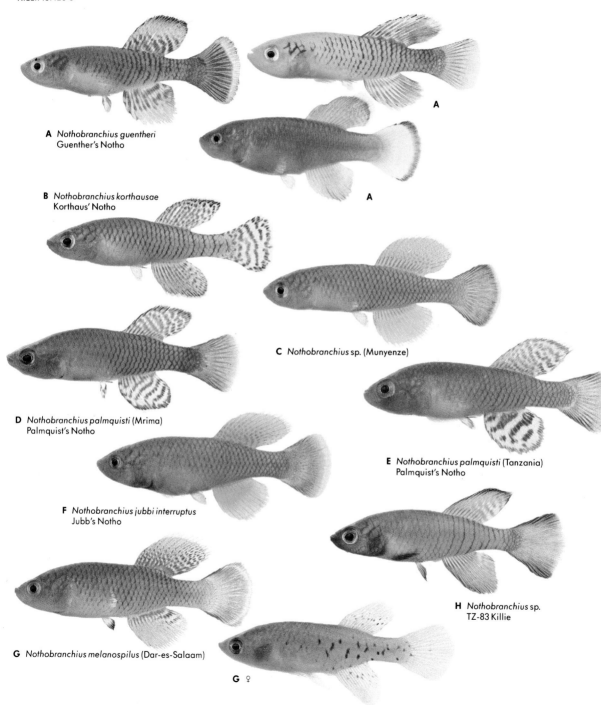

A *Nothobranchius guentheri*
Guenther's Notho

A

B *Nothobranchius korthausae*
Korthaus' Notho

A

C *Nothobranchius* sp. (Munyenze)

D *Nothobranchius palmquisti* (Mrima)
Palmquist's Notho

E *Nothobranchius palmquisti* (Tanzania)
Palmquist's Notho

F *Nothobranchius jubbi interruptus*
Jubb's Notho

H *Nothobranchius* sp.
TZ-83 Killie

G *Nothobranchius melanospilus* (Dar-es-Salaam)

G ♀

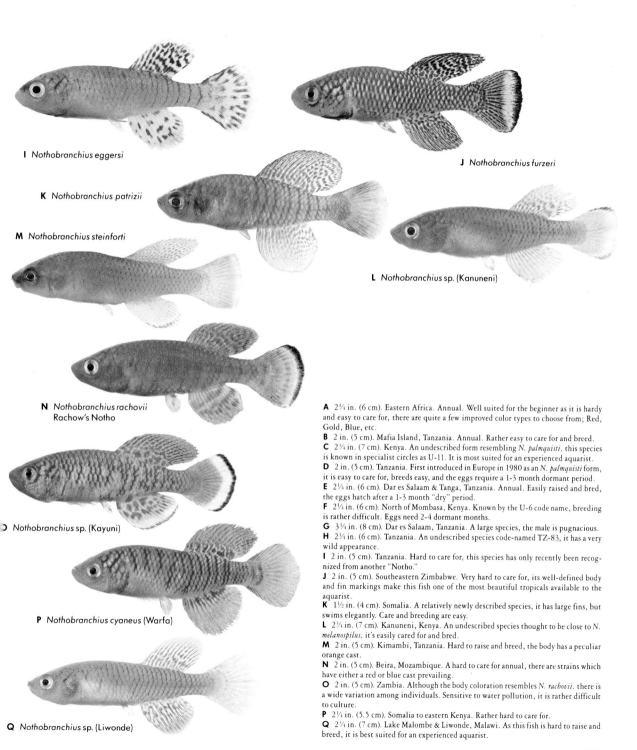

I *Nothobranchius eggersi*

J *Nothobranchius furzeri*

K *Nothobranchius patrizii*

M *Nothobranchius steinforti*

L *Nothobranchius sp.* (Kanuneni)

N *Nothobranchius rachovii*
Rachow's Notho

O *Nothobranchius sp.* (Kayuni)

P *Nothobranchius cyaneus* (Warfa)

Q *Nothobranchius sp.* (Liwonde)

A 2¼ in. (6 cm). Eastern Africa. Annual. Well suited for the beginner as it is hardy and easy to care for, there are quite a few improved color types to choose from; Red, Gold, Blue, etc.

B 2 in. (5 cm). Mafia Island, Tanzania. Annual. Rather easy to care for and breed.

C 2¾ in. (7 cm). Kenya. An undescribed form resembling *N. palmquisti,* this species is known in specialist circles as U-11. It is most suited for an experienced aquarist.

D 2 in. (5 cm). Tanzania. First introduced in Europe in 1980 as an *N. palmquisti* form, it is easy to care for, breeds easy, and the eggs require a 1-3 month dormant period.

E 2¼ in. (6 cm). Dar es Salaam & Tanga, Tanzania. Annual. Easily raised and bred, the eggs hatch after a 1-3 month "dry" period.

F 2¼ in. (6 cm). North of Mombasa, Kenya. Known by the U-6 code name, breeding is rather difficult. Eggs need 2-4 dormant months.

G 3¼ in. (8 cm). Dar es Salaam, Tanzania. A large species, the male is pugnacious.

H 2¼ in. (6 cm). Tanzania. An undescribed species code-named TZ-83, it has a very wild appearance.

I 2 in. (5 cm). Tanzania. Hard to care for, this species has only recently been recognized from another "Notho."

J 2 in. (5 cm). Southeastern Zimbabwe. Very hard to care for, its well-defined body and fin markings make this fish one of the most beautiful tropicals available to the aquarist.

K 1½ in. (4 cm). Somalia. A relatively newly described species, it has large fins, but swims elegantly. Care and breeding are easy.

L 2¾ in. (7 cm). Kanuneni, Kenya. An undescribed species thought to be close to *N. melanospilus,* it's easily cared for and bred.

M 2 in. (5 cm). Kimambi, Tanzania. Hard to raise and breed, the body has a peculiar orange cast.

N 2 in. (5 cm). Beira, Mozambique. A hard to care for annual, there are strains which have either a red or blue cast prevailing.

O 2 in. (5 cm). Zambia. Although the body coloration resembles *N. rachovii,* there is a wide variation among individuals. Sensitive to water pollution, it is rather difficult to culture.

P 2¼ in. (5.5 cm). Somalia to eastern Kenya. Rather hard to care for.

Q 2¾ in. (7 cm). Lake Malombe & Liwonde, Malawi. As this fish is hard to raise and breed, it is best suited for an experienced aquarist.

223

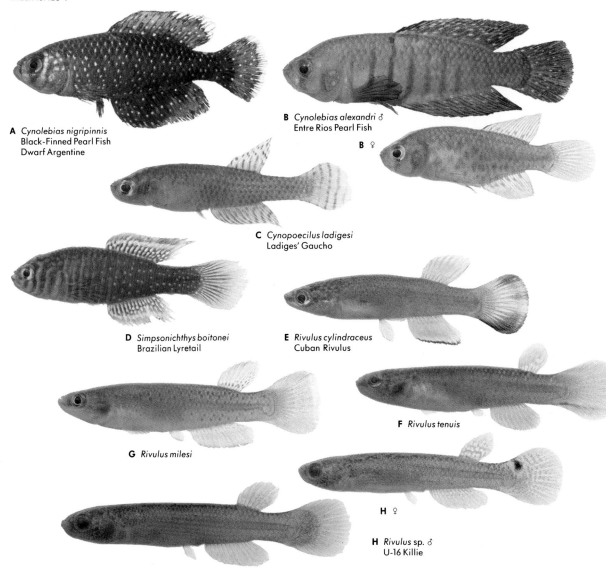

A *Cynolebias nigripinnis*
Black-Finned Pearl Fish
Dwarf Argentine

B *Cynolebias alexandri* ♂
Entre Rios Pearl Fish

B ♀

C *Cynopoecilus ladigesi*
Ladiges' Gaucho

D *Simpsonichthys boitonei*
Brazilian Lyretail

E *Rivulus cylindraceus*
Cuban Rivulus

F *Rivulus tenuis*

G *Rivulus milesi*

H ♀

H *Rivulus* sp. ♂
U-16 Killie

A 2 in. (5 cm). Parana R, Argentina. Prefers slightly acidic, soft water at 59-68°F (15-20°C). Skittish and hard to care for, it nevertheless has a matchless beauty when in top physical condition. As an annual, its eggs require a 45-day dormant period. Only shallow water, ¾ in. (2 cm) deep, should be used for hatching the eggs. A greater depth will result in the fry developing swim bladder problems.
B 2¼ in. (6 cm). Argentina. Easily recognized by its 8 or 9 vertical bands on the body. Hatching occurs after 2-3 months of dormancy.
C 1½ in. (4 cm). Northwestern Rio de Janeiro. Prefers slightly acidic, soft water. Annual. Eggs hatch after a 2-3 week dormant period.

D 2 in. (5 cm). Brazil. Close to *Cynolebias*, it lacks pelvic fins. Recent advances in understanding this fish's requirements have allowed for better care. Eggs require a 1-2 month "dry" period.
E 2 in. (5 cm). Florida, Cuba. A non-annual, it spawns on aquatic plants, with the eggs hatching after 14 days.
F 3 in. (7.5 cm). Mexico, Central America. Non-annual. *Rivulus* species, including this one, are easily raised, bred, and quite prolific.
G 2¼ in. (6 cm). Colombia to western Venezuela. A pair placed in a tank filled with fine-leaved underwater flora will readily spawn.

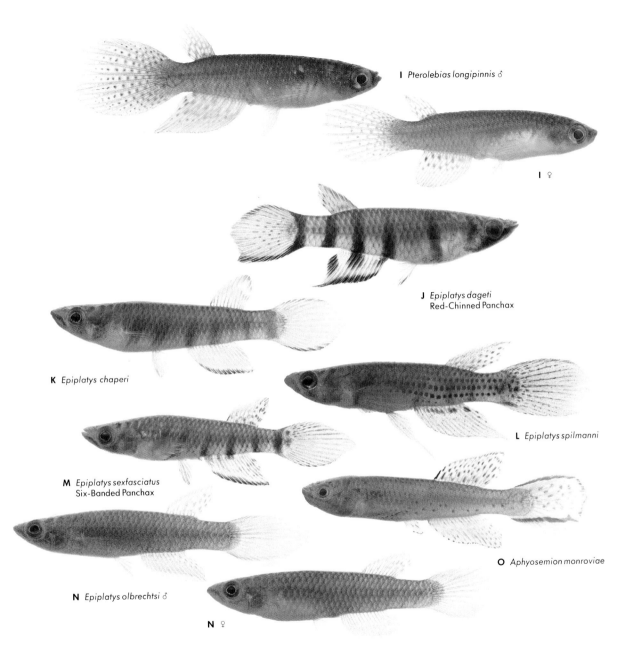

I *Pterolebias longipinnis* ♂

I ♀

J *Epiplatys dageti*
Red-Chinned Panchax

K *Epiplatys chaperi*

L *Epiplatys spilmanni*

M *Epiplatys sexfasciatus*
Six-Banded Panchax

O *Aphyosemion monroviae*

N *Epiplatys olbrechtsi* ♂

N ♀

H 2¼ in. (6 cm). Amazon. Thought to be a variant of *R. urophthalmus*. it prefers slightly acidic, soft water. Although dry food is accepted, live ones are more readily eaten.
I 4 in. (10 cm). Lower Amazon to northern Argentina. Annual. Hatching occurs after a 2-3 month dormant period.
J 2¼ in. (6 cm). Ghana, Liberia. Hardy, easy to care for and breed, this fish spawns either on aquatic plants or in a sandy substrate.
K 4 in. (10 cm). Guinea to Ghana. A rather large species, it prefers slightly acidic, soft water.

L 2¼ in. (6 cm). Ghana. Tolerant of water quality, the side stripes disappear as females mature. It is quite prolific.
M 2¼ in. (6 cm). Togo to northwestern Gabon, western Africa. This fish is easy to culture and breed.
N 2¼ in. (6 cm). Guinea, Liberia. A beautiful species, it has a shiny emerald-green color.
O 4 in. (10 cm). Monrovia, Liberia. Annual. This large species needs a good-sized tank and periodic water replacement. Fry grow quickly and mature within two months.

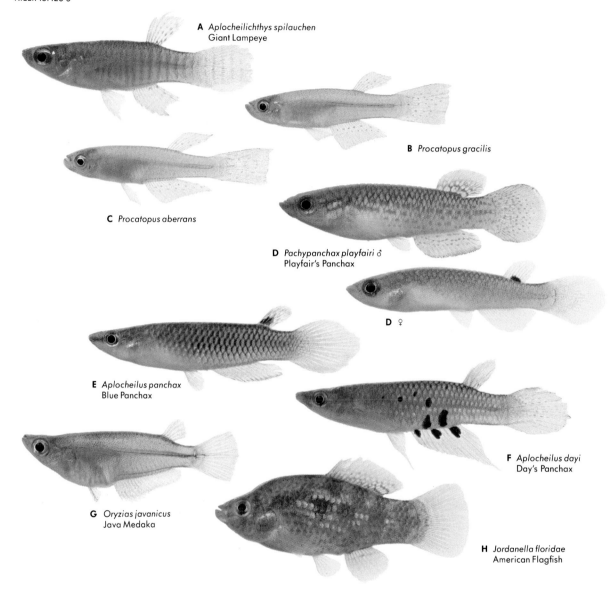

A *Aplocheilichthys spilauchen*
Giant Lampeye

B *Procatopus gracilis*

C *Procatopus aberrans*

D *Pachypanchax playfairi* ♂
Playfair's Panchax

D ♀

E *Aplocheilus panchax*
Blue Panchax

F *Aplocheilus dayi*
Day's Panchax

G *Oryzias javanicus*
Java Medaka

H *Jordanella floridae*
American Flagfish

A 2¾ in. (7 cm). Cameroon. Among the lampeyes, this species is the easiest to care for. Its eyes are not as reflective as its congeners. Breeding is rather hard however, and the fry grow slowly.
B 1½-2¼ in. (4-6 cm). Nigeria. As it matures, the body becomes a brilliant blue. Readily eating even dry foods, it coexists well with other fish.
C 1½-2¼ in. (4-6 cm). Cameroon. While its flanks have a bluish-green sheen, the tail tip is red. A school swimming in a well-planted tank is an eye catcher.
D 4 in. (10 cm). Seychelles, Zanzibar. Inhabits stagnant fresh and brackish waters. A mild-tempered fish, it coexists well with other species.
E 2¼-3¼ in. (6-8 cm). India, Burma, Thailand, Indonesia. The most popular of the

SE Asian killies, it prefers slightly acidic, soft water. Eggs hatch after 12-15 days.
F 2¾ in. (7 cm). Sri Lanka. A large, pugnacious species, it requires a good-sized tank. Eggs spawned on the roots of floating plants hatch in 12 days.
G 1½ in. (4 cm). Java, Sumatra, Malay Peninsula. A "killie-like" genus of the Order Beloniformes that is found in brooks and rice fields, this species prefers neutral to alkaline, rather hard water. The ♀ holds the eggs under her abdomen for a short while after spawning.
H 2¼ in. (6 cm). Florida and Yucatan Peninsula. A mild-mannered, native North American killifish, this prolific species is easy to care for and breed. Its eggs hatch after 5-6 days.

CATFISHES

9

FAMILY	**BAGRIDAE** **(Bagrid Catfishes)**
Genera	*Chrysichthys*
	Leiocassis
	Mystus
FAMILY	**SILURIDAE (Sheatfishes)**
Genera	*Kryptopterus*
	Ompok
FAMILY	**SCHILBEIDAE** **(Schilbeid Catfishes)**
Genera	*Eutropiellus*
	Schilbe
FAMILY	**PANGASIIDAE**
Genus	*Pangasius*
FAMILY	**SISORIDAE** **(Sisorid Catfishes)**
Genera	*Bagarius*
	Glyptothorax
FAMILY	**CLARIIDAE** **(Airbreathing &** **Labyrinth Catfishes)**
Genus	*Clarias*
FAMILY	**HETEROPNEUSTIDAE** **(Airsac Catfishes)**
Genus	*Heteropneustes*
FAMILY	**CHACIDAE** **(Squarehead or** **Angler Catfishes)**
Genus	*Chaca*

FAMILY	**MALAPTERURIDAE** **(Electric Catfishes)**
Genus	*Malapterurus*
FAMILY	**ARIIDAE (Sea Catfishes)**
Genus	*Arius*
FAMILY	**PLOTOSIDAE** **(Eeltail Catfishes)**
Genus	*Neosilurus*
FAMILY	**MOCHOKIDAE** **(Squeakers & Upside-** **Down Catfishes)**
Genus	*Synodontis*
FAMILY	**DORADIDAE** **(Thorny Catfishes)**
Genera	*Agamyxis*
	Amblydoras
	Doras
	Hassar
	Platydoras
FAMILY	**AUCHENIPTERIDAE** **(Auchenipterid Catfishes)**
Genera	*Auchenipterichthys*
	Tatia
	Trachycorystes
FAMILY	**PIMELODIDAE** **(Long-Whiskered** **Catfishes)**
Genera	*Perrunichthys*
	Pimelodella
	Pseudoplatystoma

FAMILY	**ASPREDINIDAE** **(Banjo Catfishes)**
SUBFAMILY	BUNOCEPHALINAE
Genus	*Bunocephalus*
FAMILY	**CALLICHTHYIDAE** **(Callichthyid** **Armored Catfishes)**
Genera	*Aspidoras*
	Brochis
	Callichthys
	Corydoras
	Dianema
FAMILY	**LORICARIIDAE** **(Suckermouth** **Armored Catfishes)**
Genera	*Ancistrus*
	Chaetostoma
	Farlowella
	Hypostomus
	Otocinclus
	Panaque
	Peckoltia
	Pterygoplichthys
	Rineloricaria
	Sturisoma

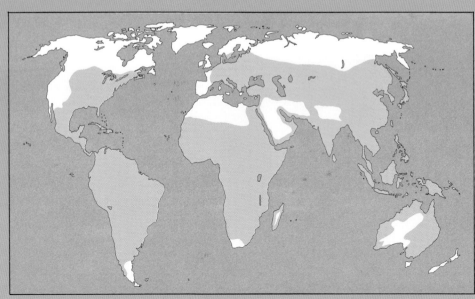

A *Corydoras paleatus.* Peppered Corydoras. **1** ♀ (top) holding eggs between her pelvic fins being pursued by three males.

CORYDORAS (DWARF) CATS

The smooth-armored catfishes of the Family Callichthyidae include the dwarf armored catfishes, which in a general sense, comprises the genera *Brochis* and *Aspidorus* in addition to *Corydoras.* There are some 90 species known at present, widely distributed throughout tropical South America, mainly within the Amazon Basin. As the speciation within these genera is an ongoing process, and much of the Amazon Basin is unexplored from an ichthyologist's

perspective, it is most probable that unidentified species may be imported with other well-known congeners.

Nijssen and Isbruecker, using body shape and habitat, divided the dwarf catfishes into five groups: Acutus, Aeneus, Barbatus, Elegans, and Punctatus complexes.

In their natural habitats, these catfishes usually swim in schools made up of the same or several often similarly colored species. *Corydoras* and their allies can live in oxygen-starved waters, such as in pools that have

almost dried up, as they can gulp atmospheric air which is absorbed into the bloodstream through their modified intestine. Even those living in rivers frequently gulp air. The obvious manifestations of such aerial respiration are the appearance of rings on the water surface accompanied by a peculiar sucking noise.

UNIQUE SPAWNING BEHAVIOR

Dwarf armored catfishes are hardy, rather long-

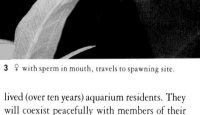

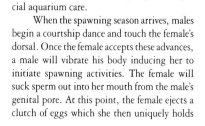

3 ♀ with sperm in mouth, travels to spawning site.

4 After sperm is sprayed onto an Amazon Sword leaf, eggs are attached.

lived (over ten years) aquarium residents. They will coexist peacefully with members of their own and other species, so they require no special aquarium care.

When the spawning season arrives, males begin a courtship dance and touch the female's dorsal. Once the female accepts these advances, a male will vibrate his body inducing her to initiate spawning activities. The female will suck sperm out into her mouth from the male's genital pore. At this point, the female ejects a clutch of eggs which she then uniquely holds between her ventral fins. Finding a suitable place, she spits the sperm out onto this site and then attaches the eggs, at which time fertilization occurs. When sperm is sucked out, it is believed that some seeps out into the surrounding water, also aiding fertilization of the eggs. During the course of this repeated series of peculiar activities, over 200 eggs may be laid. They hatch out in about three days, and feeding begins 3-5 days afterwards.

A 1 While the ♀ carries 5-6 eggs between her pelvic fins, she is followed by three males. Carrying the eggs to the selected site may take 10-30 seconds.
2 ♀ (left) sucks sperm from the genital pore of the ♂. He constantly displays near the ♀ during spawning.
3 Note the 5-6 eggs the ♀ (rt.) holds between her pelvics as she is closely followed by the males awaiting spawning of further egg clutches.
4 After selecting a suitable spawning site, in this case an Amazon Swordplant leaf, the ♀ spits the sperm in her mouth onto it. She then attaches the eggs, at which point fertilization occurs. In total, she may lay 50-300 eggs.

A *Corydoras trilineatus.* Leopard Catfish. This very pretty, long popular species is still many times mistaken for *C. julii.*

B *Corydoras* sp.

C *Brochis splendens.* Green Brochis.

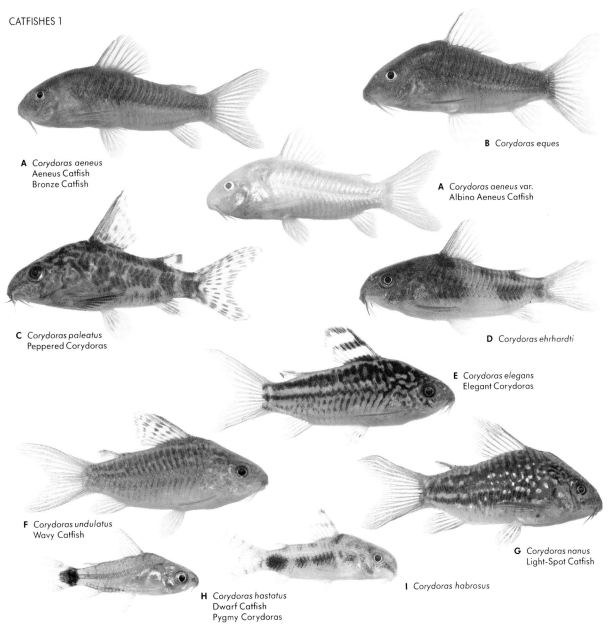

A *Corydoras aeneus*
Aeneus Catfish
Bronze Catfish

B *Corydoras eques*

A *Corydoras aeneus var.*
Albino Aeneus Catfish

C *Corydoras paleatus*
Peppered Corydoras

D *Corydoras ehrhardti*

E *Corydoras elegans*
Elegant Corydoras

F *Corydoras undulatus*
Wavy Catfish

G *Corydoras nanus*
Light-Spot Catfish

H *Corydoras hastatus*
Dwarf Catfish
Pygmy Corydoras

I *Corydoras habrosus*

A 2¾ in. (7 cm). Venezuela to La Plata R. Prefers neutral to alkaline water. The most commonly available dwarf cat, it is easy to raise and breed. An albino strain (below) is also readily obtainable.

B 2¾ in. (7 cm). Amazon R. Recently identified as distinct from *C. aenëus*, it has a beautiful greenish body and is easy to keep.

C 2¾ in. (6 cm). Southern Brazil to Northern Argentina. Prefers soft, neutral water. It is easy to care for and breed.

D Over 1½ in. (4 cm). Southern Brazil. It does best in rather low temperatures of about 68°F (20°C). Breeding is difficult.

E 2¾ in. (6 cm). Peru to middle reaches of the Amazon R. Dorsal fin markings help

distinguish it from other species. A vigorous mid-water swimmer, it is easy to raise and breed.

F 2 in. (5 cm). Argentina, La Plata R system. It is liable to be confused with *C. nanus* as the side markings within the species vary greatly.

G 2¾ in. (7 cm). Surinam, Guyana. Beautiful, its reticular markings have a golden sheen. A vigorous aquarium swimmer, even a few individuals school.

H ¾ in. (2 cm). Paraguay, Amazon R. A mid-water swimmer, in an aquarium it swims vigorously even with characins. Breeding is easy.

I ¾ in. (2 cm). Salinas R in Venezuela. It is distinguished from other corys by the wide horizontal stripe on its flank and dorsal blotches (sometimes continuous).

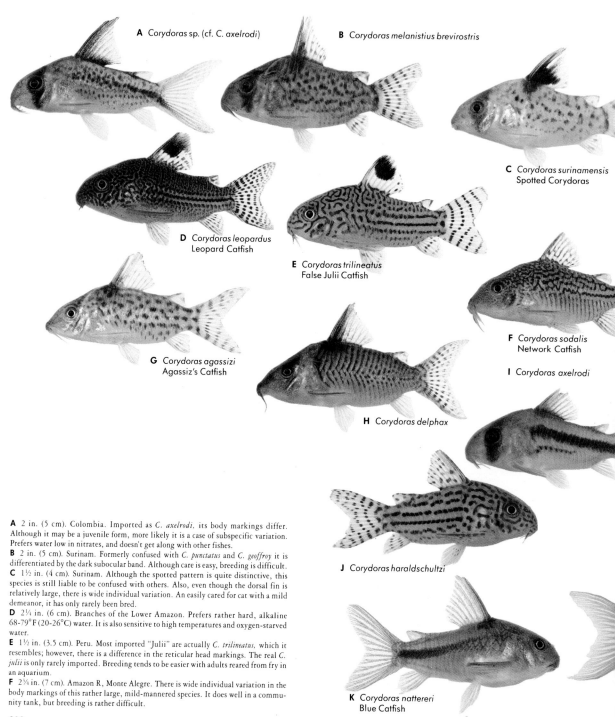

A *Corydoras* sp. (cf. *C. axelrodi*)

B *Corydoras melanistius brevirostris*

C *Corydoras surinamensis*
Spotted Corydoras

D *Corydoras leopardus*
Leopard Catfish

E *Corydoras trilineatus*
False Julii Catfish

F *Corydoras sodalis*
Network Catfish

G *Corydoras agassizi*
Agassiz's Catfish

I *Corydoras axelrodi*

H *Corydoras delphax*

J *Corydoras haraldschultzi*

K *Corydoras nattereri*
Blue Catfish

A 2 in. (5 cm). Colombia. Imported as *C. axelrodi*, its body markings differ. Although it may be a juvenile form, more likely it is a case of subspecific variation. Prefers water low in nitrates, and doesn't get along with other fishes.

B 2 in. (5 cm). Surinam. Formerly confused with *C. punctatus* and *C. geoffroy* it is differentiated by the dark subocular band. Although care is easy, breeding is difficult.

C 1½ in. (4 cm). Surinam. Although the spotted pattern is quite distinctive, this species is still liable to be confused with others. Also, even though the dorsal fin is relatively large, there is wide individual variation. An easily cared for cat with a mild demeanor, it has only rarely been bred.

D 2¼ in. (6 cm). Branches of the Lower Amazon. Prefers rather hard, alkaline 68-79°F (20-26°C) water. It is also sensitive to high temperatures and oxygen-starved water.

E 1½ in. (3.5 cm). Peru. Most imported "Julii" are actually *C. trilineatus*, which it resembles; however, there is a difference in the reticular head markings. The real *C. julii* is only rarely imported. Breeding tends to be easier with adults reared from fry in an aquarium.

F 2¾ in. (7 cm). Amazon R, Monte Alegre. There is wide individual variation in the body markings of this rather large, mild-mannered species. It does well in a community tank, but breeding is rather difficult.

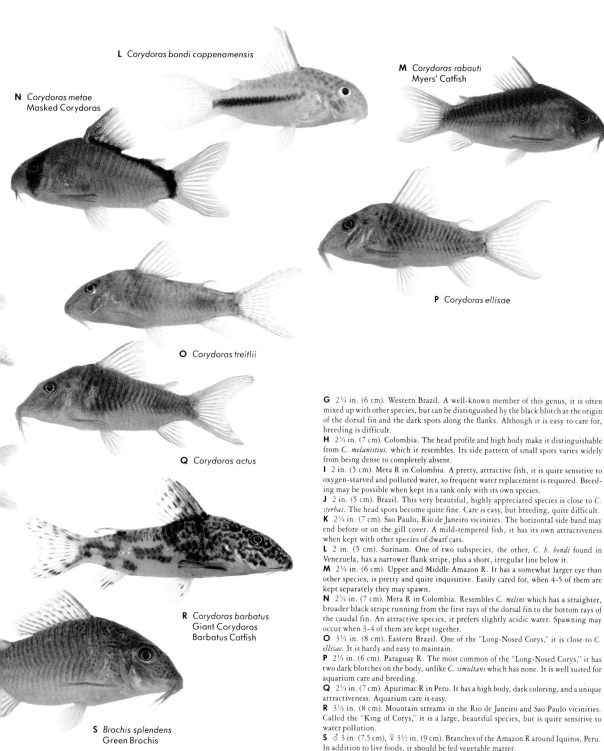

L *Corydoras bondi coppenamensis*

M *Corydoras rabauti*
Myers' Catfish

N *Corydoras metae*
Masked Corydoras

P *Corydoras ellisae*

O *Corydoras treitlii*

Q *Corydoras actus*

R *Corydoras barbatus*
Giant Corydoras
Barbatus Catfish

S *Brochis splendens*
Green Brochis

G 2¼ in. (6 cm). Western Brazil. A well-known member of this genus, it is often mixed up with other species, but can be distinguished by the black blotch at the origin of the dorsal fin and the dark spots along the flanks. Although it is easy to care for, breeding is difficult.

H 2¾ in. (7 cm). Colombia. The head profile and high body make it distinguishable from *C. melanistius,* which it resembles. Its side pattern of small spots varies widely from being dense to completely absent.

I 2 in. (5 cm). Meta R in Colombia. A pretty, attractive fish, it is quite sensitive to oxygen-starved and polluted water, so frequent water replacement is required. Breeding may be possible when kept in a tank only with its own species.

J 2 in. (5 cm). Brazil. This very beautiful, highly appreciated species is close to *C. sterbai.* The head spots become quite fine. Care is easy, but breeding, quite difficult.

K 2¾ in. (7 cm). Sao Paulo, Rio de Janeiro vicinities. The horizontal side band may end before or on the gill cover. A mild-tempered fish, it has its own attractiveness when kept with other species of dwarf cats.

L 2 in. (5 cm). Surinam. One of two subspecies, the other, *C. b. bondi* found in Venezuela, has a narrower flank stripe, plus a short, irregular line below it.

M 2¼ in. (6 cm). Upper and Middle Amazon R. It has a somewhat larger eye than other species, is pretty and quite inquisitive. Easily cared for, when 4-5 of them are kept separately they may spawn.

N 2¾ in. (7 cm). Meta R in Colombia. Resembles *C. melini* which has a straighter, broader black stripe running from the first rays of the dorsal fin to the bottom rays of the caudal fin. An attractive species, it prefers slightly acidic water. Spawning may occur when 3-4 of them are kept together.

O 3¼ in. (8 cm). Eastern Brazil. One of the "Long-Nosed Corys," it is close to *C. ellisae.* It is hardy and easy to maintain.

P 2¼ in. (6 cm). Paraguay R. The most common of the "Long-Nosed Corys," it has two dark blotches on the body, unlike *C. simultans* which has none. It is well suited for aquarium care and breeding.

Q 2¾ in. (7 cm). Apurimac R in Peru. It has a high body, dark coloring, and a unique attractiveness. Aquarium care is easy.

R 3¼ in. (8 cm). Mountain streams in the Rio de Janeiro and Sao Paulo vicinities. Called the "King of Corys," it is a large, beautiful species, but is quite sensitive to water pollution.

S ♂ 3 in. (7.5 cm), ♀ 3½ in. (9 cm). Branches of the Amazon R around Iquitos, Peru. In addition to live foods, it should be fed vegetable matter.

A *Synodontis nigriventris.* Blackbellied Upside-Down Catfish. A representative example of the upside-down catfishes.

SYNODONTID CATS

B *Synodontis acanthomias.*

Native to rivers and lakes in tropical Africa, there are some 108 reported species of the synodontid catfishes. The name "upside-down catfish" is given to this group because of the tendency of many species to swim or hover with the belly up. They are nocturnal, so remain hidden under rocks or among waterlogged branches during the daytime. Omnivorous, when they move around at night, they feed on mosquito larvae, aquatic insects, and algae on rocks, for example. Although some species coexist well with other fishes, some do not. Their nocturnal nature may prevent other fish from resting at night. This may result in the other fish developing behavioral disorders caused by insufficient rest.

Except for those species native to lakes such as Tanganyika and Malawi, they prefer slightly acidic, warm (70-82°F or 21-28°C) water. Most are considered hard to breed, so reports of successful spawnings are rare.

C *Synodontis multipunctatus.* One of the beautiful L Tanganyika upside-down cats.

D *Synodontis angelicus.* Polka Dot African or Angel Catfish.

E *Synodontis flavitaeniatus.*

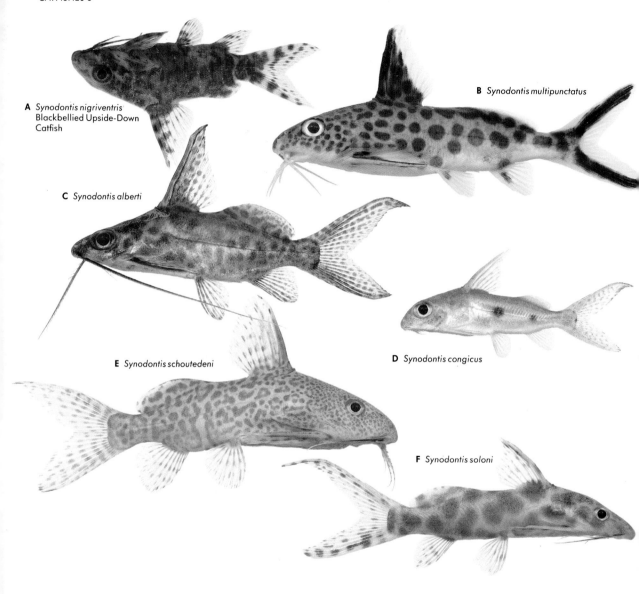

A *Synodontis nigriventris*
Blackbellied Upside-Down
Catfish

B *Synodontis multipunctatus*

C *Synodontis alberti*

E *Synodontis schoutedeni*

D *Synodontis congicus*

F *Synodontis soloni*

A 2¼ in. (6 cm). Said to abound in the Zaire and Oubangui rivers, it prefers slightly acidic, soft water. Juveniles swim normally, but begin turning upside-down when they mature. It has a dark colored abdomen. A peaceful and omnivorous species, it has been bred in aquaria, spawning in an inverted flowerpot.
B 8 in. (20 cm). Lives to a depth of 65 ft (20 m) in L Tanganyika. Prefers hard, alkaline water. Hardy, easy to care for and rather peaceful, it does well in a Lake Tanganyika cichlid community tank. Omnivorous, this catfish should be fed both live and vegetable matter. Its body spots may serve as camouflage. A brood parasite of mouthbrooding cichlids, it is one of the few *Synodontis* species that spawns regularly in captivity.
C 6¼ in. (16 cm) in nature. Zaire R. Its dorsal and caudal fins become more and more elongated during growth, plus its barbels are the longest within the genus. An active,

diurnal fish, it is mild tempered and prefers feeding on aquatic worms.
D 4 in. (10 cm). Zaire R. Often confused with *S. numifer,* a species with somewhat larger body spots, it is omnivorous, hardy and easy to maintain. Larger individuals tend to be pugnacious.
E 6 in. (15 cm). Zaire R. The rather small eyes and large barbels make it easily identifiable. As it is readily available, hardy and easy to keep, this species, together with the Upside-Down Catfish, are among the best for the beginner. Although there is no record of it being bred yet, feeding it a healthy diet of tubifex, blood and other aquatic worms, may induce it to spawn.
F 6 in. (15 cm). Zaire R. Giraffe-like markings and overall appearance closely resemble those of *S. camelopardalis.* The contrast between these markings and the background

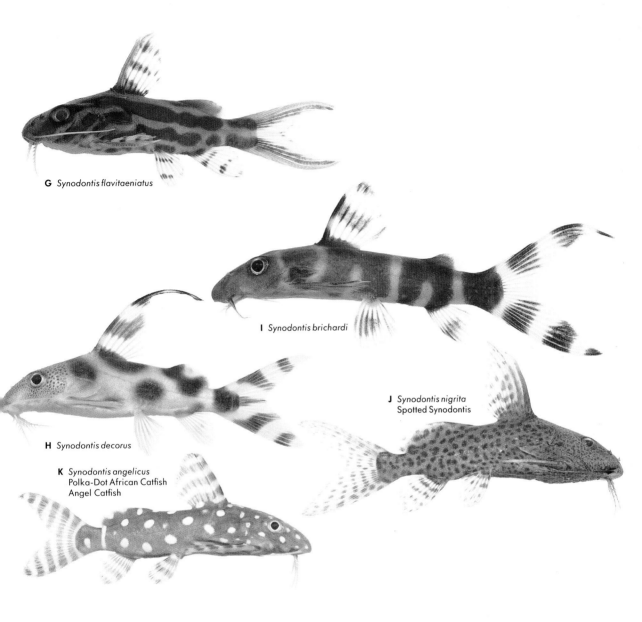

G *Synodontis flavitaeniatus*

I *Synodontis brichardi*

J *Synodontis nigrita*
Spotted Synodontis

H *Synodontis decorus*

K *Synodontis angelicus*
Polka-Dot African Catfish
Angel Catfish

become quite distinct under optimum water conditions. Mild tempered, it is easy to care for.
G 8 in. (20 cm). Zaire R. There is some variation in body markings within the species. Prefers slightly acidic, soft water. It is peaceful, but usually remains hidden behind rockwork, waterlogged wood, or within stands of aquatic plants. It thus may not eat well if kept with larger fish. No breeding recorded yet.
H 12 in. (30 cm). Zaire R. A hardy, omnivorous catfish, its body becomes grayish brown and the spots darken as it grows. It is a large, mean-tempered fish that does not even get along with others of the same species.
I 6 in. (15 cm). Zaire R. Prefers slightly acidic, soft water. Omnivorous, it should probably also be fed plant matter. Strongly territorial and an active daytime swimmer,

it should be kept either by itself or in a very large, well-planted tank (many hiding places) with only a few companions.
J 8 in. (20 cm). Coastal rivers of West Africa from Volta to Niger. Readily available as it is exported from Lagos in large numbers. This species is omnivorous and easy to keep. Quite pugnacious, this cat doesn't even tolerate others of its own species.
K 10 in. (25 cm). Zaire R. Many variations in markings can be seen, including spot size, and presence or absence of lines on the flank. Coloration may be influenced by fluctuations in water quality. Prefers slightly acidic, soft water. It readily eats dry foods, but prefers live ones such as blood worms, which should probably be supplemented with vegetable matter. Rather hot tempered, it isn't tolerant of other fish. No one has reported breeding it in an aquarium.

A *Rineloricaria* sp. (cf. *R. hasemania*). Whiptail Catfish.

B *Otocinclus* sp. Striped Otocinclus.

LORICARIID (SUCKERMOUTH ARMORED) CATS

Loricariid or suckermouth armored catfishes are found in southern Central America southward to the Rio de la Plata basin of northern Argentina. They can be found living from the upper reaches of streams down to the mangrove stands at the mouth of rivers within this region. Those species living in the upper reaches use their sucker mouth to feed off algae growing on rocks. Others live and dive into the muddy river bottoms, and reflecting this, have a rather subdued coloration for camouflage. As part of its popular name implies, the fish's body is covered with many hard, coarse bony plates. Although there is no record of anyone breeding the large Plecostomus in an aquarium, the Royal Farlowella as well as several species of *Otocinclus, Rineloricaria* and *Ancistrus* have been bred routinely in captivity. When the pair is ripe, the male develops barbel-like appendages around his mouth, and the female's belly swells somewhat. They spawn on such surfaces as stone or glass. The male cares for the eggs which hatch out within 3-5 days. A plentiful supply of boiled spinach should be fed to the fry. As they are quite sensitive to fluctuations in water quality, water replacement should be avoided.

C *Sturisoma panamense.* Royal Farlowella. Most of the loricariid cats are known to be both attractive and active algae cleaners.

A *Panaque nigrolineatus.* Royal Panaque. One of the most beautiful armored cats, there is wide variation in the yellowish brown longitudinal stripes.

B *Panaque suttoni.* Blue-Eyed Panaque.

C *Hypostomus* sp. Plecostomus.

D *Ancistrus* sp. This Bristle-Nose cat was caught in the Tocantins R, one of the southern tributaries of the Amazon R, and is very similar to *Ancistrus temminckii*.

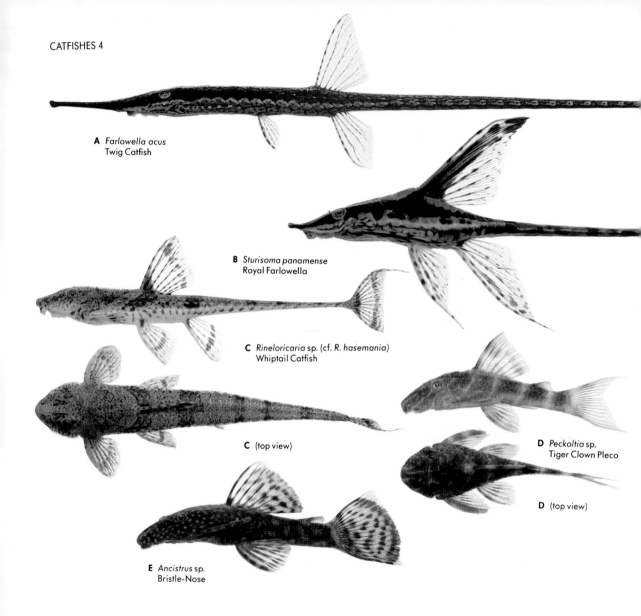

A *Farlowella acus*
Twig Catfish

B *Sturisoma panamense*
Royal Farlowella

C *Rineloricaria* sp. (cf. *R. hasemania*)
Whiptail Catfish

C (top view)

D *Peckoltia* sp.
Tiger Clown Pleco

D (top view)

E *Ancistrus* sp.
Bristle-Nose

A 8 in. (20 cm). Southern Brazil, Amazon R. Hardy and peaceful, it does well in a community tank. As it grazes on algae growing on stones, algal growth in the aquarium should be encouraged. This cat will readily take live food, so be careful to avoid overfeeding it. Reportedly, it spawns on the tank glass walls.

B 10 in. (25 cm). Rivers on the Pacific slopes of Panama to Ecuador. Prefers slightly acidic, soft aged water of over 77°F (25°C). Omnivorous, it can be fed both live and dry foods, but vegetable matter such as spinach or lettuce should be given as a supplement. A healthy pair readily spawns on the tank glass walls, and the ♂ cares for the eggs.

C 6 in. (15 cm). Magdalena R. in Colombia. Prefers slightly acidic, aged water. Occasionally water replacement may prove fatal. It is omnivorous. Not easy to breed as many mature females don't spawn, the eggs are laid on the underside of rocks or twigs, and hatch out within 3-5 days. The fry should be fed boiled spinach.

D 2¾ in. (7 cm). Amazon. A rather small, pretty species, it is an efficient aquarium algae cleaner. Their teeth make it possible for them to eat even the soft parts of floating twigs, in addition to aquatic grasses. The common name is routinely applied to what might actually be a mix of four different species, all with yellowish stripes on a dark brown base.

E 5½ in. (14 cm). Upper Amazon R. The common name is used for several regularly imported species of this genus because of the hair-like barbels on their snout or head. They like to eat boiled spinach and cabbage. This genus exhibits an unusual threat behavior of rubbing bodies. When well fed, they easily breed, and the ♂ cares for both eggs and young.

F 2¼ in. (6 cm). Peru. Prefers water of 68-73°F (20-23°C). The teeth plates on the large mouth are like files and used to scrape algae off rocks. In aquaria, however, it doesn't eat algae, so it should be fed boiled spinach or flakes as well as live foods. Care is rather difficult. There is no record of it being bred.

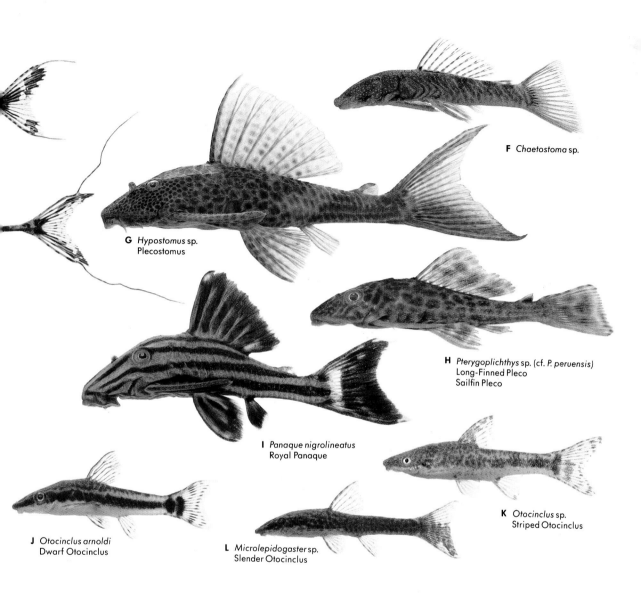

F *Chaetostoma* sp.

G *Hypostomus* sp.
Plecostomus

H *Pterygoplichthys* sp. (cf. *P. peruensis*)
Long-Finned Pleco
Sailfin Pleco

I *Panaque nigrolineatus*
Royal Panaque

K *Otocinclus* sp.
Striped Otocinclus

J *Otocinclus arnoldi*
Dwarf Otocinclus

L *Microlepidogaster* sp.
Slender Otocinclus

G Over 24 in. (60 cm). La Plata R., Venezuela, Trinidad. Found in pebbled bottoms of fast-flowing waters, this species in the wild eats algae off of rocks. In aquaria it is an efficient algae cleaner. It will also eat dry foods. As long as there are many hiding places, it does well in a community tank with large cichlids. Adults of over 12 in. (30 cm) are often bred in Bangkok. Fry are accordingly quite cheap in SE Asia.

H The common name for this genus comes from the long-based dorsal fin which has 10 or more rays. This is a distinguishing character from the genus *Hypostomus* which has a dorsal fin with 7 rays.

I 12 in. (30 cm). Upper Amazon R. The yellowish horizontal lines vary greatly; short, long, narrow, wide, spotty. Prefers slightly acidic, soft aged water. Sudden water replacement should be avoided. It eats mainly vegetable matter and will scrape algae off floating twigs. Because of its active nocturnal nature, it may cause behavioral disorders in diurnal tankmates by not letting them rest at night.

J 1½ in. (4 cm). Southeastern Brazil, around Rio de Janeiro. Prefers neutral to slightly acidic, soft water. As it grazes on algae growing on plant leaves and tank walls, but does not eat aquatic plants, it is an ideal algae cleaner. Accordingly, algae growth in its tank should be promoted. A ripe pair will lay adhesive eggs on the bottom of rocks and leaves. The eggs hatch out within 2-3 days, and the fry should be fed vegetable matter, but may eat brine shrimp.

K 2 in. (5 cm). Paraguay R, La Plata R. Prefers new water low in nitrites. It eats algae off the glass and aquatic plants, but is a ravenous eater despite its small size, so frequent feedings of boiled spinach should be given to prevent it from becoming debilitated from underfeeding.

L 1¼ in. (3 cm). A distinct species which many times is mistaken for the more commonly available *O. arnoldi*. This small fish eats algae off of aquatic plants and tank walls. It is easy to culture and breed.

Siluriform fishes or catfishes represent one of the largest groups among the freshwater fishes. There are said to be over 2,000 species in at least 31 families within the order *Siluriformes*. Taxonomic studies are still not sufficient to even estimate with precision the number of possible catfish species. Members of this order vary from a couple inches to over ten feet, plus come in a great number of shapes and coloration. Though most diverse and numerous within the Amazon Basin and its vicinity, these fishes are distributed globally within the tropical and temperate zones of North, Central and South America, Eurasia, Africa, Madagascar and Australia. Their habitats include fresh, brackish, and even marine waters.

Most species are nocturnal and solitary in nature, but on the other hand, some are active diurnal swimmers and travel in schools.

The eyes in some species, especially those that are nocturnal or inhabit turbid waters, have tended to degenerate. These catfish are almost blind. In these species, the barbels have become even more developed as alternative sensory organs, which serve to alert the fish to the proximity of prey or enemies.

The so-called "Big Cats" (those over 12 in. or 30 cm in length) are frequently treated separately from the smaller species. Before buying catfishes, the purchaser should inquire as to how large they will become. As some large species grow quite rapidly even in an aquarium, they may not be suitable for the average home aquarium. On the other hand, some people may appreciate the unique attractiveness of a substantial solitary fish in its own good-sized tank.

Certainly, siluriform fishes offer the aquarist a wide variety of body shape, pretty to odd appearance, and active to inactive behavior to choose from.

A *Perrunichthys perruno*. Sailfin Cat. Young adult.

B *Clarias batrachus* var. Albino Clarias or Walking Catfish. Its flat head is humorous.

C *Kryptopterus bicirrhis*. Glass or Ghost Catfish. Popular for its see-through body and distinct skeleton.

A *Malapterurus electricus.* Electric Catfish. A high electrical charge is passed between the head cathode and the tail anode.

B *Dianema longibarbis.* Porthole Catfish.

C *Dianema urostriatum.* Flag-Tailed Catfish.

D *Chaca bankanensis.* Frogmouth Catfish. Weirdest of the cats, one wonders if its color and body shape represent a case of mimicry.

A *Pimelodella pictus.* Angelicus Pimelodus. Members of this genus are abundant throughout Central and South America.

B *Glyptothorax major.* A SE Asian cat that is mild tempered despite its appearance.

A *Callichthys callichthys*
Slender Armored Catfish

B *Dianema urostriatum*
Flag-Tailed Catfish

C *Dianema longibarbis*
Porthole Catfish

E *Pimelodella* sp. (cf. *P. blochi*)

D *Pimelodella pictus*
Angelicus Pimelodus

F *Perrunichthys perruno*
Sailfin Catfish

G *Pseudoplatystoma fasciatum*
Tiger Shovelnose Catfish

A 7 in. (18 cm). Widely distributed throughout tropical South America, it may be frequently seen gulping surface air which can be used by the intestinal breathing apparatus similar to that in loaches. Omnivorous, it is hardy and easy to care for. Keeping the water temperature at 68°F (20°C) may induce spawning. The ♂ builds a bubble nest among floating plants in which 100-150 eggs are spawned, and continues to care for them during the 2-3 days they take to hatch. Larvae become free swimming in about a week.

B 3½ in. (9 cm). Branches of the Amazon near Manaus. Nocturnal, hidden behind rocks or among floating wood during the daytime, it is a rather peaceful fish that coexists well with characins. It likes to eat aquatic worms.

C 3½ in. (9 cm). Widely distributed throughout the Amazon, it is hardy, and care is like the above species.

D 4 in. (10 cm). Colombia. Tolerant of water quality, it is hardy, easy to care for, and an active daytime swimmer in an aquarium. Omnivorous, it prefers aquatic worms. Care should be taken when handling it as the dorsal and pectoral spines are sharp.

E 6 in. (15 cm). South America. An active aquarium swimmer, it grows larger than *P. pictus*.

F 18-20 in. (45-50 cm). The color in adults becomes darker and the markings less distinct. Pretty when small, it voraciously consumes small fish and crustaceans as it grows, reaching 12 in. (30 cm) in a year. Large individuals are pugnacious, so are probably best kept alone.

G 28 in. (70 cm). Amazon Basin. The large variation in markings might have some geographical aspect and depend on their place of origin. Most popular of the large catfish, it is omnivorous, and does well with other large fishes if there is sufficient food. A very large tank is needed.

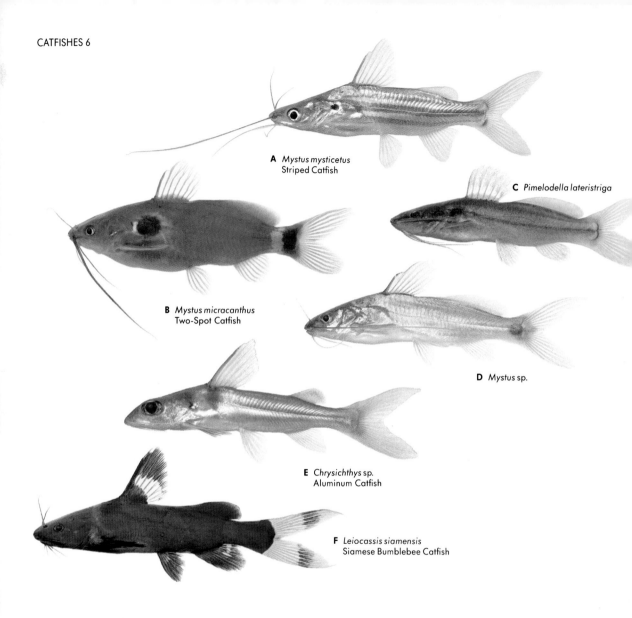

A *Mystus mysticetus*
Striped Catfish

C *Pimelodella lateristriga*

B *Mystus micracanthus*
Two-Spot Catfish

D *Mystus* sp.

E *Chrysichthys* sp.
Aluminum Catfish

F *Leiocassis siamensis*
Siamese Bumblebee Catfish

A 6 in. (15 cm). Thailand, Indochina. Omnivorous and a schooler, in Thailand it tends to congregate where garbage is dumped. Rarely exported, this peaceful fish does well with others, and its care is easy. Of the four striped species of *Mystus* in Thailand, this one had slightly more anal fin rays and a very lateral eye which can be viewed from below the head. In the hobby it is often confused with *M. vittatus* (of which *M. tengara* is a junior synonym), only found in India.

B 6 in. (15 cm). Sumatra, Java, Borneo. All *Mystus* species in SE Asia are small (less than 6 in. or 15 cm) and well suited for aquaria. They are peaceful, and may appear quite shy when swimming. Aquatic worms are the preferred foods.

C 2¾ in. (7 cm). Max. unknown. S America, mainly Amazon R. Although it has a black longitudinal stripe on its side similar to *P. gracilis* and *P. linami*, it can be distinguished by the spot above the pectoral fin. Not sensitive to, but prefers neutral or

slightly acidic, soft water. It has a rather mild demeanor, and care is easy.

D 3¼ in. (8 cm). Max. unknown. Thailand. The fin ray count of this species indicates it belongs in the genus *Mystus* of which some 18 species have been identified to date. Care is easy, and it prefers live foods.

E 3½ in. (9 cm). Max. unknown. The very large-eyed, silvery young of this fish from the Zaire R. are exported under this common name. As they grow, reaching over 8 in. (20 cm) in length, the body color darkens. Fresh water and aquatic worms are preferred.

F 7 in. (18 cm). Thailand. While the brown color and markings are quite distinct in the young, they become muddy as they grow. Nocturnal by nature, they are mild tempered and coexist well with other fish too large to be easily swallowed. Aquatic worms and small fish are the preferred foods.

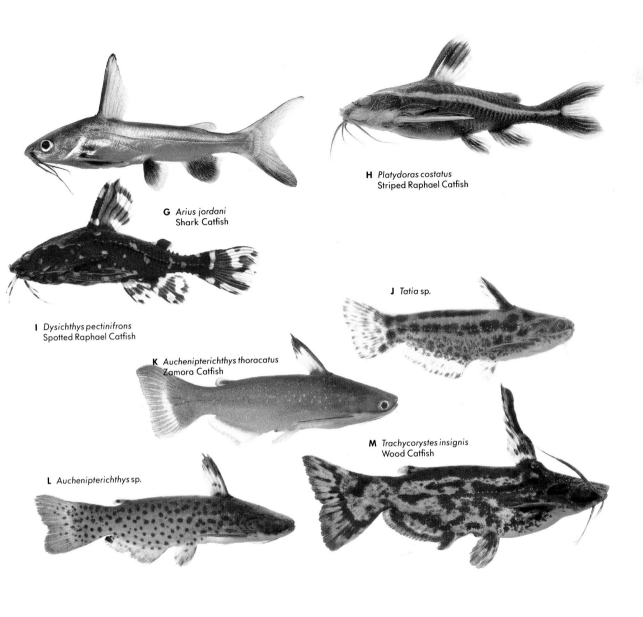

G Arius jordani
Shark Catfish

H Platydoras costatus
Striped Raphael Catfish

I Dysichthys pectinifrons
Spotted Raphael Catfish

J Tatia sp.

K Auchenipterichthys thoracatus
Zamora Catfish

M Trachycorystes insignis
Wood Catfish

L Auchenipterichthys sp.

G 12 in. (30 cm). Brackish waters from the Gulf of Panama to Peru. Many species of this predatory marine catfish genus are sold as aquarium fish. Prefers brackish water, rather than fresh water. Live foods are best. A mouthbrooder, they swim in groups of 3-4.
H Over 6 in. (15 cm). Putumayo, Amazon R. Mild tempered, it remains hidden behind stones or among floating wood during the daytime. If handled without care, the mild toxin which can be injected by the spine on the inner side of the pectoral fins can be harmful. It also produces a talking-like sound by rubbing these pectoral fins.
I 6¼ in. (16 cm). Ecuador. As the fish gets larger, the entire body becomes black except for some white spots on the belly. Hardy and easy to care for, it has a mild demeanor. Although it prefers live foods, dry ones are also accepted. Its spawning behavior is unknown.

J 4 in. (10 cm). Amazon R. Similar to the Wood Catfish. Mild tempered and easy to care for, it prefers live foods such as tubifex and blood worms.
K 4 in. (10 cm). Northern Amazon R to eastern South America. Omnivorous, it prefers live but eats dry food. It is also hardy and easy to care for.
L 7 in. (18 cm). In the Amazon around Iquitos. Close to the above species, but it has black spot on the body. Peaceful, it does well with other fish including its own species. Care is easy, and it likes to eat tubifex, blood worms and other live food.
M Around 4 in. (10 cm). Amazon R. Normally nocturnal, smaller ones swim in a school all day. This species is known to fertilize its eggs internally. The ♂ holds the ♀ between his dorsal fin and head when copulating. Eggs hatch out after 5 days.

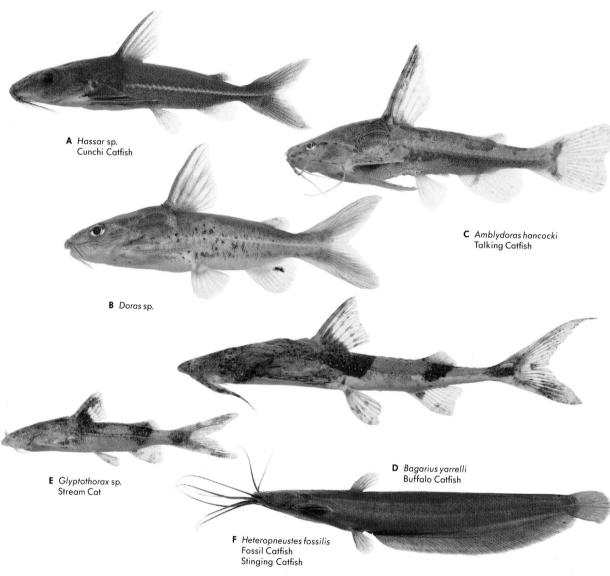

A *Hassar* sp.
Cunchi Catfish

C *Amblydoras hancocki*
Talking Catfish

B *Doras* sp.

E *Glyptothorax* sp.
Stream Cat

D *Bagarius yarrelli*
Buffalo Catfish

F *Heteropneustes fossilis*
Fossil Catfish
Stinging Catfish

A 8 in. (20 cm). Amazon R. This species, and occasionally *H. otestis* which has a grayish brown body and a black spot on the dorsal fin, are imported. Rather mild tempered, they coexist well with other fishes.

B Over 4 in. (10 cm). Amazon R. It burrows in sandy bottoms, so because of this behavior it can remain hidden during the daytime.

C 6 in. (15 cm). Peru, Bolivia, Guiana. Popularly known as the "Talking Cat" because of the grunting noise it makes when leaving the water. Easy to care for, it prefers live foods.

D About 16 in. (40 cm) in aquaria, 40 in. (1 m) in nature. SE Asia. A food fish that is however, more peaceful than South American catfishes similar in appearance. The wide, thick barbels are a strong diagnostic character. Frequently resting on the tank bottom, it prefers to eat small fishes and crustaceans.

E 4 in. (10 cm). Burma, Thailand. Young are similar to the above species. It lives in

mountain streams, and prefers 68-86°F (20-30°C) water with strong aeration. In aquaria, it tends to remain hidden in refuges.

F 28 in. (70 cm). Eastern India, Sri Lanka, Burma, southern Vietnam. Inactive in aquaria, it is pugnacious, so should be kept by itself or as a pair. It prefers live foods, but can also be fed vegetable matter. Breeding reports state that the pair digs a hole to spawn in, then cares for the eggs and young.

G Over 20 in. (50 cm) in aquaria, 28 in. (70 cm) in nature. India, Sri Lanka, Malay and Indochinese Peninsulas, Philippines. Nocturnal, it is an active, voracious fish that requires a good-sized tank. Notorious for its movement across land from ponds to other places, it can live out of water for a long time if its body remains wet, as it has a specially adapted gill apparatus for breathing air.

H 6 in. (15 cm). Endemic to northern and eastern Australia. Other congeners also suitable for aquaria include the small "White Tandan" and *N. hyrtlii*, which grows to

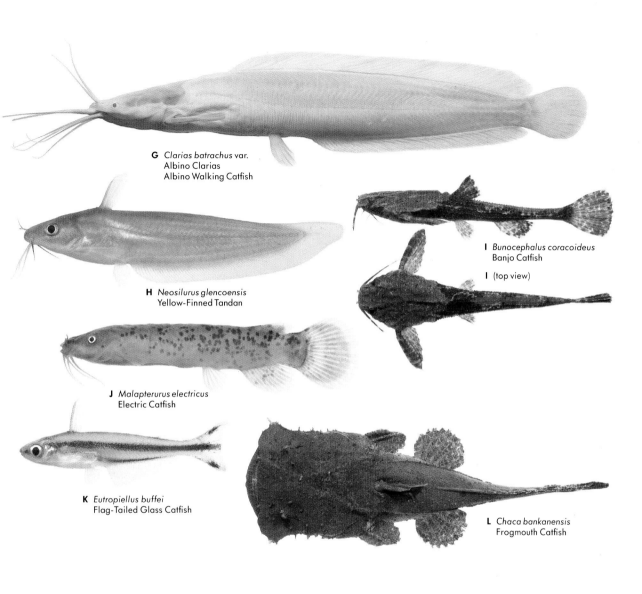

G *Clarias batrachus* var.
Albino Clarias
Albino Walking Catfish

H *Neosilurus glencoensis*
Yellow-Finned Tandan

I *Bunocephalus coracoideus*
Banjo Catfish

I (top view)

J *Malapterurus electricus*
Electric Catfish

K *Eutropiellus buffei*
Flag-Tailed Glass Catfish

L *Chaca bankanensis*
Frogmouth Catfish

approx. 16 in. (40 cm). As exports are strictly controlled, they are all only rarely available.

I 4¾ in. (12 cm). Western Amazon to Ecuador. Tolerant of water quality, it remains healthy as long as the water temperature remains 68-86°F (20-30°C). Usually inactive, remaining behind rocks or in pebbles, when it moves, water is forced from the gill slits, causing it to skip along. It prefers worms such as tubifex. The pair spawns on rocks and cares for the eggs until they hatch out.

J 12 in. (30 cm) in aquaria, about 40 in. (1 m) in nature. Tropical Africa. The ability to generate a powerful electrical current is the property for which this species is famous. There are electric organs on both sides of the body. Some 100-300 V is produced by cutaneous cells (rather than muscles as in other electric fishes). It is said that this high power charge is mainly to catch prey and secondly for defense, but others say it acts as a kind of radar. When water is replaced, care should be taken to avoid receiving an electrical jolt. Although spawning behavior hasn't been observed, Zairean fishermen claim it is a cave spawner. A voracious eater of small fish and blood worms, large individuals are pugnacious and should be kept by themselves.

K 3¼ in. (8 cm). Southern Nigeria. Known in African fisheries as the "Glass Cat," it is quite sensitive to water quality, preferring slightly acidic, aged water. Care is fairly difficult. It favors live foods such as tubifex worms. There is no breeding record. *E. debauwi,* a less attractively striped congener, is also sometimes exported from Zaire.

L 12 in. (30 cm). Malaysia, Indonesia, Thailand. Tolerant of water quality, it is hardy and peaceful, yet being piscivorous, eats small fish. Capable of surviving long fasts, it is generally inactive, hiding behind stones or in sand, and grunts when touched. Its color pattern and queer shape appear to mimic a fallen leaf.

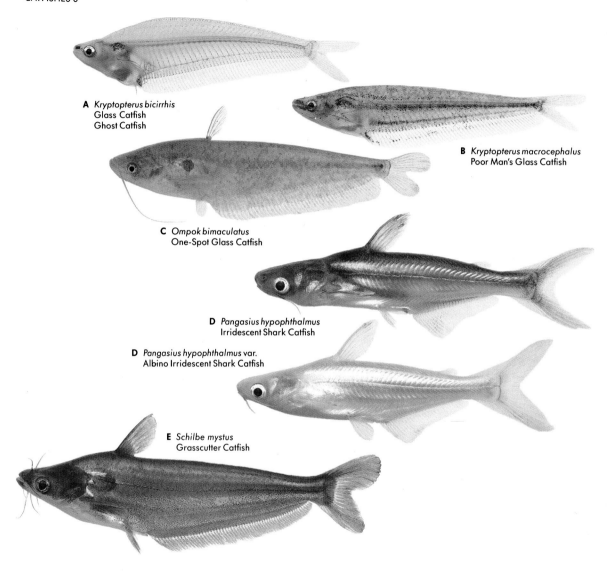

A *Kryptopterus bicirrhis*
Glass Catfish
Ghost Catfish

B *Kryptopterus macrocephalus*
Poor Man's Glass Catfish

C *Ompok bimaculatus*
One-Spot Glass Catfish

D *Pangasius hypophthalmus*
Irridescent Shark Catfish

D *Pangasius hypophthalmus* var.
Albino Irridescent Shark Catfish

E *Schilbe mystus*
Grasscutter Catfish

A 4¾ in. (12 cm) in aquaria, 6 in. (15 cm) in nature. Thailand, Malay Peninsula, Sumatra, Borneo. As it lives in running water, circular water movement should be maintained in the aquarium. It forms a school even with a few individuals. Well suited for a community tank, it prefers live foods such as mosquito larvae. Just imported fish are prone to White Spot disease. No record of spawning.
B 6 in. (15 cm). Sumatra, Java. Found in shaded portions of running waters, there are about 10 species known. Care is easy, but there is no record of them being bred in aquaria.
C 18 in. (45 cm). Java, Borneo, Indochinese Peninsula, Malaysia. A type of glass catfish, its body is blackish and not all that translucent. The spot behind the gill cover is a diagnostic character.

D 40 in. (1 m) in nature. Widely distributed on the Indochinese Peninsula, it has been introduced throughout SE Asia where it is now an important food fish. Water quality is of little concern. Care is easy, and although omnivorous, it doesn't attack other fish, so can be kept in a community tank housing cyprinids. Recently, an albino form shown here has been produced in Bangkok and widely exported.
E 18 in. (45 cm). West and Central Africa. Closely related to the above species, it also serves as a food fish in countries where it is native. Care is easy. It prefers carp pellets over live foods.

RAINBOWFISHES
AND BRACKISHWATER FISHES

10

FAMILY	**BATRACHOIDIDAE**
	(Toadfishes)
Genus	*Halophryne*
FAMILY	**ATHERINIDAE (Silversides)**
SUBFAMILY	BEDOTIINAE
Genus	*Bedotia*
SUBFAMILY	PSEUDOMUGILINAE
Genera	*Popondetta*
	Telmatherina
SUBFAMILY	MELANOTAENIINAE
	(Rainbowfishes)
Genera	*Glossolepis*
	Melanotaenia
FAMILY	**ANABLEPIDAE**
SUBFAMILY	ANABLEPINAE
	(Four-Eyed Fishes)
Genus	*Anableps*

FAMILY	**BELONIDAE (Needlefishes)**
Genus	*Xenentodon*
FAMILY	**HEMIRAMPHIDAE**
	(Halfbeaks)
Genus	*Dermogenys*
FAMILY	**SYNGNATHIDAE**
	(Pipefishes & Seahorses)
SUBFAMILY	SYNGNATHINAE
	(Pipefishes)
Genus	*Microphis*
FAMILY	**CENTROPOMIDAE**
	(Snooks)
SUBFAMILY	LATINAE
Genus	*Lates*
FAMILY	**AMBASSIDAE**
Genus	*Chanda*

FAMILY	**TOXOTIDAE**
	(Archerfishes)
Genus	*Toxotes*
FAMILY	**MONODACTYLIDAE**
Genus	*Monodactylus*
FAMILY	**SCATOPHAGIDAE (Scats)**
Genus	*Scatophagus*
FAMILY	**ELEOTRIDAE (Sleepers)**
Genera	*Hemieleotris*
	Mogurnda
	Oxyeleotris
FAMILY	**GOBIIDAE (Gobies)**
Genera	*Brachygobius*
	Periophthalmus
FAMILY	**TETRAODONTIDAE**
	(Puffers)
Genus	*Tetraodon*

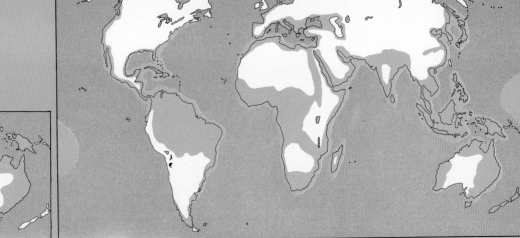

RAINBOWFISH   BRACKISHWATER FISH

BRACKISHWATER FISH

Brackishwater fishes is a general name given to the ichthyofauna living basically within estuarine systems where both fresh and salt waters meet and mix. It is believed that some of these fish were originally fresh water species, while others migrated from marine environments.

Estuaries within the tropical to subtropical zones usually are well populated by mangrove trees. It is an active ecosystem in which muddy deposits rich in nutrients can be found, along with an abundance of organisms such as plankton, crustaceans and fishes. Examples of the last two include fiddler crabs and schools of mudskippers found along the mud flats, plus fingerfishes and archerfishes within the mangrove roots. This is the biotope, the environment that is home to the brackishwater fishes.

Most of the brackishwater fishes for sale in pet shops are those considered to prefer fresher water. Even these, however, do best when a small quantity of salt is added to the tank. Others require conditions closer to sea water to maintain them in peak shape and bring out their best coloration. In over half of the species included here, spawning and hatching occur in sea water.

As a general rule, these fish should be kept in an aquarium filled with 80% alkaline fresh water and about 20% (natural or artificial) sea water. Crushed coral should be spread to cover the bottom. Although tropical species should be kept in 68-86°F (20-30°C) water, others may do better at lower temperatures. The tank should be large enough to ensure sufficient swimming room, and also be provided with strong aeration or water circulation.

Some omnivorous species may prefer a ready supply of algae, so in this case, such growth should be promoted by placing the tank where it receives strong sunlight. Most of these fish also relish feeding on aquatic worms and even smaller fishes.

A *Anableps anableps.* Four-Eyed Fish. **1** Lower half of eye is clearly visible.

2 While lower half looks under water, the upper half shown here looks out above the water surface.

B *Toxotes chatareus.* Seven-Spot Archerfish spits water to knock a worm down. ◗

A *Xenentodon cancila*. Silver Needlefish. **1** Close-up shows it catching a small fish.

B *Halophryne trispinosus*. Freshwater Lionfish. Numerous tentacles make its face comical.

2 This member of the Family Belonidae, has a streamlined body ideally suited for rapid movement to catch prey.

C *Scatophagus multifasciatus*. Silver Scat.

E *Tetraodon nigroviridis*. Spotted River Puffer.

D *Brachygobius doriae*. Doria's Bumblebee Goby.

F *Mogurnda mogurnda*. Purple-Striped Gudgeon.

A *Telmatherina ladigesi.* Celebes Rainbowfish. Courting ♂ (rt.). This beautiful fish comes from Celebes (Sulawesi) Island.

RAINBOWFISH

Despite the great breadth of the Australian continent, its freshwater fish fauna is rather limited. Among those fish considered to be genuine freshwater fishes are the Australian Lungfish (*Neoceratodus forsteri*) plus the Spotted and Northern Barramundi (*Scleropages leichardi* and *S. jardini* respectively). According to continental drift theory, Australia separated from Gondwanaland about 150 million years ago when only the ancestors of these three fish lived. Other freshwater fishes such as the characoids, cyprinids and cichlids evolved much later, so are not distributed in Australia.

Fishes that are believed to have migrated from the sea to Australian fresh waters are the atherinomorph fishes which include the rainbowfishes and their allies. In support of this theory, many of these fishes may be found in a wide range of habitats ranging from freshwater to marine with brackish waters in between.

Australasian rainbowfishes belong to the family Melanotaeniidae and are found only in Australia and New Guinea. The telmatherinid

B *Popondetta connieae.* Connie's Blue-Eye.

C *Bedotia geayi.* Madagascar Rainbowfish.

D *Glossolepis incisus.* New Guinea Red Rainbowfish.

E *Melanotaenia splendida fluviatilis.* Splendid Australian Rainbowfish. Pair.

sailfin silversides of the Subfamily Pseudomugilinae are restricted to the Celebes Islands, while the Subfamily Bedotiinae are endemic to Madagascar. Genus and species distribution patterns vary greatly, some being found widely, others being endemic, and still others being discontinuous. Their habitats also vary greatly; from stagnant to swiftly moving waters and even in small intermittent ponds that become desiccated during the dry season. Some are found in hard, alkaline waters, while others occupy soft, slightly acidic brook water. Although water quality closest to the original habitat would be best, rainbowfishes are quite tolerant and will adapt to a broad range of water conditions. Most species are omnivorous, but some prefer plant matter such as spinach.

A well-planted aquarium is preferred for breeding. The male induces the female to spawn by quivering and displaying by spreading his fins. Spawning continues over several days. Once the pair is spent, they should be removed to another aquarium to prevent them from eating their brood. Adhesive strings coming from the eggs attach to the aquatic plants, hatching taking place 7-10 days later. At first, the fry should be fed infusoria.

A *Toxotes jaculatrix*
Archerfish

B *Toxotes chatareus*
Seven-Spot Archerfish

E *Scatophagus multifasciatus*
Silver Scat

C *Scatophagus argus argus*
Spotted Scat

D *Scatophagus argus atromaculatus*
Red Scat

F *Monodactylus sebae*
Mono Sebae
African Angelfish

G *Monodactylus argenteus*
Silver Mono

A 10 in. (25 cm). SE Asia, India, Philippines, Australia. Found in fresh to estuarine waters within mangrove stands or jungle, it prefers alkaline brackish water. It shoots out a jet of water to knock down flies, worms, other insects and even tiny animals on land. The pair spawns close together at the water surface. About 3,000 floating eggs are laid in a single spawning, and hatch out in about 12 hrs.

B 12 in. (30 cm). Widely distributed throughout SE Asia, requirements are the same as **A**.

C & D 12 in. (30 cm) in nature, 6 in. (15 cm) in aquaria. Freshwater to estuarine and coastal waters in India, Indonesia, Thailand, Vietnam. Keeping it in salt water rather than freshwater tends to keep it healthier and with better coloration. Omnivorous, it should be fed vegetable matter such as lettuce or spinach, which it relishes. No record of it being bred.

E 4¾ in. (12 cm). Coastal waters, except southern Australia. Prefers hard, alkaline brackish water. Small, beautiful and docile, it should be given lettuce, spinach and live foods.

F 8 in. (20 cm). Estuaries of the Zaire and Senegal R. The tank should be filled with 5 parts fresh: 1 part salt water, and the bottom covered with crushed coral. Omnivorous, its care is rather difficult. A pair swims round and round, spawning a few thousand eggs which hatch out in 2-3 days.

G 10 in. (25 cm). SE Asia, Australia, Red Sea, East African coast. Same as **F**, but no record of breeding.

H 6 in. (15 cm). India, Burma, Malaysia, Thailand. Add salt to the water. Omnivorous, it frequently may nip at other fishes' fins.

I 8 in. (20 cm) in nature. SE Asia. Common even in fresh waters.

J 2¼ in. (6 cm). India, Burma, Thailand fresh waters. Easy to care for, it has a delicate appearance and a mild demeanor. The pair spawns in an upside-down manner with the floating eggs hatching out within a day.

K 12 in. (30 cm) in nature, 6 in. (15 cm) in aquaria. India, Thailand, Malaysia, Java, Sumatra. Prefers alkaline water. Usually staying on the tank bottom, it feeds only on live foods such as aquatic worms or small fishes, and is definitely not tolerant of other fish. Although its breeding behavior is unknown, some claim it is a mouthbrooder, while others claim the ♂ cares for the eggs.

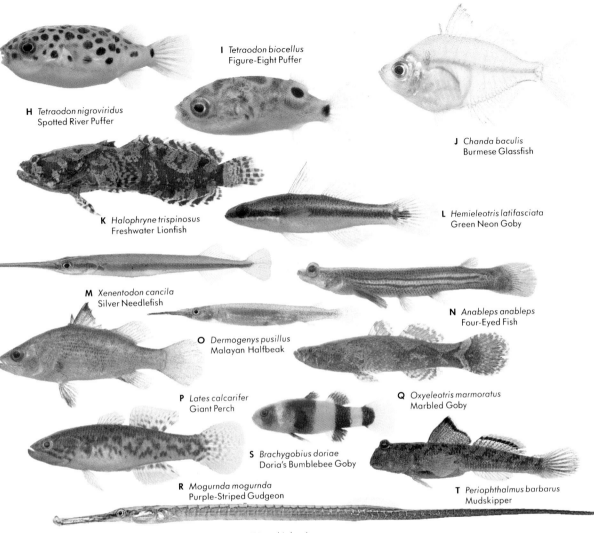

H *Tetraodon nigroviridus*
Spotted River Puffer

I *Tetraodon biocellus*
Figure-Eight Puffer

J *Chanda baculis*
Burmese Glassfish

K *Halophryne trispinosus*
Freshwater Lionfish

L *Hemieleotris latifasciata*
Green Neon Goby

M *Xenentodon cancila*
Silver Needlefish

N *Anableps anableps*
Four-Eyed Fish

O *Dermogenys pusillus*
Malayan Halfbeak

P *Lates calcarifer*
Giant Perch

Q *Oxyeleotris marmoratus*
Marbled Goby

S *Brachygobius doriae*
Doria's Bumblebee Goby

R *Mogurnda mogurnda*
Purple-Striped Gudgeon

T *Periophthalmus barbarus*
Mudskipper

U *Microphis boaja*

L 4 in. (10 cm). Pacific coast of Costa Rica, Panama, Colombia. An eleotrid with characteristic parallel horizontal black and metallic green stripes. It is mild tempered, and care is easy.

M 8 in. (20 cm). India, Sri Lanka, Thailand, Malaysia. Prefers slightly brackish, alkaline water. A surface swimmer, it eats small fish and crustaceans.

N 8 in. (20 cm). Atlantic coast of Central and South America. Prefers brackish water. Small crustaceans and aquatic worms are the desired foods. This specialized livebearer has its eyes divided into upper and lower halves allowing for simultaneous viewing both above and below the water's surface.

O ♂ 2 in. (5 cm), ♀ 2¼ in. (6 cm). Thailand, Malaysia, Sumatra, Borneo. Prefers brackish water. An ovoviviparous surface swimmer, it is highly inquisitive about things on the water's surface. The female gives birth to 10-50 fry, but may eat them.

P Max. 40 in. (1 m), 24 in. (60 cm) in aquaria. Philippines and SE Asia to Australasia. Prefers fresh alkaline water which should be made brackish after the fish reaches 20 in. (50 cm). Similar to the Nile Perch, it too is a voracious predator. Worms and dry shrimp are its favorite foods. While the young have brown markings, after reaching 8

in. (20 cm), they become uniformly silver.

Q Over 16 in. (40 cm) in nature, 8 in. (20 cm) in aquaria. Thailand, Malaysia, Indonesia. Tolerant of water conditions, it is nocturnal, easy to care for, and a voracious eater of smaller fish and crustaceans.

R 4 in. (10 cm). Eastern and northern Australian rivers. Prefers brackish to fresh water. Care and breeding are easy. The eggs are deposited on a smooth, often vertical, surface. The ♂ cares for his clutch until the fry hatch.

S 1½ in. (4 cm). Thailand, Malay Peninsula, Sumatra, Borneo. A small, colorful fish, it must be kept in brackish water, while a shallow tank depth is preferred. Spawns on shells or stones. As with most gobies, the ♂ cares for his clutch until the fry hatch.

T 6 in. (15 cm). India, Australia, eastern Africa. Sensitive to changes in water quality, brackish water is preferred. It is territorial in aquaria. Care is difficult, but worms are its favored food.

U 7 in. (18 cm). Thailand, Malaysia, Indonesia. Prefers aeration-free, alkaline, brackish water. A rare, minutely mouthed species, it should be fed brine shrimp or very small worms. Eggs hatch out within the male's abdominal brood pouch.

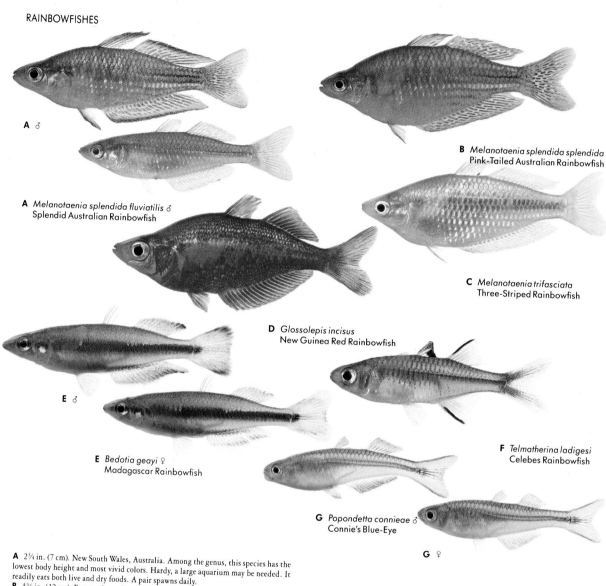

RAINBOWFISHES

A ♂

A *Melanotaenia splendida fluviatilis* ♂
Splendid Australian Rainbowfish

B *Melanotaenia splendida splendida*
Pink-Tailed Australian Rainbowfish

C *Melanotaenia trifasciata*
Three-Striped Rainbowfish

D *Glossolepis incisus*
New Guinea Red Rainbowfish

E ♂

E *Bedotia geayi* ♀
Madagascar Rainbowfish

F *Telmatherina ladigesi*
Celebes Rainbowfish

G *Popondetta connieae* ♂
Connie's Blue-Eye

G ♀

A 2¾ in. (7 cm). New South Wales, Australia. Among the genus, this species has the lowest body height and most vivid colors. Hardy, a large aquarium may be needed. It readily eats both live and dry foods. A pair spawns daily.
B 4¾ in. (12 cm). Eastern Australian rivers. Best known of the rainbowfishes, it has a mild demeanor, so is well suited for community tanks. Although it prefers live worms, dry foods will be accepted. Spawning will begin after it reaches 2¾-3¼ in. (7-8 cm), but to increase its longevity and get it to grow over 4 in. (10 cm) long, the water must be replaced monthly.
C 2¾ in. (7 cm). Queensland, Australia. Easily distinguished by its wide horizontal black stripe and red caudal fin. This species is a relatively recent addition to the ranks of ornamental fishes. Care is the same as **A** & **B**.
D 6 in. (15 cm). New Guinea. While it can be kept in soft, slightly acidic water, alkaline water will produce a more intense body coloration; ♂ is red, ♀ is grayish brown. Omnivorous. It spawns on fine-leaved aquatic plants, but producing a large number of young is difficult. The fry feed on infusoria or mashed egg yolk.
E 4 in. (10 cm). Tolerant to water conditions, but prefers hard, alkaline water. Omnivorous, its care is easy. A few eggs are laid daily on fine-leaved aquatic plants. Caring for the fry which hatch out in about 5-8 days is easy.

F 2¾ in. (7 cm). Celebes (Sulawesi). Prefers neutral, hard water. Omnivorous, it likes floating foods best. Shoal maintenance is desirable. A few eggs are laid daily on fine-leaved underwater flora, and these hatch in 12-14 days. Since the fry are really tiny, minute foods are needed. Fry grow really slowly. The fish shown is a ♀ as the second dorsal is elongated in males.
G 2 in. (5 cm). Papua New Guinea. Prefers alkaline water, and is omnivorous. This is a small, beautiful and easily cared for fish. It should be kept in a well-planted tank with weak aeration. Sexing is done using the anal fin as the diagnostic character. A few eggs are spawned daily, but the fry should be removed as soon as they hatch out.

FAMILY	**POTAMOTRYGONIDAE** (River Stingrays)	**FAMILY**	**PANTODONTIDAE**	**FAMILY**	**CHANNIDAE (Snakeheads)**
Genus	*Potamotrygon*	Genus	*Pantodon*	Genus	*Channa*
FAMILY	**ACIPENSERIDAE** (Sturgeons)	**FAMILY**	**NOTOPTERIDAE** (Knifefishes or Featherbacks)	**FAMILY**	**ACHIRIDAE**
SUBFAMILY	ACIPENSERINAE			Genus	*Achirus*
Genus	*Acipenser*	Genera	*Notopterus*	**FAMILY**	**CERATODONTIDAE** (Australian Lungfishes)
FAMILY	**POLYODONTIDAE** (Paddlefishes)		*Papyrocranus*		
			Xenomystus	Genus	*Neoceratodus*
Genus	*Polyodon*	**FAMILY**	**MORMYRIDAE** (Elephantfishes)	**FAMILY**	**LEPIDOSIRENIDAE**
FAMILY	**POLYPTERIDAE (Bichirs)**			SUBFAMILY	LEPIDOSIRENINAE (S. American Lungfishes)
Genus	*Polypterus*	Genera	*Campylomormyrus*	Genus	*Lepidosiren*
FAMILY	**LEPISOSTEIDAE (Gars)**		*Gnathonemus*	SUBFAMILY	PROTOPTERINAE (African Lungfishes)
Genus	*Lepisosteus*		*Hippopotamyrus*		
FAMILY	**AMIIDAE (Bowfins)**		*Marcusenius*	Genus	*Protopterus*
Genus	*Amia*		*Mormyrus*	**FAMILY**	**ESOCIDAE (Pikes)**
FAMILY	**OSTEOGLOSSIDAE** (Bonytongues & Arapaimas)		*Pollimyrus*	Genus	*Esox*
		FAMILY	**GYMNARCHIDAE**	**FAMILY**	**MASTACEMBELIDAE** (Spiny-Eels)
SUBFAMILY	HETEROTIDINAE	Genus	*Gymnarchus*		
Genera	*Arapaima*	**FAMILY**	**GYMNOTIDAE** (Knifefishes)	Genus	*Mastacembelus*
	Heterotis			**FAMILY**	**CENTRARCHIDAE** (Sunfishes & Freshwater Basses)
SUBFAMILY	OSTEOGLOSSINAE	SUBFAMILY	STERNOPYGINAE		
Genera	*Osteoglossum*	Genus	*Eigenmannia*		
	Scleropages	SUBFAMILY	APTERONOTINAE	Genus	*Enneacanthus*
		Genus	*Sternarchella*		

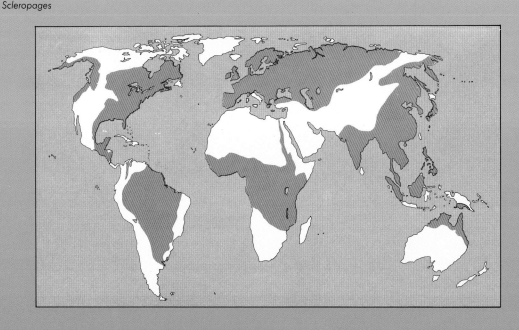

A *Scleropages formosus.* Asian Arowana. A dignified swimmer, this species is now protected under CITES.

B *Scleropages jardini.* Silver Barramundi. An Australian arowana.

AROWANAS

The arowanas belong to the Family Osteoglossidae of which three species are known from South America, one or possibly two from SE Asia, two from Australia, and one from Africa. Also included in this family is the Arapaima or Pirarucu, found throughout the Amazon. All of these freshwater fishes closely resemble each other despite the fact that they are found distributed across many continents separated by oceans. This is considered to be supporting evidence for Wegener's Continental Drift Theory, first put forth in 1912. Under this theory, Africa, Southeast Asia, Australia and the Americas were united eons ago in one super continent called Gondwanaland. The ancestors of today's bonytongued

fishes inhabited this super continent's waters, and as the mass split, became dispersed across the globe. Fossil evidence shows that ancestors of these fish were even more widely distributed to include North America, Europe and India, but probably died out due to environmental changes.

Included in the Order Osteoglossiformes are the aforementioned family, plus the Pantodontidae, Hiodontidae, Notopteridae, Mormyridae, and Gymnarchidae. Fossil records of close relatives of these primitive fish go back some tens of millions of years ago. Today's descendants retain many of the ancient characters found in the fossil records, and so are called "living fossils."

Arowanas either deposit their eggs in a nest of plant material or are mouthbrooders. All tend their mobile young diligently, but are not very prolific. They are thus vulnerable to overexploitation, and several species are threatened with extinction. Under CITES, the Asian Arowana cannot be imported into any of the signatory countries. Australia has prohibited export of its two endemic arowana species, as have countries from which the Pirarucu comes. Thus the availability of most of these fishes is severely limited.

A *Osteoglossum bicirrhosum*. Silver Arowana. Representative of Amazonian fishes, young are exported from S America annually from December to February.

B *Pantodon buchholzi*. Butterfly Fish. A small osteoglossiform fish that catches floating foods.

C *Osteoglossum ferreirai*. Black Arowana. Just imported larvae still retain a large yolk sac.

A *Polypterus ornatipinnis.* An ancient African fish with a diagnostic dorsal fin composed of independent spiny elements.

B *Polypterus palmas.* Green Polypterus.

C *Polypterus lapradii.*

D *Protopterus annectens.* African Lungfish. **1** Growing to 40 in. (1 m) in length, this fish lives in African ponds and swamps, breathing with its lungs.

2 Aestivating fish encased in its muddy mucus cocoon.

3 Placed back in water, the fish breaks out of its cocoon.

LUNGFISHES

There are six known species of lungfishes; four in Africa (*Protopterus aethiopicus, P. amphibius, P. annectens, P. dolloi*), one in South America (*Lepidosiren paradoxa*), and one in Australia (*Neoceratodus forsteri*).

Most fish exchange gas through their gills, but the gills in lungfishes have degenerated and a modified swim bladder closely resembling lungs allows for atmospheric respiration. Except for the Australian Lungfish, they all aestivate. Living in climates that alternate between rainy and dry seasons, as the dry season begins, they burrow into the mud and form a mucus capsule around themselves which inhibits dessication. While aestivating, they draw on the nutrients stored within their body.

A *Amia calva*. Bowfin. About 32 in. (80 cm) in length, this ancient fish lives in North America. Its ancestors first appeared in the Permian Period and later lived during the time of dinosaurs.

NORTH AMERICAN FISH

Most aquarium fishes come from tropical to subtropical waters, while those from temperate to arctic waters are rare. Generally unappreciated in their homeland, some North American fishes have long been sought after by European and Japanese aquarists. On occasion, such scientific oddities as bowfins and paddlefishes are exported. Treated as curiosities

or novelties, they are not really suited for the usual home aquarium as they grow quite large. On the other hand, there are many North American fish well suited for home aquaria, such as shiners, darters, minnows and other small cyprinids. As these rather subtle colored, yet attractive fishes are seldom available through commercial channels, European and Japanese aquarists must rely on person-to-person contact with their American counterparts to secure these species. It may be desirable that hobbyists thus develop international ties through shared interest in their native fishes.

273

A *Esox lucius.* Northern Pike. This so-called "River Gangster" found in temperate to subarctic waters can exceed 40 in. (1 m) in length.

B *Polyodon spathula*. Paddlefish.

C *Lepisosteus oculatus*. Spotted Gar just catching a sunfish.

D *Acipenser transmontanus*. White Sturgeon.

A *Channa micropeltes.* Red Snakehead.

B *Potamotrygon* sp. A Freshwater Stingray from S America.

C *Papyrocranus afer.* A large, mild-tempered knifefish, some individuals have white markings on their flanks.

D *Gnathonemus petersii*. Peter's Elephant Nose. Representative of the African mormyrid fishes, it gets its name from the elongated snout.

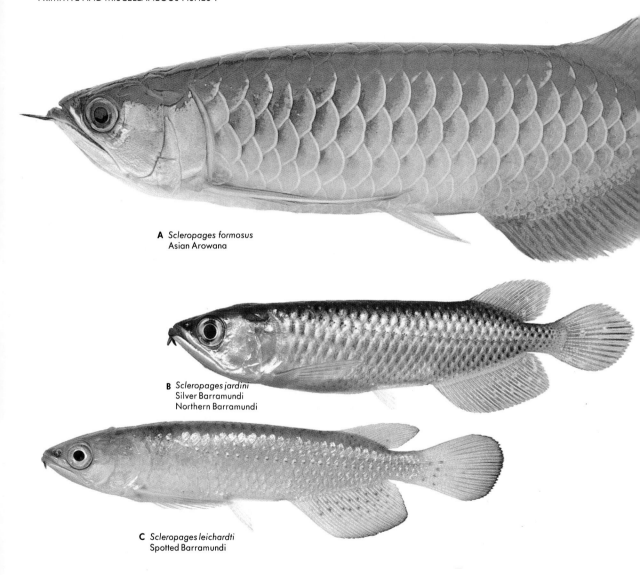

A *Scleropages formosus*
Asian Arowana

B *Scleropages jardini*
Silver Barramundi
Northern Barramundi

C *Scleropages leichardti*
Spotted Barramundi

A 28 in. (70 cm). SE Asia. Prefers neutral to slightly acidic water. Some fin rays may be missing due to self-inflicted injury caused by madly dashing about when frightened such as during sudden water replacement. This species is highly piscivorous. Care of the congeneric Green Arowana is the same, and both are paternal mouthbrooders. Export, import and trade in wild caught fish are prohibited under CITES, therefore trade should be limited to fish hatched in captivity.

B 16-20 in. (40-50 cm). Northern Australia, Papua New Guinea, West Irian. Adults have a strong orange cast. A piscivorous paternal mouthbrooder, it spawns 50-200 eggs ⅜ in. (10 mm) in diameter which hatch out within 10-14 days.

C 16-20 in. (40-50 cm) in aquaria, 36 in. (90 cm) in nature. Fitzroy R. in NW Australia. It has one or two orange spots on each scale. Sensitive to water pollution, care of this piscivorous paternal mouthbrooder is more difficult than for *S. jardini*. Not bred in aquaria yet.

D Max 40 in. (1 m). Amazon R. Just imported juveniles prefer slightly acidic, soft aged water. Tolerant to water quality, it grows over 12 in. (30 cm) in a single year, readily feeding on blood worms, other aquatic worms or small fish. It is also a paternal mouthbrooder.

E Less than 40 in. (1 m). Rio Branco tributary of the Rio Negro. Juvenile (seen here) and adult coloration are quite different as adults resemble the Silver Arowana. It prefers slightly acidic water, and the young are quite sensitive to water quality. Hardy

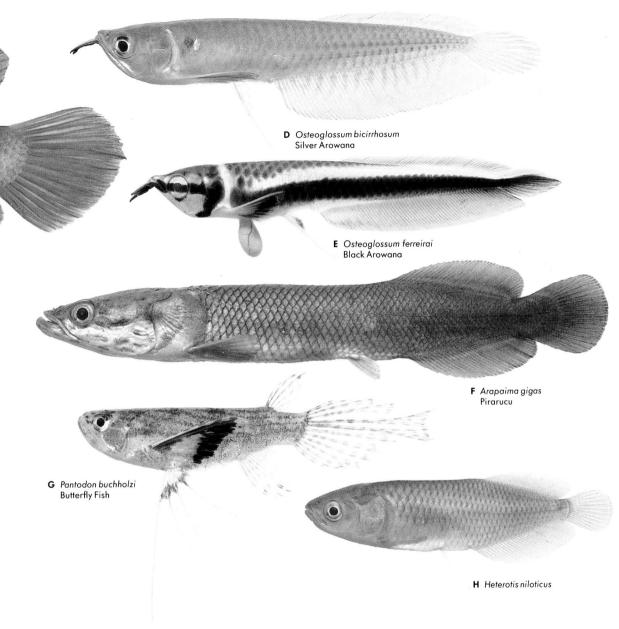

D *Osteoglossum bicirrhosum*
Silver Arowana

E *Osteoglossum ferreirai*
Black Arowana

F *Arapaima gigas*
Pirarucu

G *Pantodon buchholzi*
Butterfly Fish

H *Heterotis niloticus*

after it reaches 12 in. (30 cm), this piscivorous fish is best kept by itself. Rather skittish compared to the Silver Arowana.

F Max 8 ft (2.5 m) in aquaria, 16 ft (5 m) in nature. Amazon R, Orinoco R. Prefers slightly acidic, aged water. Its potential size should be considered in choosing the tank, and as it's a frequent jumper, the tank should be covered. Commercial trade of this piscivorous fish is prohibited in Brazil, but juvenile fish are sometimes exported from Colombia and Peru. It is a nest breeder that practices protracted defense of its mobile young.

G 4¾ in. (12 cm). Tropical rain forests from Nigeria to Zaire. Tolerant to water quality. It catches insects on the water surface, but will not eat food from the tank bottom. The pair prefers slightly acidic, soft 82°F (28°C) water for spawning. They swim round about each other, spawning over a long period of time, but 3-8 floating eggs in each clutch. These eggs hatch out within 36-48 hours, and the fry take brine shrimp at the water surface.

H Max 36 in. (90 cm). Not sensitive to water quality, it is a plankton feeder in nature, but omnivorous in aquaria. It is a nest breeder characterized by long-term male defense of the mobile young.

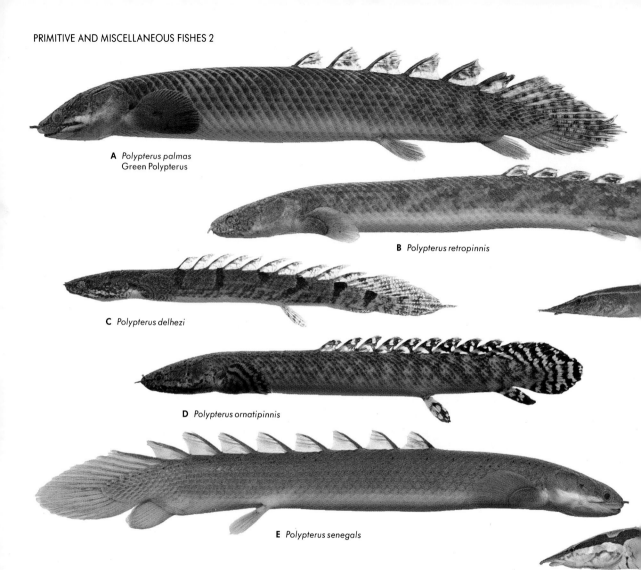

A *Polypterus palmas*
Green Polypterus

B *Polypterus retropinnis*

C *Polypterus delhezi*

D *Polypterus ornatipinnis*

E *Polypterus senegals*

A 12 in. (30 cm). Sierra Leone, Liberia, Zaire. Care is easy. Although tolerant of other fish, it will catch those of edible size. Its modified swim bladder for breathing atmospheric oxygen allows it to live a long time out of water (as long as its body remains wet), plus move on wet ground.

B 10 in. (25 cm). Aruwimi R of the upper Zaire R. A rather smallish lobe-finned pike with a slender, yellowish body, it is peaceful and easy to care for. Preferred foods include tubifex, blood worms and dried shrimp.

C 14 in. (35 cm). Middle and upper Zaire R. Prefers neutral to alkaline, hard water. It will feed on small fishes and dried shrimp. Care is easy, but it is pugnacious, definitely intolerant of others. No record of being bred in aquaria.

D 16 in. (40 cm). Kasai R, middle to upper Zaire R. Variation exists in markings. Nocturnal by nature, it is mild tempered and tolerant of other fish, but may eat smaller tankmates. The fish has been reported to spawn by vibrating its entire body.

E 16 in. (40 cm). Widely distributed from the Nile R to Senegal in W Africa. Hardy and mild mannered, it is easy to maintain. As many are exported from Lagos, it is readily available. Foods include small fish and dried shrimp. Recently it has been bred in captivity, so young with external gills have also become available.

F Exceeds 30 in. (75 cm). Senegal, Niger. Tolerant of changes in water quality, this easily cared for large fish grows quite fast, reaching about 18 in. (45 cm) in two years. It feeds on small fish, fish fillets and dried shrimp.

G 16 in. (40 cm). Upper reaches of the Zaire R. in Shaba Province. The body has 7 or 8 vertical stripes which fade as the fish grows. A peaceful, easily maintained fish, it is often misidentified as *P. palmas*. but can easily be distinguished by its shorter body and dorsal fin origin being closer to the head.

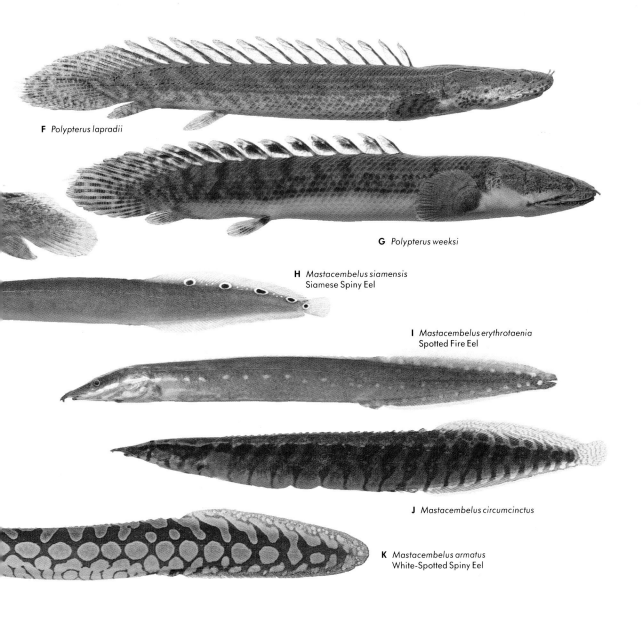

F *Polypterus lapradii*

G *Polypterus weeksi*

H *Mastacembelus siamensis*
Siamese Spiny Eel

I *Mastacembelus erythrotaenia*
Spotted Fire Eel

J *Mastacembelus circumcinctus*

K *Mastacembelus armatus*
White-Spotted Spiny Eel

H 15 in. (38 cm). India, Sri Lanka, Thailand, Malaysia, Sumatra. Tolerant to water quality, it prefers slightly brackish water. Nocturnal by nature, during the daytime the fish remains hidden in a refuge. Its long snout and mouth are used to catch worms, but acclimated individuals will eat dry food. The tank should have a well-fastened cover as this fish has been known to escape from aquaria. No record of breeding.

I 30 in. (75 cm). India, Sri Lanka, Thailand, Sumatra. This large, beautiful fish tolerates any kind of water quality and is easy to care for. Noctural in the wild, acclimated individuals become diurnal and even solicit their owner for food. Omnivorous, live foods are preferred. Spawning among fish over 20 in. (50 cm) long has been reported.

J 16 in. (40 cm). Thailand, Malay Peninsula, Sumatra. A nocturnal fish that remains buried in the sand during the daytime, both it and *M. erythrotaenia* are commonly

exported. It prefers live food such as earthworms and blood worms, but acclimated individuals will eat dry pellets. This fish should not be kept with smaller fish.

K Exceeds 28 in. (70 cm). India, Sri Lanka, Thailand, Sumatra. Largest of the spiny eels, there is a wide variation in its markings which resemble a tire tread. Hardy and easy to care for, it prefers to eat earthworms and large, live fish. Not suited for an aquascaped tank, this fish is a sand diver that destroys aquatic plants.

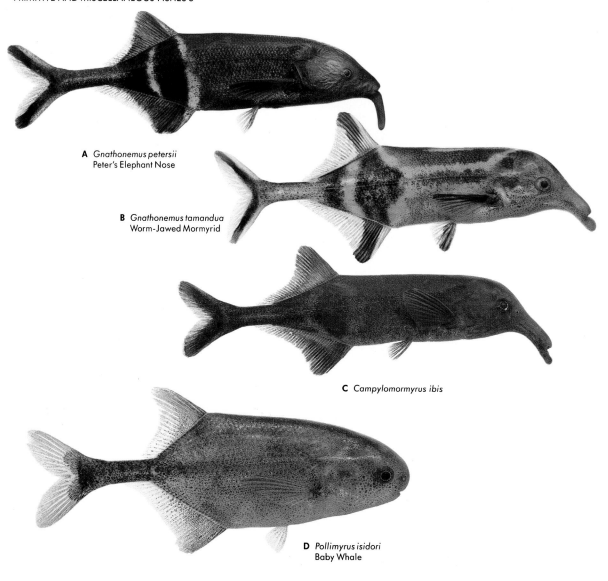

A *Gnathonemus petersii*
Peter's Elephant Nose

B *Gnathonemus tamandua*
Worm-Jawed Mormyrid

C *Campylomormyrus ibis*

D *Pollimyrus isidori*
Baby Whale

A 8 in. (20 cm). Nigeria, Cameroon, Congo, Zaire, Lake Victoria. Although tolerant of alkalinity, it prefers slightly acidic, soft water. An electrical organ on this fish's caudal peduncle emits pulses of mild voltage that form an electrical field around its body. Changes in this field are sensed by the head, allowing it to swim quickly in dark or turbid waters to catch prey or escape enemies. Normally a nocturnal fish that can exist peacefully within a community tank, once acclimated however, it becomes an active diurnal feeder that may disturb its tankmates. Rather solitary by nature, a large, well-planted aquarium is best as it may pester other fishes in one that is too small. Tubifex and blood worms are among its preferred foods, but it will eat dry food as well. There is no record of it being bred.

B 16 in. (40 cm). Zaire R. Strongly territorial and pugnacious to others of the same species or other mormyrids, it is best kept by itself or with large cichlids. Live food is preferred.

C 6 in. (15 cm). Ubangi R of the upper reaches of the Zaire R. Only rarely exported. It prefers slightly acidic, soft water. Nocturnal by nature, solitary care is best, and the tank should include a plastic pipe for refuge. When the water quality is suitable it readily eats earthworms and blood worms, and is otherwise easy to care for.

D 4 in. (10 cm). Lower reaches of the Nile, upper reaches of the Zambezi R. A mild-tempered fish tolerant of the same or other species, in nature it lives in schools. A water temperature of 82°F (28°C) is preferred.

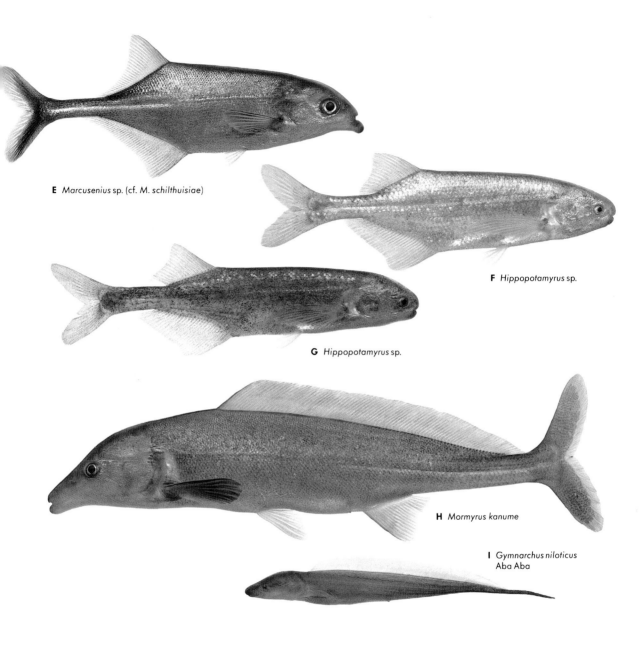

E *Marcusenius* sp. (cf. *M. schilthuisiae*)

F *Hippopotamyrus* sp.

G *Hippopotamyrus* sp.

H *Mormyrus kanume*

I *Gymnarchus niloticus*
Aba Aba

E 6 in. (15 cm). Africa. A short-nosed mormyrid with a protruding lower jaw, this fish may be *M. schilthuisiae*. It prefers slightly acidic, soft water, and if the water quality is not suitable, it will become quite thin even if well fed.

F 12 in. (30 cm). Congo, Zaire, Cameroon, Gabon. Prefers slightly acidic to acidic, soft water. Sometimes sold under the name *Gnathonemus moorii,* it should be kept by itself in a medium-sized tank.

G Fish shown was 4 in. (10 cm), but max. size is unknown. Similar to the above, but the body height and distance from the dorsal to caudal fin are different. Care is the same, however.

H 20 in. (50 cm). Nile R. Nocturnal in the wild, when acclimated, it becomes an active diurnal swimmer, preferring live food. A large, quite aggressive species, it should be kept by itself.

I 6 ft (2 m). Nile R, Zaire R, much of W Africa. Pugnacious, making cohabitation with even other large fishes impossible. It prefers live food, large individuals feeding on small fishes. A floating nest is made using aquatic grasses. About 1,000 eggs are laid in a spawning, and these hatch out in 3-4 days. The pair cares for the eggs and larvae. The larvae have a large yolk sac and external gills (similar to *Polypterus*), and become free swimming when they reach about 5/16 in. (7.5 mm) in 5 days. They serve as food fish in the above locations. Juveniles are regularly exported from Lagos. Occasionally, an albino variant is available.

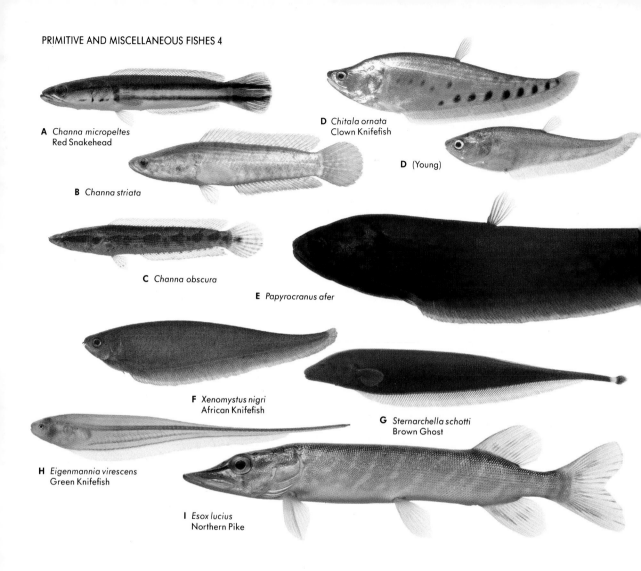

A *Channa micropeltes*
Red Snakehead

B *Channa striata*

C *Channa obscura*

D *Chitala ornata*
Clown Knifefish

D (Young)

E *Papyrocranus afer*

F *Xenomystus nigri*
African Knifefish

G *Sternarchella schotti*
Brown Ghost

H *Eigenmannia virescens*
Green Knifefish

I *Esox lucius*
Northern Pike

A Exceeds 40 in. (1 m) in aquaria. SE Asia. While young fish have a black and yellowish lion-like appearance, adults become blacker and more ferocious looking. Juveniles prefer slightly acidic, aged water, but adults are tolerant even of alkaline conditions. Hardy, it will voraciously consume small fish and crustaceans, growing fast. Fishes of the Family Channidae have an accessory respiratory organ that allows them to survive for a long time in oxygen-starved water. Entwined by the ♂ (like with gouramis), the ♀ will spawn about 2,000 eggs near the water surface. They will both care for the eggs and young fry.

B Exceeds 40 in. (1 m). SE Asia. Rarely exported, care is the same as the above species.

C 14 in. (35 cm). Widely distributed throughout Africa, it's not fussy about water quality. Easy to care for, this fish is a voracious piscivore, even consuming unsuspecting large fish. An acclimated individual may eat fish fillets.

D Reaches 40 in. (1 m) in nature. India, Burma, Thailand. Active at dawn and twilight, quiescent and hidden during the daytime, it prefers live foods, larger individuals eating small fish. The pair will spawn on a stone or on floating twigs with the

♂ guarding the eggs and juveniles which hatch out in 6-7 days.

E 24 in. (60 cm). Zaire to Senegal. Prefers slightly acidic, soft water. Piscivorous and nocturnal, it remains hidden during the day. As it is aggressive and dislikes company, it is best kept by itself.

F 8 in. (20 cm). Nile R to Liberia. Recognizable by the absence of a dorsal fin, it is hardy, peaceful and easily adapts to aquaria. Long-lived, a varied diet of live foods will keep it healthy. When expelling air from its swim bladder, a peculiar sound is emitted. There is no record of it being bred.

G 7 in. (18 cm). Amazon Basin. A nocturnal, electric fish, pipes or rock refuges should be prepared for it in the tank. As it does not readily accept dry food, live foods are preferred. Although it will sometimes coexist peacefully with other fish, it will attack closely related species. This fish's behavior of sometimes laying still, other times swimming by undulating its long anal fin, is quite wondrous.

H 18 in. (45 cm). Tropics of S America. Inhabits stagnant waters like grassy ponds and brooks. Prefers slightly acidic, soft water. Omnivorous and easy to care for, it does well with other peaceful fishes in a planted community aquarium.

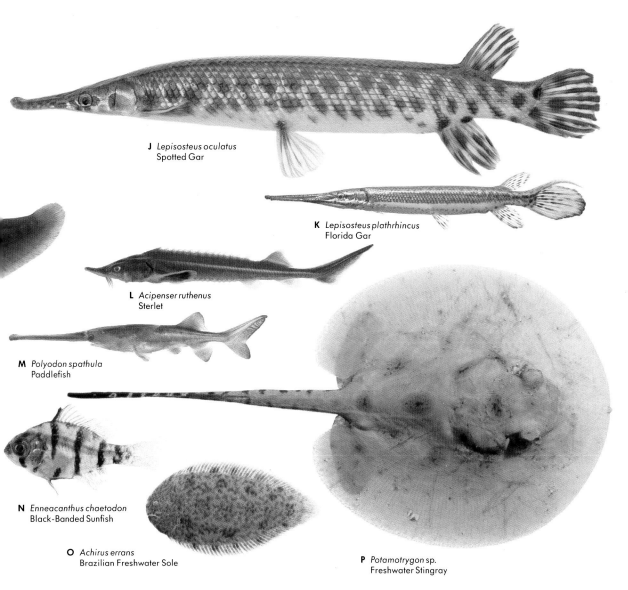

J *Lepisosteus oculatus*
Spotted Gar

K *Lepisosteus plathrhincus*
Florida Gar

L *Acipenser ruthenus*
Sterlet

M *Polyodon spathula*
Paddlefish

N *Enneacanthus chaetodon*
Black-Banded Sunfish

O *Achirus errans*
Brazilian Freshwater Sole

P *Potamotrygon* sp.
Freshwater Stingray

I ♀ 5 ft (1.5 m), ♂ 3 ft (90 cm). Widely distributed in Europe, N America, Asia. Piscivorous, it waits in ambush among aquatic grasses. In Europe, the fish spawns in grassy shallows in March or April, a large ♀ laying about 300,000 eggs. The larvae grow fast, and cannibalism among the young has been reported.

J Exceeds 28 in. (70 cm). Mexico to Great Lakes Region in N America. It is found in fresh to marine waters. Although piscivorous, it is peaceful and can coexist with other large, mild-tempered fishes. Equipped with a swim bladder that acts as an accessory respiratory organ, it will sometimes take in air at the water's surface. In N America, it spawns in March or April.

K 5 ft (1.5 m). Around Florida to Mexico. Named for its snout which is longer than the above species. Hardy, it requires a large aquarium as it grows fast, just as does the Alligator Gar (*L. tristoechus*).

L Reaches 40 in. (1 m) in nature, 20 in. (50 cm) aquaria. Danube R to Siberia. It eats voraciously at low temperatures, sucking earthworms and blood worms out of the sandy substrata. This fish requires a big, wide aquarium.

M Reaches 5 ft (1.5 m). Mississippi R. A close relative to China's *Psephurus gladius,* it

is a plankton feeder, although in a tank it may accept flake foods as they sink. It frequently starves to death in captivity.

N 3½ in. (9 cm). N America, New Jersey to northern Florida. Prefers alkaline, new water. It feeds on live foods. After the ♂ digs a hole in the substrata, he induces the ♀ to spawn eggs that adhere to the gravel. Once spawning's over, the ♀ should be removed. The ♂ will care for the eggs and fry.

O 2-4 in. (5-10 cm). Amazon R, Paraguay R. Prefers slightly acidic, aged water kept at a high temperature. Rather weak, it is difficult to keep for any length of time. Live foods such as earthworms and blood worms are preferred.

P 24 in. (60 cm). One of about a dozen species native to the rivers of S America, this viviparous fish prefers slightly acidic, aged water. Sudden water replacement may prove fatal. Peaceful, rarely attacking other fish, it eats food from the bottom of the tank, and while small is a good aquarium cleaner. Care should be taken in handling it as the tail barb is toxic and can inflict excruciatingly painful, slow-healing wounds.

A typical underwater forest of green. Fish and plants are set off by ample lighting.

TROPICAL FISH & AQUATIC PLANTS

Many materials such as rocks or stones, floating wood, and sand on the bottom can be used in laying out the aquarium's interior. These all serve as a background for the stars of the aquarium, the fishes themselves. On the other hand, recently plants have become equally appreciated. Aquatic plants have been used to supply oxygen, take up dissolved nitrogenous wastes, and even as food for the fish, but now they can be enjoyed in their own right.

In recent years, more plants from around the world have become accessible to the aquarist so that everybody can lay out the aquarium according to his or her taste and design. With great improvements in lighting apparatus, plus newly developed equipment and fertilizers, anyone can raise a wide assortment of aquatic plants. One may now say that this underwater flora is an essential part of today's aquarium.

1	*Hygrophila stricta.* Ragged Leaf Hygro.
2	*Bacopa caroliniana.* Giant Bacopa.
3	*Echinodorus amazonicus.* Amazon Swordplant.
4	*Rotala rotundifolia.* Dwarf Rotala.
5	*Hygrophila angustifolia.* Temple Plant.
6	*Vallisneria* sp. Val.
7	*Hygrophila difformis.* Water Wisteria.
8	*Egeria densa.* Argentine Anacharis.
9	*Aponogeton undulatus.*
10	*Lilaeopsis norae-zelandiae.*
11	*Anubia barteri* var. *nana.*
12	*Echinodorus osiris.* Melon Swordplant.
13	*Ludwigia* sp. Ludwigia.

A	*Poecilia reticulatus* var. Guppy.
B	*Rashora heteromorpha.* Harlequin Fish.
C	*Hyphessobrycon scholzei.* Black-Lined Tetra.

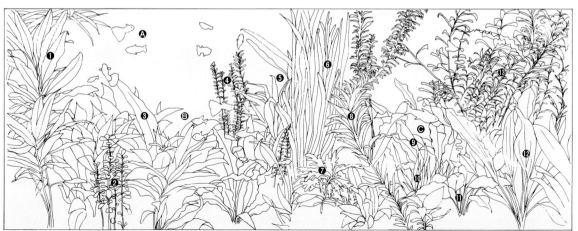

Such a scene will add to the interior design of any living room.

1   *Spatiphyllum wallisii.*

2   *Saururus cernuus.*

3   *Vallisneria asiatica* var. *biwaensis.* Corkscrew
    Vallisneria.

4   *Echinodorus quadricostatus.* Chain Amazon Swordplant.

5   *Sagittaria graminea.* Giant Sagittaria.

6   *Echinodorus major.* Ruffled Swordplant.

A   *Hyphessobrycon herbertaxelrodi.* Black Neon Tetra.

B   *Paracheirodon axelrodi.* Cardinal Tetra.

C   *Petitella georgiae.* False Rummy-Nose Tetra.

D   *Otocinclus arnoldi.* Dwarf Otocinclus.

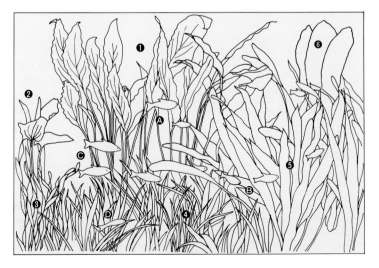

SCIENTIFIC NAME INDEX

Scientific name is followed by common name.
Page numbers in bold refer to illustrated species.

COMMON NAME INDEX

Common name is followed by scientific name.
Page numbers in bold refer to illustrated species.

First published in the United States in 1993 by Chronicle Books.

Copyright © 1985, 1991 by Atsushi Sakurai, Yohei Sakamoto, Fumitoshi
Mori. All rights reserved. No part of this book may be reproduced in any
form without written permission from Chronicle Books.

First published in Japan by Yama-Kei Publishers Co., Ltd.

Printed in Singapore.

Library of Congress Cataloging-in-Publication Data

Sakurai, Atsushi.
    Aquarium fish of the world : the comprehensive guide to 650
species / Atsushi Sakurai, Yohei Sakamoto, Fumitoshi Mori.
      p.   cm.
    Translated from Japanese.
    Includes index.
    ISBN 0-8118-0269-8 (hardcover)
    1. Aquarium fishes. 2. Aquarium fishes -- Pictorial works.
I. Sakamoto, Yohei. II. Mori, Fumitoshi. III. Title.
SF427.S25 1992
639.3'44 -- dc20   92-16784
                                   CIP

Cover design: Earl Office
Composition: On Line Typography

Distributed in Canada by
Raincoast Books
112 East Third Avenue
Vancouver, B.C. V5T 1C8

10 9 8 7 6 5 4 3 2 1

Chronicle Books
275 Fifth Street
San Francisco, California 94103